MY CITY, MY LOS ANGELES

Also by Jeryl Brunner

My City, My New York: Famous New Yorkers Share Their Favorite Places

MY CITY, MY LOS ANGELES

Famous People Share Their Favorite Places

Jeryl Brunner

Guilford, Connecticut

All the information in this book is subject to change. We recommend that you call ahead to obtain current information before traveling.

To buy books in quantity for corporate use or incentives, call **(800) 962-0973** or e-mail **premiums@GlobePequot.com.**

Photos on pages i (Griffith Park Observatory), vii, vii-ix, and xii Licensed by Shutterstock.com
Photos on pages ii-iii and xv Licensed by Thinkstock.com

Editor: Amy Lyons
Project Editor: Tracee Williams
Layout Artist: Maggie Peterson
Cover Design: Bret Kerr
Text Design: Lisa Reneson, Two Sisters Design

Library of Congress Cataloging-in-Publication Data

Brunner, Jeryl.
  My city, my Los Angeles : famous people share their favorite places / Jeryl Brunner.
    pages cm
  Includes index.
  ISBN 978-0-7627-8422-6
  1. Celebrities—Homes and haunts—California—Los Angeles—Guidebooks. 2. Los Angeles (Calif.)—Guidebooks. 3. Los Angeles (Calif.)—Biography. I. Title.
  F869.L83B78 2013
  979.4'94—dc23

                                                              2012050358

Printed in the United States of America

10 9 8 7 6 5 4 3 2 1

To Jodie Berlin Morrow, Ph.D., my teacher, guide, mentor and friend who sees with her heart

"To look at a thing is very different from seeing a thing. And one does not see anything until one sees its beauty."
—Oscar Wilde

And for my nephews, Curt Brodner and Eli Brodner

"There is something you must always remember. You are braver than you believe, stronger than you seem, and smarter than you think. . . . Even if we're apart, I'll always be with you. If there ever comes a day when we can't be together, keep me in your heart, I'll stay there forever."
—A.A. Milne

Stay curious.

Love,

Aunt Jeryl

* I'm from LA, second generation on both sides. I love the fact that a half hour away you can be in the snow, at the beach. I love how spread out it is. When you're an Angeleno you know how to get around the little back sides and find the little historic sections—the El Salvadorian parts of town, Koreatown, I love all that ethnicity of it. I love the diversity.

—Bonnie Raitt,
Grammy-winning artist, guitarist, singer, and songwriter

CONTENTS

Acknowledgments   xiii
Introduction   xvi

Beaches, Gardens, Hideaways & Secret Spots 1

Jessica Chastain • Nicholas Kristof • Molly Shannon • Steve Rabineau • Alexander Ludwig • Mark Nicholson • Erika Anderson • Shaun White • Mark Morrison • Edward Zwick • Jimmy Smits • Noah Emmerich • Luanne Rice • Tracie Bennett • Pat Haden • Judy Kameon • Melora Hardin • Penelope Spheeris • Eric Garcetti • Andrew R. Tennenbaum • Piers Morgan • Robert S. Anderson • Dan Klass • Sharon House • David Marciano • Richard Abramson • Sang Yoon • William Brien, MD • Mia Lehrer • Selena Gomez

LA Eats 29

Lucy Liu • Eric McCormack • Tony Danza • Ken Howard • Jewel • Kathryn Fiore and Gabriel Tigerman • Richard Dreyfuss • Marc Blucas • Anna Kendrick • Michael Irby • Amy Ryan • Adrien Brody • Ruth Vitale • Michael Shannon • Anthony Mackie • Lisa Ling • Robert and Audrey Loggia • Josh Groban • Anjelica Huston • Brooke Lyons • Gene Simmons • Jenny Wade • Candy Spelling • Jennifer Morrison

• Meiko • Scott Conant • Wilmer Valderrama • Carrie Brownstein • Patrick J. Adams • Bow Wow • Zach Pollack • Colin Egglesfield • Claude Kelly • Michael Feinstein • David Alan Basche and Alysia Reiner • Bonnie Raitt • Paige Morrow Kimball • Jonathan Cheban • Jerry Springer • Ken Paves • Robert Wuhl • Doris Roberts • Constance Zimmer • Denis O'Hare • Ana Martinez • Loris Kramer Lunsford • Jeffrey Dean Morgan • Janet Montgomery • Dan Angel • Angela Lansbury • Nick Cannon • Chris Nichols • Clark Gregg • Ciara • Josh Charles • Jennifer Westfeldt • Olga Garay • Jeff Skoll • Bryan Batt • Gulla Jonsdottir • Donald De Line • David Hallberg • Merle Ginsberg • Ne-Yo • Jack Black • Chris Riggi • Frances Fisher • Karen Schaler • Cindy Williams • Sacha Gervasi • Christopher Gorham • Da'Vine Joy Randolph • Neal Fraser • Kristin Chenoweth • Fisher Stevens • Eve Plumb • Camila Alves • Lauren Miller • Tonya Pinkins • Lisa Lillien • Dylan Baker • Tyler Perry • Scooter Braun • NiRé All'Dai • Thomas Matthews • Chad Greer • Giuliana Rancic • Gabourey Sidibe • Debi Mazar and Gabriele Corcos • Tracee Chimo • Bill Borden • Chloe Flower • La La Anthony • Craig Zadan • Illeana Douglas • Richard Kind • Tena Clark • Kirsten Segal • Valentin Chmerkovskiy • Cheryl Cecchetto • Lisa Gilbar, ACSW, LMSW • Martin Papazian • Stephen Schwartz • Jonathan Krisel • Sang Yoon • Ezra Doner • Max Jacobson • Matt Lanter • Zane Buzby • Elizabeth Much

Nocturnal Los Angeles 103

Susan Sarandon • Michael Stuhlbarg • Corbin Bleu • Ilse Metchek • Kellan Lutz • Ruth Vitale • Laraine Newman • Bobby Moynihan • Toni Trucks • Justin Long • Merle Ginsberg • Art Streiber • Adriano Goldschmied • Tracie Thoms • Adrian Salamunovic • Tova Laiter • Laura Lane • Nick Karno • Julia Gogosha • Steve Walter • Barbara Fairchild • Chris Clark • Anne Bartnett • David R. Carpenter • Debby Ryan • Thom Andersen • Offer Nissenbaum • Retta • Peter Cambor • Jonathan Cheban • Erica Moller-Islas

Stores, Markets & Spas 129

Jennifer Love Hewitt • Mandy Patinkin • Heather Graham • Vanessa Hudgens • Kim Kardashian • Audra McDonald • Ne-Yo • Laraine Newman • Josh Lobis • Nicholas Jarecki • Stephanie Austin • Jesse Tyler Ferguson • Merle Ginsberg • Gurmukh • Kirsten Segal • Ilse Metchek • Retta • Allison Williams • Suzanne Goin • Cheryl Cecchetto • Joachim Splichal • Susan B. Landau • J Mascis • Elizabeth Stewart • Debi Dumas • Christopher Gartin • Robert Wuhl • Kimba Hills • Jacklyn Zeman • Jerome Dahan • Selma Blair • Ruth Vitale • Mohan Ismail • Melora Hardin • Lainie Kazan • Suzanne Tracht • Jonathan Cheban • Mary Vernieu • Molly Shannon • Ryan Patterson • Mae Whitman • Natalie Compagno • S. Irene Virbila • Glynis Costin • Zane Buzby

Superstar Structures, Sexy Spaces, Beatific Bridges & Pockets with Panache . 163

Dustin Hoffman • Antonio R. Villaraigosa • Ben Stiller • Candace Nelson • Matthew Rolston • Constantine Maroulis • Adrian Salamunovic • Dan Mazeau • Paige Morrow Kimball • Richard Bloom • Jenica Bergere • Carol Martinez • NiRé All'Dai • Marco Reed • Sam Russell • Olga Garay • Darin Moiselle • Ken Levine • Gigi Levangie Grazer • Robert Wuhl • Cassie Steele • Sir Richard Branson •

Gale Anne Hurd • Michael Barlow • Michael Tilson Thomas • Dave Barry • Eric Ripert • Duff Goldman • Ken Burns • Lou Diamond Phillips • Patrick Dragonette • Gulla Jonsdottir • Geraldine Knatz • Art Streiber • Amadea Bailey • Tom LaBonge • Hannah Simone • Ilene Angel • Martin Cooper • Hans Ulrich Obrist • Fred Armisen • Jerry R. Schubel, PhD • Margy Rochlin • Nick Karno • Betty Buckley • Nancy Davis • Jean-François Piège • Max Casella

Saunters, Sails, Rides, Hikes & Drives **213**

Cheryl Tiegs • Usher • Kellan Lutz • Ryan Seacrest • Guy Webster • Nancy Silverton • Hugh Jackman • Frances Fisher • Jane Fonda • Sanaa Lathan • Edward Mady • Byata Cousins • Mark Ruffalo • Arlene Nelson • Chynna Phillips and Billy Baldwin • Jon Cryer • Kelly Lynch • Gabriel Macht • Charles Brunner • Marion Cotillard • Carol Bishop • Gina Marie Lindsey • Gail Midgal Title, Esq. • Tova Laiter • Dayle Reyfel • Patrick Dragonette • Dan Klass • Mehdi Eftekari • Ella Thomas • Cristin Milioti • Eugene Pack • Lucy Hale • Peter Theroux • Graham Russell • Peter Greenberg • Ezra Doner • Jeff Klein • Annie Gilbar • Sylvia Lopez • Mark Mothersbaugh • Scott Allen • Julian Sands • David O. Russell • Amy Schiffman • Denise Flanders • Adrian Salamunovic • Leven Rambin • Brit Marling • Christopher Reynolds • Susan Feniger • Jenny Wade • Tena Clark • Merle Ginsberg • Dr. Ava Cadell • Kim Marshall • Rocky Malhotra • Jill-Michele Meleán • Bernard Markowitz, MD FACS • Karen Zambos • Paul Herman • Zane Buzby • Lorraine Bracco

Index   259
About the Author   268

ACKNOWLEDGMENTS

Los Angeles is known as the City of Angels. But who knew that so many "angels" in and outside LA not only had my back, but encouraged, inspired, and rallied like crazy on my behalf. I am truly overwhelmed and humbled by the generosity and kindness of these angels.

Karissa Fowler, Kelly Nagle, Mark Morrison, Betsy Israel, Cheryl Kramer Kaye, Abbie Kozolchyk, Margy Rochlin, Tina Reine, Patrick Dragonette, Skelly Holmbeck, Hayley Doner, Carla Schwam, Karina Arutyunyan, Steve Rabineau, Bryan Bantry, Jodi Lobis, Eugene Pack, Dayle Reyfel, Luba Kanor Abrams, Ron Abrams, Sarah Evans Thelen, Greta Vanhersecke, Karen Tina Harrison, Max Jacobson, Trisha Cole, Nadia Al-Amir, Kim Marshall, Gulla Jonsdottir, Rachel Axler, Tammy Peters, Julie Besonen, Aik Wye Ng, Gigi Schilling, Dave Carpenter, Tova Laiter, Hillary Zuckerberg, Barbara Zuckerberg, Arlene Winnick, Bonnie Reuben, Marian Gerlich, Jane Summer, Shelly Howell, Lisa Gilbar, Lainie Munro, Molly Shannon, Ilene Angel, Heather Gary, Lloyd Zuckerberg, Karen Jones, Jennifer Cooke, Danielle Patla, Leslie Lefkowitz, Nora Walsh, Gail Migdal Title, Deborah Glusker, Jodie and Bruce Morrow, Tena Clark, Katrin Sosnick, Patti Adcroft, Marina Morrison-Keiler, and Nancy Winston.

To Chad Greer. Thank you for your extraordinary photography and profound and amazing commitment to this book.

To Carol Martinez who got *My City, My Los Angeles* early on and reached out to so many on my behalf.

To Rick Newman who is as talented as he is kind. You are a rock star!

To Rick Guidotti who sees so much magic in people and captures them like no other in his photos.

To Karen Schaler for your beautiful devotion and for being so stellar. And Clint Page Henderson, I'm still speechless! Thank you!

To the 582 and Hamptons lovelies: Dana Lowe, Kevin Allen, Sarita Varma, Nicole Deutsch, Lisa Tucker, Lynn Sadofsky, Dina Goldfinger, Laura Begley Bloom, Jonathan Bloom, and Zahra Elmekkawy for your support, kindness and for making me feel so special.

Thank you, Jenica Bergere, for your giant heart and for getting so many people excited about *My City, My Los Angeles.* I am astounded by all you did on my behalf.

To Paige Morrow for your beautiful wisdom, guidance, talent, and for being such an extraordinary and generous connector. You are a treasure..

Zach Pollack, not only are you a stupendous chef and writer, you are such an unbelievably kind soul. WOW! Thank you!

To the incredibly talented Josh Lobis. Thank you for talking up my book to so many cool people (like you).

To Ruth Vitale for believing in me so much, your can-do unstoppable-ness and all around amazingness.

Thank you, Dina Zuckerberg, for caring so much for *My City, My Los Angeles* and for being such a great friend.

Simon Baitler, Carla Migdal, and Lily Baitler you are superstars! Where do I begin? You took me in, shared the treasures of your city. You gave of yourselves, shared your family, your friends. Then you gave some more. And Simon, I don't know what this book would be with without you. But I do know that my mother thanks you too.

Thank you to my family, extended family and their loved ones: Sherry, Bonnie, Curt, and Eli Brodner, Charles and Claire Brunner, Naomi, Hal, Adam, Kathryn, Brianna and Nicholas Kaufman, Marsha and Fred Drachman, Alise Drachman Beccaria, Pat Beccaria, Chuck, Bruce and Stephanie Bernzweig, Andrea Brunner Behrens, Jack, Emma, and Noah Behrens, Renee, Andrew, Rebecca and Michael Paratore.

Thank you to my associate, Laura Cain. You are terrific. What a pleasure to work with you!

To CarolLee Kidd and the staff of CLK Transcription—a truly talented bunch!

To the wonderful and devoted people at Globe Pequot. To my editor, Amy Lyons and to Tracee Williams, Joanna Beyer, Bret Kerr, Sheryl Kober, John Spalding, Amy Alexander, Anita Oliva, Lisa Reneson and Laurie Kenney.

To my agent, Jessica Regel, who continues to nurture my voice. And to Tara Hart, Laura Biagi, and the fantastic Jean V. Naggar Literary Agency staff.

To the many people who shared their passion for Los Angeles and lent their beautiful voices to this book. I am honored to include you.

As the writer and director Luciano De Crescenzo said, "We are each of us angels with only one wing, and we can fly only by embracing each other." Thank you for holding me up and letting me fly.

INTRODUCTION

For a young Angeleno named Norma Jeane Baker (aka Marilyn Monroe), pure bliss was spending hours at the exotic Egyptian Theatre on Hollywood Boulevard escaping into the world of movies. In later years, heaven was a bowl of chili at the LA comfort food joint, Barney's Beanery. Jessica Chastain and Jimmy Smits find their groove by the long stretches of beach in Santa Monica. For Jane Fonda happiness is hiking along Runyon Canyon, a tranquil spot high up above the city. These places hold a special connection.

But my special tie to Los Angeles began before I ever got there.

From the time I was a very little girl, I dreamed of becoming an actress. Not a superstar. An actress. I've heard that actors are so passionate about their work because when they play a new character, they find a new identity, a new part of themselves. Edward Norton once said, "I always felt that acting was an escape, like having the secret key to every door and permission to go into any realm and soak it up. I enjoy that free pass."

Well, I wanted that free pass too. I was born with a birth defect called a unilateral cleft lip and palate. So instead of lip, teeth and gums, I had a giant gap on the upper left side of my mouth. Part of my nose and lip had to be constructed. When I first learned to talk, I sounded like Donald Duck. After more surgery, people mistakenly thought I had a very bad cold.

My nose and lips were asymmetrical, smooshed and scarred from many surgeries. I'd get on the school bus longing for two empty seats. If I had to sit next to someone, they'd yell that they didn't want to catch my cooties. "Don't touch her. Don't touch her." they chanted to one another.

I'd come home completely defeated, look into the mirror, and rub my finger against the scars wishing they would disappear. Or what if *I* could disappear? What if I was an actress like Judy Garland and could become Dorothy in *The Wizard of Oz*? Or I'd imagine being Debbie Reynolds, playing Kathy in *Singin' in the Rain* and tap dancing with Gene Kelly. Then I could step into someone else and be rescued from myself.

But how? From what I recall, no one in my family was an actor or even remotely trying to be an actor or even knew actors or knew people who knew actors. One day, my teacher announced they were holding auditions for the next school play and asked who wanted to try out. My arm shot up quickly. My big chance! She looked at my earnestly raised hand and fell silent. While everyone colored at their desks, she quietly led me to a corner in the room and kneeled down, so her eyes met mine. A forlorn expression fell over her. "You can't audition, Jeryl, she said. "No one would understand you."

So the closest I got was hearing my mother tell the story about Lana Turner's great discovery and entrée into the movie business. As my mother told it, Lana Turner was just a regular sixteen-year-old school kid when she walked into Schwab's drugstore and sat on a stool by the soda fountain. Then poof, a Hollywood director who also happened to be there took notice. He was so blown away by this Hollywood High School student, he offered a screen test on the spot. By the time she left Schwab's, Turner's career was launched. An actress was born.

Never mind that my mother got several details wrong (many others did too). As I later learned, the director who "discovered" Lana Turner was probably the publisher of the *Hollywood Reporter*. He offered an introduction to super agent Zeppo Marx. And in fact, the place wasn't Schwab's. It was the Top Hat Cafe. And never mind that Lana Turner was one of those rare specimens—a lucky winner of the beauty gene lottery blessed with drop-dead gorgeousness.

The most important detail, the one that stuck with me always, was where it all happened. In my little girl mind, there was only one place in the world where people walked into drugstores and came out actors.

At the time we lived just outside New York City. My parents had been divorced since I was a baby and my mother had recently remarried. While we spoke regularly by telephone, I hadn't seen my father in a year when my sister and I got the call. Were we up for a two week visit with my dad who lived in . . . where else?

And so began my trip of firsts. My first airplane trip (and without grown-ups no less). First adventure so far from home. First time visiting Los Angeles. And, I was convinced, my first Lana Turner–style Hollywood discovery.

So my nine-year-old sister and I boarded a super groovy TWA 747 at JFK with a groovy bar with sweet flight attendants serving unlimited sweet sodas. And we flew into the mythic land of eternal sunshine.

When we arrived, the air was dry, humid-free, and completely liberating. The sky was huge, set against red blue-ish mountains. And thus began our LA odyssey. Nights were spent by the rooftop pool high up on top of my father's hipster adults-only apartment on Lafayette Park Place. LA twinkled and glowed. I thought of Tinker Bell spreading her pixie dust and wondered when some of it would fall on me.

We met the Sierra Club for one of their regular walks through Griffith Park and saw the sun set upon the city. We took a sailboat from the Port of Los Angeles in San Pedro. We walked up tony Rodeo Drive. Surely, I thought, someone *has* to discover me on this glitzy street. But to no avail. We hit the beach in Santa Monica. The expanse of sand from the water to the pavement was so vast, it wouldn't stop. I struck every pose I could—hoping and hoping. But no director or casting agent ever appeared.

We ended up at the La Brea Tar Pits. As far back as 50,000 years ago, animals would get stuck there in the hot sticky asphalt seeping out of the ground and were trapped like flies on flypaper. Over time, fossils of these extinct animals greatly accumulated, like the 44,000-year-old saber-toothed cat and a 46,800-year-old coyote. Several million fossils have been discovered in the pits, from the twelve-foot-tall Columbian mammoth to the water flea. In fact, fossil discoveries have been so comprehensive and vast, paleontologists have been able to understand and reconstruct the entire prehistoric ecosystem from many, many years ago.

I studied the bubbling black goo and was utterly flummoxed, mesmerized.

The La Brea Tar Pits were full of bewildering marvel and worlds to be revealed. They seemed to hold so many riches and answers. But it was more than I could possibly understand. And maybe that was the point? Somehow, I understood that just like those tar pits, there was so much in my seven-year-old universe yet to be unfolded. And at that moment in time, it was way beyond my realm of comprehension. The astonishing awaited. I had so much to learn. As Hamlet would say, "there is more in heaven and earth than is dreamt of in your philosophy."

So maybe Hollywood and Los Angeles weren't really about getting discovered. It ignited to my discovery of possibilities and wonder. My salvation wasn't about being found by a casting director. It was about finding joy in all that was waiting and could set me free.

BEACHES, GARDENS, HIDEAWAYS & SECRET SPOTS

✳ My favorite place is the Santa Monica beach walk. I live near there and I like to walk my dog. I get a tea in the morning from my private spot at a place on Main Street and just walk around. The walk is amazing and beautiful.

—Jessica Chastain, Academy Award- and Golden Globe-nominated actress

Greg Bonann was practically born swimming. His lifeguard career started when he was seventeen. "When you're a kid from Palisades High School growing up ten feet from the sand, becoming a lifeguard is a rite of passage, a no brainer," he says. "I was just coming off my high school swim team; everyone went down and did it."

His first day on duty was at Will Rogers State Beach, a tranquil stretch of sand tucked into the Santa Monica Bay. "It's an icon of Los Angeles and the kind of place that you really never get tired being around. It changes every hour. It's gorgeous." He explains, "It's close to the road. It's thin and narrow, it's got dangerous spots, it's got safe spots. It's got good surf. It's got bad surf. It's got surfboarding areas. It's got swimming areas. And people don't realize that the sun there comes up on the left, shines on the beach all day long and sets on the right. Just for one little beach, it's one of the most unique places in Los Angeles."

And from that lifeguard station at Tower 18, Bonann got the inspiration for a show called *Baywatch,* which centered on the lives and travails of LA County lifeguards. "In my business you write what you know. It's simple," he explains.

Baywatch debuted on NBC in 1989, but was cancelled after one season. However, instead of floating away, the series had a renewed life in first run syndication. Yet with new opportunity came challenges. "We had to reinvent the show and do things smarter, cheaper, and better," says Bonann.

So Bonann turned to the beach he knew so well and adored. He sought permission to create a *Baywatch* set at Will Rogers State Beach.

"I went down to my lifeguard buddies and said, 'Can we build a set on top of these headquarters?'" They agreed. Of course it helped that he spoke their language. "They never would have allowed a non-lifeguard to do it because a non-lifeguard wouldn't have known that you have to shut things down when emergencies happen, which I knew didn't happen very often," he shares. "So, when they said, 'Listen, you can't be shooting when we have a code three. Your stuff has to be second priority to our business.' I said, 'Okay. No problem.'"

So they placed the camera on top of the building and shot down the beach "We had the real deal," says Bonann. Having a TV set at a location rather than a soundstage was not only groundbreaking but enabled them to do things that would simply be unaffordable by any other means. Sometimes dolphins swam by. If they wanted actors to run from the top of headquarters down to the beach into the water, they could do that too. Also, because of the natural light, they only shot from sunrise to sunset. Most television shows start earlier in the morning, going well past sundown because they're indoors and have to light everything.

The toughest piece was working around the real lifeguards who shared the headquarters facility. They had real emergencies including code three situations. Boats came by. Helicopters landed. Sirens went off. And the production team would have to stop filming, stop recording audio, and let them do their business until they were finished.

"It was terribly exciting," recalls Bonann. "Working at this lifeguard headquarters, which I'd been a lifeguard at for, at that time, twenty years and being a director at the very same headquarters was great." What's more, they embraced the massive crowd of onlookers, seeing them as an asset. "We loved the crowd," he adds. "You could see the glass as half empty or half full. Most people in Hollywood see a crowd as problematic. I saw them as free extras."

Ultimately, the series that had been cancelled by the network was not only a colossal hit, but made an indelible mark on how the rest of the world viewed the beachy Southern California culture and fire engine red Speedo. *Baywatch* has been seen in 144 countries. "When you're in front of that many people, you easily and quickly become a very watched television show," says Bonann. In fact, according to the *Guinness Book*, *Baywatch* is the most watched TV show with more than 1.1 billion viewers. In China alone, it's distributed in three languages: Mandarin, Cantonese, and Chinese. "The show appeals to all audiences in almost any language. It doesn't matter what they're saying. You get it," Bonann explains. Although he says that it never really occurred to him that the show was that popular, adding "I was just doing what I did."

Bonann continues to be a lifeguard at Will Rogers State Beach. "Probably some of the greatest memories that I have were all there," he says. "It's where I grew up from a teenager into a man." When asked to list his greatest Will Rogers memories, paramount is being a lifeguard. Having the place as the home of a television show comes in as a close second. "I started lifeguarding there in 1970 and we didn't shoot the show there until 1989. Of my forty-two years there, the show was only about twelve of them," he explains. "I saved a lot of lives at that beach. It changed my life."

. . . .

Nicholas Kristof, *New York Times* columnist and author

[My wife] Cheryl and I met in LA back in 1986. And so we were both young reporters there. And LA has a huge emotional value for that reason. I love Santa Monica Beach. When I was working in LA, the *New York Times* followed East Coast deadlines. And I would get done early, and occasionally I would be able to go to Santa Monica Beach in the late afternoon. And it always seemed so cool to have the beach right there and to be so accessible and so close. I liked just walking along the beach and the pier.

Santa Monica Pier, 200 Santa Monica Pier, Santa Monica; (310) 458-8901; http://santamonicapier.org and santamonica.com

....

Molly Shannon, Emmy-nominated actress and author

The Annenberg public pool in Santa Monica is one of my favorite places. William Randolph Hearst built the estate for actress Marion Davies. I love the idea that I'm swimming in the mistress's pool. Whenever I swim in it, I think about their relationship. There's something exciting about swimming in a mistress's pool. The deep end is so fantastic and deep and it's right on the ocean and I think it's the most gorgeous place. I'm always telling people about it who don't know it. It's just the loveliest pool with a great snack bar.

Annenberg Community Beach House, 415 Pacific Coast Highway, Santa Monica; (310) 458-4904; www .annenbergbeachhouse.com

....

Steve Rabineau, partner and senior agent, United Talent Agency

I grew up going to the beach in Los Angeles, body surfing and surfing. And my favorite place is Topanga Beach, either at daybreak or as the sun is setting over Los Angeles. I have a really diverse group of friends that I have known since seventh grade and they are doctors, lawyers, carpenters, and painters. And we all converge there every morning as the sun comes up and watch the sun rise over LA. And we surf and enjoy. We surf for as many days as there are waves breaking there. So if there's ever a swell, I will go every day or every night. Very early or late it's a really beautiful transition time.

Why this spot? It's a great surf break, there is a very particular sort of wave there. And for me, it gets back to the people who gravitate towards it. We don't really get together at any other surf spot or social place. We don't dine together. We don't surf at Venice together. We don't surf at Malibu together. That place brings us together every morning or every night, and it's sort of like *Cheers* at the beach in a weird way. People are just standing, looking, and complaining about how it used to be better.

Our gathering is a unique experience. You get a melting pot of people that you don't normally get. It's a convergence of a lot of different people doing what I love most which is surfing. Spending time there brings me back to being a kid when most of my life was oriented to the beach. And just being in the water is so soothing and fun. There is a sense of freedom. A joy. Being in the water makes me feel alive. It connects me to my youth when growing up here was easier, less crowded, less complicated.

Topanga State Beach, 18700 Pacific Coast Highway, Los Angeles; (310) 305-9546

....

Alexander Ludwig, actor (*The Hunger Games*) and musician

Whenever I go surfing in Huntington Beach or Malibu, just being out there is what I live for. Whenever you hit that water and going into a big set, you're always reminded about just how small you are. You're reminded of how insignificant all the bulls#@t is that happens in Hollywood. Excuse my language. You realize, all the craziness, none of it matters. I'm just doing what I love.

I like Huntington Beach because it's often less crowded. As a surfer, the way the waves break is perfect. It usually gets biggest there, which I like. It's just such a spiritual experience for me when I'm surfing. That and skiing are my main sports.

Huntington Beach, www.huntingtonbeachca.gov

....

Mark Nicholson, executive and head of development, Storyline Entertainment

I have a nineteen-month-old daughter and we recently discovered the Annenberg Beach House in Santa Monica. It has come to be one of our favorite spots in the summer just to go for the day. It's around ten bucks per adult and four bucks for a kid, but you get so much for what you pay.

The pool is beautiful and has been redone and what I love is that it's limited to a number of people, so it's never crowded. They have beautiful washing and changing rooms that are always clean. So you have this gorgeous beach and sitting area. You're right on the beach. You can go into the ocean, or explore the beach, come back, you never lose your spot. It's the best day in Santa Monica as a family.

We arrive rather early because it's competitive. It opens at 10:00, there's usually a line-up at 9:30 on the weekends. We grab a couple chairs and an umbrella and create a base. I took my daughter swimming there and she loves it. They have wonderful areas for kids with a splash pond, sand castles and shade. There's restaurants and we spend the entire day there.

The Annenberg Beach House also has a rich history. The property was originally built in the 1920s by William Randolph Hearst for actress Marion Davies. So you can tour the original guest house that's open during the days. There are events like yoga and paddleboarding. And I just love the water and beach. It's endless. It just feels like it can go on forever.

Annenberg Community Beach House, 415 Pacific Coast Highway, Santa Monica; (310) 458-4904; www.annenbergbeachhouse.com

. . . .

Erika Anderson, publisher, *Los Angeles Magazine*

I grew up in Santa Monica, and while I was not necessarily a beach person, I loved living in a beach community and being near the water. As an adult, I learned to row in Marina del Rey. I am currently rowing at LA Rowing Club, and appreciate the opportunity to be on the water with others who are just as passionate about the sport as I am.

Over the past twelve years, I have been on the water in the early morning hours, four to five days per week, year-round. I may be up to about 2,500 sunrises sitting in a rowing shell. Seeing Los Angeles when most of the city is still asleep is such a special experience. It's quiet, the sea lions are still sleeping, the birds are just starting to dive for breakfast, and occasionally a pod of wayward dolphins swims into the channel.

It encourages me to see the water enthusiasts out there: paddlers, kayakers, sailors and rowers, all enjoying a uniquely Los Angeles resource. It's a great reminder that while our sprawling city features eclectic and unique urban communities, it is also home to diverse and thriving outdoor experiences.

LA Rowing Club, All skill levels for sweep and sculling rowing; www.larowing.com

Phins Water Sports Club, Whithall-designed rowboats and stand-up paddleboarding, 14045 Panay Way, Marina del Rey; (310) 822-7600; www.phinsclub.com

UCLA Marina Aquatic Center, Single sculling available; 14001 Fiji Way, Marina del Rey; (310) 823-0048; http://marinaaquaticcenter.org/Rowing/

....

Shaun White, Olympic gold medal snowboarder and skateboarder

My family is in the San Diego area. The mountains that I ride are close by. I ride Northstar, at Tahoe. So, it's super close to where I live in LA. It's an hour flight maybe, and I'm there. I can ride and come right home. It's all centralized around there and where I grew up.

I like going to the beach in Malibu. I surf. So, there are a bunch of different breaks out there that are really fun. It gets really hot in the city. So, I'll cruise out there once in a while to surf. There's a place called Big Dume and Little Dume. They are two points where the waves are really good. Little Dume is a private beach, so you've got to be friends with someone there or kind of like, buddy up. But Big Dume is open to anybody who wants to go, and it's really fun. And there is a beach around the corner, Zuma, that's really nice and gorgeous.

Surfing is just relaxing. I mean there's something calming about just going in the water. There is something strange about the sport because the mentality is kind of aggressive. It's territorial. If you're not in the right place, and you don't know the right people, it can be intimidating. But, when you're just out with your friends and you're just sitting in the water you do this, "wow, life is pretty great. Things are good." It's where I get to decompress, and nobody is expecting me to be really good. I could just surf and have fun. No one is saying, "oh, what's he going to do?" Like, "impress us."

Santa Monica Beach, Big Dume; www.santamonica.com

Zuma Beach, 30000 Pacific Coast Highway, Malibu; www.ci.malibu.ca.us

....

Mark Morrison, longtime entertainment journalist and editor

If you drive north on Pacific Coast Highway and go through Malibu, past Cross Creek and Pepperdine, past Point Dume and Zuma, you begin to leave the city and Santa Monica Bay behind. About ten minutes past Malibu's laid-back civic center, cliffs rise from sandy beaches below; there is a series of three super-scenic but low-key beaches, the first of which is El Matador.

Follow the signs and pull into a small parking lot ($8 for the day) that sits on a grassy bluff overlooking a jaw-dropping coastal panorama that is possibly unparalleled in Southern California—pelicans fly past as the sun glitters on the ocean while an occasional boat or paddleboarder cruises by. Take the trail down to the beach (there is a flight of stairs to make it easier) and you can stroll among giant rock formations, hunting for shells and sea glass. Or you can stroll along the surf down toward Broad Beach and check out the rarefied real estate.

I like to stop first at Malibu Kitchen in Cross Creek Shopping Center and pick up some sandwiches and snacks and picnic at one of the bluff-top tables that overlook the sea. It's an instant getaway from LA life without ever leaving town. And the view is so vast, the sense of nature so strong, that all the stress of daily life begins to fade, while a sense of calm and balance is restored. The view is so dramatic that there is no need for words or conversation—you can just stare and space out and enjoy the solitary beauty. And if you're lucky, you may even spot some dolphins cavorting in the surf, which is always good for a smile.

El Matador Beach, 32215 Pacific Coast Highway, Malibu; (310) 377-0360; www.ci.malibu.ca.us

Malibu Kitchen & Gourmet Country, 3900 Cross Creek Road, Malibu; (310) 456-7845

....

Edward Zwick, Academy Award– and Emmy-winning and Golden Globe-nominated director, producer, and writer

These past twenty-five years, my favorite thing has been the staircases of Santa Monica Canyon. The secret walkways connect one street to the other, leading eventually to the beach. They were all built during the 1930s as part of the WPA. In the 30s Santa Monica was a rather louche place. When Cole Porter said "hates California. It's cold and it's damp" he's referring to Santa Monica. And when Raymond Chandler was talking about Bay City, that place where these rather disreputable figures hung out, he was really more or less talking about Santa Monica, I think.

And so these staircases evoke that period. They're a little world unto themselves. I don't know how many there are; a couple of them have been adopted by exercise fanatics who climb from Entrada back up to Adelaide. Up there at the top you see trainers, ripped bodies and cut girls, and all of that going on there.

But there are also the guys from the fire department, and track teams. But those are only a small subsection of these staircases. People don't know about most of them. Some of them are in disrepair, some of them are still fantastic, and you have to really walk and take a walking tour to actually see them.

Often what I'll do with people when we're working together is walk through the canyon. It's almost like a game of Chutes and Ladders. They connect one street to the other, and then back up and around. And there seems to be no rhyme or reason as to why they were built, exactly, except that they provide this public access from the very top of the canyon all the way down to the beach.

Ultimately, when you climb up to the top you'll see an ocean view. It's often the glimpse of the top of Santa Monica Bay as it appears and disappears as you walk. But, it's just for the ambient feel of people's homes. Many of them are restored from the 30s, and even earlier. We happen to live in a house that was part of something called the Up Lifters Ranch, which was a drinking fraternity for the rich guys in East Hollywood and Pasadena. So they had a place to keep their polo ponies, and their mistresses. They would come out on the weekends from their respectable lives, and they would drink and f#@k and put on little drag shows at the park right across the street in Rustic Canyon, which is one of the destinations of the staircases.

Will Rogers's house is in Will Rogers Park is a wonderful place in Santa Monica. His house is still standing on it. It's a museum that you could tour. He was a member of this group.

The funny thing is that I've lived in this area now for twenty-five to thirty years. The stairs were shown to me by somebody when I first moved there. I don't know if they're mapped. You'd have to get a very close careful map of Santa Monica Canyon. Some of them are obvious, the ones right off of Entrada go up to the beach. You'll see hard bodies there day and night going up and down the stairs, and that's one of them. My guess is they're about a dozen of these staircases or more.

The 30s were a really interesting time in Santa Monica. All the German immigrants moved there. It's where Bertolt Brecht, Kurt Weill, and Christopher Isherwood lived. It was cheap. And then it became a kind of hippie community in the 60s, and it stayed rent controlled for a long time. So, people moved in and they started upgrading and gentrifying the neighborhood, as it happened every place in cities.

One of the nice things about Santa Monica is that it's mostly shaded, so you can really go anytime of day. It's nice early morning or late afternoon. There is something particular to Santa Monica after the rain, which happens less and less frequently these days. There are mists in and out all the time. When those mists part, and the sun comes out it's very sparkly, and things are very wet. It's usually ten to fifteen degrees cooler in that canyon than most places in Los Angeles, and oftentimes twenty-five to thirty times cooler than places like the Valley, because it's a little microclimate.

Most places are defined by your friendships and work.

Very early I formed very close collaborations in Los Angeles. And then my children formed friendships. And the nice thing about my life is that I've been able, because of the work that I do, to spend a lot of time in a lot of other places too. I make movies all around the world, and so, I have extended periods away, and then I come back always. Also I've figured out a way to make LA a little bit of a smaller place. We were able to make an office in Santa Monica. My kids went to school there. So, it became a much more circumscribed universe. So, I wasn't battling traffic every day, I couldn't do that.

When I first came to Los Angeles, I was very young and living in the city. And I was invited out to Santa Monica to some intimidating party. I left, started walking around, and discovered this whole, very magical place. So, my romance with Santa Monica began concurrent with my time in Los Angeles. I think one of the things that just kept me here is the feel of this particular place.

Santa Monica Stairs, Adelaide Drive between 4th and 7th Streets; Santa Monica

....

Jimmy Smits, Emmy- and Golden Globe–winning actor

When I came to Los Angeles, I worked at Fox and was doing *LA Law.* And then I got to work at Fox again when I was on *NYPD Blue.* The first film I actually did was on the west side of Los Angeles at MGM. So I've always lived near the beach, whether it be West LA, Brentwood, or Santa Monica. I've always been closer to that side of Los Angeles. That whole area from the Santa Monica Pier all the way up to where Malibu begins gives me great memories about life in Los Angeles or the blessings that Los Angeles has given me.

So whether it's looking at a sunset on Ocean Avenue where that pier is, or just running to keep myself fit—and being able to do that in December and January.

My folks always call and say, "what is it, seventy degrees again?" It is always just really a nice temperature. I remember taking my kids through the years to the amusement park there at the pier or seeing Cirque du Soleil, or sitting out on the beach. That whole little area to me, although they say that the water levels are atrociously bad, that area for me is enchanting. It just is. To look at the bluffs and the palm trees. You can get some really cool sunsets on the bluffs over there. I've seen some beautiful sunsets, but I've been there early in the morning too. I've helped give food out. There is a big homeless population that lives in that little area.

Depending on what time you get there, time of year, and the distance, sometimes you see dolphins in March. People are out there actually whale watching. You have surfing. I just look out into the horizon and see the beautiful water and I'm not thinking about the toxicity levels. I came from the East Coast and was in Brooklyn. I used to sit on Canarsie Pier in Brooklyn and now I'm on the other side of the country on the West Coast.

I've been lucky to work. I've gotten to go to some really nice places whether it's Morocco, New England, Australia, New Mexico—wherever the job takes you. But that little area has great memories. It reminds me of blessings. I'm sure there are a lot of much nicer places and canyons and Malibu and all that stuff, but that place for me is cool.

The beach in Santa Monica, www.santamonica.com

....

Noah Emmerich, actor

I went out to LA with a national tour of *A Few Good Men*. I was living in New York and I got the job there and I'll never forget it. LA was such a foreign culture and a foreign world. I had so many images of it in my head, but I had never been there. It was so sunny and easy and gentle and warm and relaxed and calm. And there is so much good food and produce and restaurants. It felt incredibly abundant without any of the dirt or the grit or the frenetic or the kinetic energy of New York. So it was a very bizarre combination of the diversity and resources of a city with the energy of the country. To me it felt like the energy was more of a pastoral energy.

And you know what I love about LA? I'm a giant fan of the ocean. So I would go to the ocean every day. But I just couldn't believe how many people in Los Angeles didn't appreciate or didn't even acknowledge it, and didn't go. It's one of the great resources and jewels of LA.

I really like the beach at the north end of Santa Monica where it gets quieter, right by the Palisades. Dusk and dawn are my two favorite times, either really early morning at sunrise or sunset. I find it very peaceful and contemplative and reassuring and poetic in different ways.

The beach in Santa Monica, www.santamonica.com

....

Luanne Rice, best-selling author

I love the wild part of Malibu, the wilderness aspect of it. The Santa Monica Mountains come right down to the Pacific Ocean and so there are so many hikes and viewpoints. You can hike in Solstice Canyon and then go cool off and take a swim at Westward Beach.

One of my favorite things to do is to walk on Westward Beach and climb the path that goes up to Point Dume, to the headland. And if you go there during whale season, you can see gray whales passing very close to the coastline. They migrate from the north to Mexico and if you go during certain times in the spring, the wildflowers are just magical. I think that that's what I love most about this part of California in general is nature and how big it is and inspiring.

I would go either early in the day or just before sunset, when it's not so hot and it's not too crowded. The waves and the light are so interesting. I think the light in LA in general is very romantic and very beautiful. It's just the hue, especially along the ocean. Certain times of year, there's a lot of crystal fog and the sun comes through the fog and it's very silvery. And then at night, when the sun sets, the way it sets into the clouds is spectacular and it's the brightest colors. I just love that.

I remember going on this trail many years ago when I was visiting California with my sister. We're both Connecticut natives. We grew up on the beach on Long Island Sound, where it's a really beautiful beach. The Long Island Sound is sort of my home waters, where I learned to swim and love salt water.

But I remember I was out here working on a movie and my sister came with me. We just were in awe just of the enormity of everything—the Pacific Ocean and the trail going up onto a very majestic headland that juts out into the sea. And I'm not sure if that was the first time I saw this spot. Maybe it was because I had actually been there before. But being able to show it to my sister and knowing it was her first time, made it so special.

Solstice Canyon, Malibu, Corral Canyon Road; www.nps.gov/samo/planyourvisit/solsticecanyon.htm

....

Tracie Bennett, Tony-nominated actress

I've been going on and off to Zuma Beach for twenty years. An ex-boyfriend of mine took me. It's really gentle. You can totally relax. It's peaceful and idyllic and it's not packed. Every time I've been there's hardly anything there except seagulls.

There's a great restaurant nearby called the Beau Rivage. It's French, just past the beach and not too busy. You have a great day on the beach thinking and then go to the Beau Rivage. The food is magnificent. There's a great wine list. The staff is wonderful. What a day of heaven.

Zuma Beach, 30000 Pacific Coast Highway, Malibu; www.ci.malibu.ca.us

Beau Rivage Restaurant, 26025 Pacific Coast Highway, Malibu; (310) 456-5733

....

Pat Haden, athletic director at the University of Southern California and former quarterback for the Los Angeles Rams

I live in the Pasadena area and one of my favorite things is visiting Huntington Library Gardens. It's a spectacular point, and I go often. I'll go there by myself or take my wife, my grandkids. And a. it's close, b. it's beautiful, and c. it's ever-changing. It's the one place that I visit most.

Either my second or third date with my wife was at the Huntington Gardens. And so that was my first recollection of visiting. I was going to school and living at USC and we drove out there. It's actually in San Marino, which is a town contiguous to Pasadena. In those days I had no money and it was free.

The Huntington Library Gardens was originally Henry Huntington's home in Southern California. He was a railroad magnate. Now it's a research institute. USC has a collaboration with them where the Institute of the West, headed by a Professor Bill Deverell, does incredible research, so they have incredible archives including historical manuscripts and original documentation about the history of California. So it's a great research and teaching facility. Also, it has many, many acres of beautiful gardens with all kinds of plant species of Southern California. And then it has some of the most famous art in the world. Most famously, I guess are *Pinkie* and *The Blue Boy.* It's just a spectacular place.

Huntington Library, Art Collections and Botanical Gardens, 1151 Oxford Road, San Marino; (626) 405-2100; http://huntington.org

. . . .

Judy Kameon, landscape designer, Elysian Landscapes

My background is in fine arts and I'm a painter. And as a landscape designer, I've been completely self-taught. So, when I started my own private education, one of the things I would do is visit botanical gardens to learn about plants, trees, and garden-making.

In Los Angeles, we're lucky to have several botanical gardens like the Los Angeles County Arboretum and the Descanso Gardens. But the Huntington Gardens are really unique and special. They were one of the first gardens that I visited when I was starting my own education as a landscape designer.

At the Huntington Gardens, the Desert Garden really grabs my heartstrings. It's one of the original gardens there and over a hundred years old. That particular garden really celebrates the beauty of desert plants. It has all kinds of succulents and cacti. It's several acres with over five thousand species. But it's not just the size or the quantity of plants. The way they've been arranged and the planting compositions are exquisite. The use of color and form, texture and scale is magnificent.

It is like a living painting. It has these meandering paths and you wander through different landscapes that are very other-worldly. The planting areas are mounded and rolling. Then the topography of the plants themselves really creates a really dynamic environment.

The aloes are spectacular. They're gorgeous because they send up these beautiful orange candelabras in the winter that last several months. And the flowers attract hummingbirds, so it's just a really delightful place.

It's interesting because it's not lush in the typical sense of a leafy environment. But it is lush in that it's very rich with plants and very fulsome. And you see beautiful layering and integration of palms and other desert plants. Unlike so many gardens, which are best visited in the spring, the Desert Garden is wonderful to visit in the winter because a lot of the desert plants bloom in the winter.

Huntington Library, Art Collections and Botanical Gardens, 1151 Oxford Road, San Marino; (626) 405-2100; http://huntington.org

. . . .

Melora Hardin, actress, director, and singer/songwriter who stars in *Wedding Band*

About twice a year, my husband and I love taking stay-cations. We'll check into a hotel in town and never leave. Shutters on the Beach is at the very top of our list. We check in as early as we can and spend time by the pool which is intimate and small. We eat our meals there. There's something special about staying within the hotel for a night or two. Our kids might join us for the second day and get to swim. They love room service, so they get spoiled too.

There's not a bazillion people walking around Shutters. The thread count of the sheets is pretty incredible. Their lobby is really lovely and inviting and there's all those wonderful chairs and fireplaces. They have a piano playing. And their restaurant is really good. The food is delicious. The view is amazing and you really do feel like you've gotten away and transported to somewhere else.

I also love the Beverly Hills Hotel because you really feel a sense of Old Hollywood there circa 1930. You could be in old Miami, in the heart of glamorous. The Bel-Air Hotel which just reopened is also another extraordinarily beautiful place and great for stay-cations. During Christmastime, they would decorate their bar and have a roaring fire, in their bar area. Now that it's totally redone, I'm not sure if they are still doing that.

I was born in Houston, Texas. Since both my parents are actors, their work drew them here, so we came when I was five. And I went to Sarah Lawrence College in New York so I've been back and forth. I just love it here. As far as caring for yourself: preventative body care, being spiritual, it's so cutting edge, progressive and forward thinking. Also, LA is a humongous city with an incredible cross section of people: from staunch Republicans to liberal Democrats. Ethnicity is really varied. People come from all walks of life. It's a hugely inspiring melting pot and I really like that cross section of difference. And I kind of like the car culture. I enjoy driving. I tend to write a lot of songs when I'm in the car.

Shutters on the Beach, 1 Pico Boulevard, Santa Monica; (310) 458-0030; www.shuttersonthebeach.com

The Beverly Hills Hotel, 9641 Sunset Boulevard, Beverly Hills; (310) 276-2251; www.thebeverlyhillshotel.com

....

Penelope Spheeris, Grammy-nominated film director, producer, and screenwriter

I can imagine that most people would think that my favorite place in LA would be some crazy rockin' joint like The Rainbow, or some other Sunset Strip thing. But no, that's really not my favorite place.

If I have a free moment at all, I go to the Japanese Garden. It's really quite a unique pleasure, and near the Sepulveda Dam. The Japanese Garden is an amazingly tranquil and beautifully manicured place right in the middle of the valley where you would never expect it. The garden is in the strictly Japanese tradition. Different parts of the garden that have different meanings. If you read about it it's pretty interesting. There's the Dry Garden, a tea house, a lake. And then there are lots of bridges, some gingko trees, and waterfalls. And the cool thing is there's really a lot of wildlife there, like cranes and a lot of koi of course.

I discovered the Japanese Garden years ago. It has been around for quite a while. My second love next to moviemaking is building houses. It's a really creative process, I've got four houses in LA, one in Santa Monica. It's just always an adventure fixing it up. So, I was working with an architect, Alan Bernstein who was helping me design one of my other homes here. I told him that I was thinking of having something Japanese. He said, "well go visit the Garden." And so I did. I just was in shock because nobody knows about it. And it's so just sort of unexpected. I think it must be county subsidized, and there's a water recycling station in there which is actually kind of cool because it's a building with a moat around it. They also have a really cool bonsai garden, where they have potted bonsais that you can look at that are so old and so little.

I think there's a small charge to go in, but it's worth every cent, It's so peaceful, so zen, so gorgeous. I like to sit and think there. There are these moments where you feel totally in touch with nature and your life, and then everything is all good, that's what I feel there.

The Japanese Garden, 6100 Woodley Avenue, Van Nuys; (818) 756-8166; www.thejapanesegarden.com

....

Eric Garcetti, Los Angeles City Council member

Movies like *Grease* and *Terminator 2* made the Los Angeles River famous for its waterless, concrete bed. Today, major portions of the fifty-two-mile channel have been transformed into green waterways, lined new bike and pedestrian paths, and dotted with new park areas.

The LA River runs along the Elysian Valley and Atwater Village neighborhoods that I have represented on the City Council. Over the last two decades, these areas have become greener, cleaner, and great places to bicycle or go for a run without having to navigate LA streets.

The river was an important part of our city's founding back in 1769 when the city's founding pobladores arrived and settled next to it. I love going to the river not only to enjoy nature, but to think about the Los Angeles River's place in our city's history and to envision its great place in our future.

Los Angeles River, http://lariver.org

....

Andrew R. Tennenbaum, motion picture producer (the Bourne films, *Water for Elephants,* and others)

There's an area in West Los Angeles called Westwood. And aside from being the home of UCLA, go Bruins!, it was the movie house capital of Southern California. This is where all the great movie theaters were before they divided them into multi-plexes. They were single-standing great movie houses. Westwood Village was the capital of moviegoing, not for just people who worked in the movie industry, but for people who lived in Los Angeles.

There were about a dozen single freestanding movie houses with balconies. It's what it used to be to go to the movies. On any Friday or Saturday night, it was crowded, and hard to park, all those things that we rue. But at the end of the day it was a village. You could walk from theater to theater and if one was sold out. This was before you bought tickets online or over the phone. And it was THE place to be on Friday and Saturday nights. It was fun. You had the mix of families, dates, college students.

Everyone would converge in Westwood, and that was my favorite place to be on Friday and Saturdays. It reminded me of why I went into the movie business. You don't go into the movie business to make movies, you go into the movie busi-ness to watch movies. And that used to be my favorite place, but now it's different. It's not the capital of the movie house anymore.

Freestanding theaters have given way to multiplexes, to twelve to fifteen screens in a building. So for the last twelve to fifteen years, my favorite thing in LA has been replaced by something much more organic, and I'm sure, much more of a cliché: the beach. One of my favorite beaches is Colony Beach, which is where my family has lived for thirty-six years. So I've seen the sands come up, and go down, I've seen the water levels rise and decrease.

As far as I know, Malibu Colony Beach is the only private beach in California. But if you go a little farther down the beach, there's Carbon Beach, nicknamed Bil-lionaire's Beach, because it's just populated with billionaire after billionaire. Carbon is not a private beach. It's purely public. You can walk along the waterline. As you walk down the beach on one side you have your friends and their kids. They're playing and barbecuing. You're called up for a drink. Run into someone. Strike a deal. On the other side, is the most majestic thing, the ocean. It's something we can't control. It's not tame-able.

When you drive west down Wilshire or Sunset Boulevard to the Pacific, you not only hit the end of the boulevard, you don't just hit the end of the city, you don't just hit the end of the county, or the end of the state, or the end of the country. You hit the very end of the continent. That is the line. It puts things into a little bit more perspective. You're not just having to cross that red light to go to the beach. It is the very end of the continent. This is arguably the most successful country in the world. It's pretty cool. You want out? Dive on in and go for a swim.

Carbon Beach, 22601 Pacific Coast Highway, Malibu

....

Piers Morgan, host of CNN's *Piers Morgan Tonight*

My favorite place in LA is Manhattan Beach. It's an intimate, friendly little beachside city within a city—smaller than most of its neighbors, so it reminds me of a British seaside resort. I like to buy some crab salad from one of the delis [Manhattan Meats], near the promenade, and an armful of newspapers, then head down right to the water's edge, so I can lie on a towel munching my lunch, digesting world news, and plotting global domination, as the waves crash in a few feet away. Or, if my three teenage sons are in town, we'll play some cricket on the flat harder sand where the water breaks, just to really confuse the locals!

Manhattan Beach, www.ci.manhattan-beach.ca.us/
Manhattan Meats, 1111 Manhattan Avenue, Manhattan Beach; (310) 372-5406

....

Robert S. Anderson, author, *The Beverly Hills Hotel and Bungalows: The First 100 Years* and official historian of the *Beverly Hills Hotel*

My great grandmother built the Beverly HIlls Hotel. Growing up, I would see Fred Astaire and Gene Kelly walking around. The Beverly Hills Hotel is so interconnected with the entertainment industry. Jeffrey Katzenberg said that anybody in show business has either made or is going to make a major deal in the Polo Lounge or by the pool.

On my perfect day, I would drive up to Paradise Cove, in Malibu. It's a bit of a drive but the trip along the coast is beautiful and the beach there is gorgeous. The air is clean and it's not crowded like it is further down. I was there the other day and the pelicans were flying in flocks. There's kelp beds. It's a whole different world.

Then I would come home from the beach and see a film at the ArcLight movie theater where you can reserve seats beforehand. I like to sit in the middle, above the floor. And I reserve the seats on either side of me so that I have room to put my popcorn and I'm not fighting over the arm rest. For an extra twenty bucks, I can be a big shot.

LA is really a beautiful place to live in and Beverly Hills is especially so. Now, if you could do something about the traffic, I'll vote for you.

Paradise Cove, 28128 Pacific Coast Highway, Malibu

....

Dan Klass, humorist, actor, pioneering podcaster, and author

I live near the beach now, but I grew up inland, in the 70s and 80s. My most common association with sand is not from the beach but from seeing it in all the ashtrays at the mall. So, whenever I'm at the beach, sitting in the sand, I feel at any moment someone will snuff out their cigarette on me on the way to Spencer's Gifts.

Now I have a family and we live near the beach. As you can imagine, I am occasionally dragged there, to sit in the sand. Often to dig. Yes, we find cigarette butts. It doesn't help. Anyway, the point is, we'll end up going to Playa del Rey, which is near the house, or Manhattan Beach, which my wife prefers, because the houses along the beach there are more huge and expensive and the town's name has the word "Manhattan" in it. We'll drag towels and umbrellas and buckets and bodyboards and all sorts of junk down near the water's edge, and my wife will finally choose where we should set up camp (invariably blocking some other family's view of the ocean).

She and I sit. I will have a moment of clear-headed calm. It doesn't last. Just about the time I'm really diving into some serious self-loathing, beating myself up for not loving the beach (I should love the beach, everyone loves the beach, why can't I just be normal like other normal people and love the damned beach?), the kids will decide that it's time for me to get in the water. The cold, cold Pacific water. Suddenly, sitting on a dry towel in the warm sand chatting with my wife doesn't really seem like such a hardship. But, I have to be "Super Dad," so I put on a good show of wanting to join them. The truth is I'm hoping the temperature of the ocean will scare the kids off. Who am I kidding? Absolutely no one.

Honestly, the first shock of the cold doesn't last long, and soon my feet are completely numb. Wonderful. Then, it's onto the knees. Those are easy. The big commitment comes when the water is lapping up around my, well, lap. The bathing suit area is sometimes the last part of your body you'd like to be bathing. There are, frankly, certain temperature-regulating systems built into the male anatomy that I'm never eager to engage.

But then I'm in. And there's nothing like it.

I love being in the ocean, fighting the waves, trying to stay standing, keeping the kids from drowning. Somehow it disconnects me from my brain and connects me to the rest of the planet. It is relaxing and invigorating and private and communal all at the same time. It is like no lake or river or pool or reservoir. It is the ocean. It is a return to the womb, a disconnecting from the Matrix. I can now see the sand, and the beach and the waves. The sailboats that silently make their way in and out of the marina. The palms that outline the lagoon that was once part of a resort of bygone days. It is silent and roaring, I can hear everything and nothing. I become exhausted, with boundless energy. I am alive. And I need that.

Manhattan Beach, www.ci.manhattan-beach.ca.us/

. . . .

Sharon House, Much and House Public Relations

Saturday mornings are reserved for a leisurely Santa Monica stroll with my dog Pinky. Palisades Park, on the bluff overlooking the Pacific Ocean, is what dreams are made of. I park in the residential area, usually around 11th Street and follow the ocean breeze down Alta Avenue toward the ocean. The avenue itself is wide and quiet, flanked by an array of architectural styles, from early 1900s Craftsman and

Spanish to sleek, modern, and contemporary. And if you are lucky there is a chance for a celebrity sighting. Once we cross Ocean Avenue and enter Palisades Park, I am instantly energized and simultaneously relaxed.

Locals, tourists, retirees, students, couples with their arms entwined, fitness buffs, families enjoying time together, singles with their canine companions—the park beckons an array of visitors. Bike- and pet-friendly paths with new benches, clean public bathrooms, and plenty of drinking fountains festoon the park, which overlooks the ocean. The Arcadia Bandini de Baker rose garden with dozens of fragrant varieties, ringed by benches with poignant dedications is to my left, providing a few minutes of sweet solitude. Pinky and I usually turn right for a vigorous thirty-minute loop that takes us down toward Entrada Canyon, past the C. Walter Todd totem pole, dedicated in 1926, and if we are lucky, we are able to sight a small pod of dolphins enjoying the surf, just yards away from Santa Monica Beach swimmers.

No walk is complete without lunch and Montana Avenue, which parallels Alta, is a foodie paradise—from my favorite dog-friendly Kreation Kafe at 11th Street and Father's Office, famous for their burgers, to the eclectic Babalu. My appetite is always quenched on Saturdays with Pinky.

Kreation Kafe, 1023 Montana Avenue #B, Santa Monica; (310) 458-4880

Father's Office, 1018 Montana Avenue, Santa Monica; (310) 736-2224; www.fathersoffice.com

Palisades Park, Ocean Avenue (from Colorado Avenue to San Vicente Boulevard); www.santamonica.com

....

David Marciano, actor (*Homeland*), writer, director

There's a little par 3 golf course at the bottom of Los Feliz Boulevard just before you get to Atwater. I love to walk through there and play a little nine holes of golf. Anybody can go. What I like most about it is that it's dense with trees. You feel like you're in a forest, or in a cathedral.

I originally landed in Northern California because I came out for school. The Drama Studio of London at Berkeley and San Francisco were my first tastes of California. And it was, wow, this place is pretty cool. I had my first café latte with brown sugar in it.

When I first got to LA, I was staying with friends, sleeping on couches. And I was just floating around trying to find my way. We hung out a lot. I had a little Austin Healey convertible. I'd drive around all day with my top down, hang out with other actors, and go to acting class. The Improv on Sunday nights had dance night. That's where you would meet a lot of people. They'd put the dance tape in, we all would look for celebrities, hang out and dance, and see what the world had to offer.

My first big job was a guest star lead on *Wiseguy* in 1987. I had only been in LA about a year and a half. I did not understand the magnitude of the situation. When I auditioned there were only two scenes to audition. I was very naive at the time. I'd only been in LA eighteen months and I thought that was my whole part, those two scenes. Then when I got the job and they sent me the script I was on almost every page. I thought, I can't do this. How am I going to do this? I'm the main guy. I'm the star in this freaking episode. But of course, I took the job.

Los Feliz Municipal Golf Course, 3207 Los Feliz Boulevard, Los Angeles; (323) 663-7758

. . . .

Richard Abramson, partner with Gene Simmons, Simmons Abramson Marketing and cofounder, Cool Springs Life

One of my favorite places which I like to visit several times a year is a small public park in Point Dume, Malibu. You climb up and when you get there, there's almost never anybody around, maybe five or six people at the most.

A small trail leads up to a promontory point on a triangle. When you get up, there's a 360-degree view, which is incredible. The ocean goes around something like 200 degrees. Then you turn around and see the mountains of Malibu. It's just perfect. It's quiet, peaceful, and wonderful. On a clear day, you can see for hundreds of miles.

I used to live in Malibu and so every month or so I like to drive there to watch the ocean and turn around and watch the mountains. Not many people know or care about it. If there was a restaurant up there, it'd be so expensive. If you could build a house up there, the house would be worth millions and millions of dollars, because it's the single best view of anything I've ever visited. Fortunately, that'll never happen.

Los Angeles is the center of popular culture for the world. The number one export of the United States of America isn't aerospace, steel, or lumber. It's filmed entertainment, and it has been for years and years and years. People don't realize that it's not food. It's obviously not oil. It's not all those things. Then on top of that, add music entertainment, and most of it emanates from here. LA is the home of popular culture, and I'm a big believer in popular culture. It's a phenomenal place to live.

Point Dume Natural Preserve, Westward Beach Road, Malibu; (310) 457-8143; www.parks.ca.gov

....

Sang Yoon, head chef and owner of the gastropubs, Father's Office, in Santa Monica and Los Angeles, and Lukshon by Sang Yoon

I grew up on the west side so many of my favorite places are the hiking trails. One I keep returning to is the Los Liones trail in the Pacific Palisades. The views are spectacular. It starts off very narrow, windy and really green and lush. It's almost tropical, like you're walking through a forest. Then it opens up to a really spectacular vista of the ocean. It's a really beautiful top of the world view and literally a couple of minutes from my house. I've lived in lots of different cities around the world, and I don't know any city where you can just, within a couple of minutes, be in a place that doesn't feel like you're in a city at all. It's really nice to have that connection to an urban place where you can look over it and yet live in it at the same time. I like to go late afternoon, as the sun is in its last third of its day. The shadows get a little deeper. The lighting gets a little more dramatic. It's not as hot. The place gets more beautiful as the sun is retreating. You see ocean. What I like about that trail is all the wildlife. I've seen coyotes, lots of deer, lots of snakes, lots of living things that you don't associate to living in the city.

Los Liones Canyon, Topanga Canyon State Park, West Sunset Boulevard and Los Liones Drive, Los Angeles; (310) 455-2465; www.parks.ca.gov

....

William Brien, MD, mayor of Beverly Hills

The Beverly Gardens Park spans from Santa Monica and Doheny to Wilshire and Santa Monica. It actually goes a little bit around the corner up towards Whittier and Wilshire, but it's bordered on each side by two beautiful old fountains. The park was built back in the 20s. It's a beautiful walking park with mature trees. It has the wonderful history of the Electric Fountain, which is at Wilshire and Santa Monica. It used to have eighty different types of water displays coming out of it.

Also, in the park is the famous Beverly Hills sign that was just put back up by Beverly Hills Rotary that matched the original sign. But the reason that I love that park is that it takes me back to my childhood days when there used to be a lily pond in front of the Beverly Hills sign.

I used to hang out there as a kid. I even tried to catch some fish there and never was successful. Back then, there was a beautiful cactus park. And there still is a cactus park, although it's not as beautiful. But the reason why I love it is that we're now in the process of working to completely redo our parks, like the Beverly Gardens Park.

And we are going to bring back the lily pond. We're going to restore the cactus park. We're bringing back incredibly lush and colorful cacti beds like we used to have. And we're going to redo the fountains and bring back the eighty different water elements on the Electric Fountain and put some tender loving care on the fountain on the east side at Doheny. And we're going to redo all the parks in between. And the beauty of it is that it's a restorative process so it's not changing the parks or the character. It's just restoring them to the way they were in the 20s.

The lily pond was something that was unbelievable. You had a beautify lily pond with lily pads, fish, frogs. It was just a really fun place to just go hang out as a kid with my family and my brother and sister. We used to go in the cactus park on most weekends and there were places where you could walk through the cactus garden, where you could crawl under some cacti. My sister once came up a little early and got a back full of cactus. But my brother and I didn't think that was bad.

This is where we used to play football—just pickup games with friends in the park during the day and during the weekends. As I got older and I'd walk and jog through the park, it was just always a tranquil peaceful place in the middle of a busy urban city. And it's just a wonderfully beautiful place to go into your thoughts.

One of the things that we've worked really hard on is not only restoring the parks, but creating a cultural heritage commission. We can landmark buildings in the city that retain grand old architecture that were at risk and on the verge of being lost. People don't realize that we actually want to preserve the beauty of the past.

In fact, I am the mayor who had the first landmark building occur in the last month, the Beverly Hills Hotel. It was the first major structure. It is now one hundred years old. It was actually built before the incorporation of the city. It's a spectacular building that needs to be preserved architecturally.

And we're about to landmark some of our buildings that are already on the National Historic Landmark so we're preserving our wonderful history. Our post office building right across the street from the Beverly Gardens Park is a historic building. It's on the national registry. It's going to be put on the local registry very soon. That's being restored for our new cultural center with the Wallis Annenberg Cultural Center. We're going to be landmarking the Saban Theater, which is in the southeast part of Beverly Hills.

My grandfather [Earl Warren] was a three-term governor of California and then became Chief Justice of the United States. He lived in the north and then he went to Washington, DC after that. So he has some fond memories of visiting us down in Southern California. Back in those days, you could go to the pharmacy and if you didn't have enough money to buy a hot dog, they'd say, "Just pay me next time."

But Beverly Hills remains a wonderful community with incredible schools, police and fire departments. Some of my friends have been saved by the fire department and paramedics. It's interesting. You know it when you grow up enough to leave. But then you realize how great it is when you get to come back.

Beverly Gardens Park, Santa Monica Boulevard and Wilshire Boulevard; www.lovebeverlyhills.com

....

Mia Lehrer, landscape designer and president of Mia Lehrer + Associates, an international landscape architecture firm

What I love about LA is that you could be in the core of the city, kind of in the grit, and you can get away. If I close my eyes, I think of an area within the Ahmanson Ranch which is in the county of Los Angeles within twenty miles of downtown. You go into the mountains and find beautiful soft hills and gigantic oak trees. And I'll walk there with my family and my dogs.

At other times, I walk along the LA River. People ask, is it really a river? I love that juxtaposition between the infrastructure and the concrete and the occasional patch of green and the waterfowl that somehow find a way of enjoying nature in the city.

The majority of the river was channelized. The Corps of Engineers were so excited when they discovered concrete in the 1930s. They were responsible for keeping people safe and built these walls to keep the water out. So it disrupted the natural function of the river. But now there is an effort to make the river function better by allowing more plants and water to flow through in a more natural way. That doesn't mean that you're going to turn it into a natural river.

I particularly love the area by the river which we call Frogtown. The plants have poked through and survived on their own. It's wide enough so you feel a little lost. The concrete is still there. I happen to like the infrastructure aspect of it, but you also see trees and mountains, so you feel pretty sequestered.

Another spot I love is the Huntington Gardens on the estate of Mr. Huntington who was an oil baron. It contains his original house and a few wonderful galleries with very well curated shows.

They also have a few places to actually eat including an old little tea house where afternoon tea is served. It's a great family destination. They also have plant sales and it operates like a botanical garden. They have lots of summer programs with concerts and picnics. If you're a member there's other special events.

I think about the experience of going through the Arroyo Parkway to the Huntington Gardens. Or riding along PCH through Malibu or ending up at the Ahmanson Ranch, experiencing beautiful hillsides with amazing oak trees and having a picnic. Or being by my river with my dogs. Those are all things that I love. I feel connected and disconnected all at once.

Huntington Library, Art Collections, and Botanical Gardens, 1151 Oxford Road, San Marino; (626) 405-2100; http://huntington.org

Los Angeles River, http://lariver.org

. . . .

Selena Gomez, actress, recording artist, and fashion designer

If I have a chill day, I like to go to the beach. It's really nice going there and just a 15-minute drive. So it's pretty easy. I love the noise of the beach, the vibe. I love all of it.

LA EATS

It's funny. I trick myself into thinking that anything
with the word "organic" doesn't have calories.

—Anna Kendrick, Academy Award– and
Tony-nominated actress

Zach Pollack was a twenty-year-old student at Brown University studying art and historic architecture in Florence. It was wintertime and there he was on the Via dell'Ariento, when smack, he ran into his great love. And he hit it hard.

The moment he laid eyes on the breathtaking gastronomic treasures at the San Lorenzo Mercato Centrale, this Jewish boy from Southern California was smitten.

"For a kid who grew up with plastic-wrapped, unrecognizable cuts of meat and Kraft singles, the market was an overload of culinary stimulation," Pollack recalls. Imagine a virtual explosion of local cheeses, dried pasta, spices, truffles, prosciutto, olives, fish—you name it. Each stall contained unique riches to discover.

Pollack liked that in Italy people specialized in their craft. He found the culinary environment utterly riveting. "Modern cooking can be somewhat arbitrary, too often based on the prevailing trends and fads of the day," he explains. "In Italy, cooking is an intuitive exercise and strongly rooted in the economic, geographical, even political context of a particular locale. Take Trapani, for instance. Couscous is one of the city's most popular dishes, not because of some avant garde North African fusion, but because of Sicily's history as a political doormat for Mediterranean civilizations, among them the Arabs. When a people and their food evolve together over hundreds of years, they tend to reflect one another. What's the expression? You are what you eat? That's very true in Italy."

Before the Mercato Centrale encounter, Pollack had barely ever dabbled in his mother's kitchen and was never a professional. He remembers crafting a bizarre concoction—linguine with smoked salmon, asparagus, and lemon cream. "It turned out to be as revolting as it sounds," he recalls. But with the bounty he scored at the market, Pollack got seriously juiced to cook in his little apartment making dishes like pici with wild boar and pork arista from scratch. With each ingredient, Pollack discovered an opportunity to explore how to ultimately make it better. "Take pancetta. If you take the time to source the best possible pork belly and cure and age it yourself, you're going to end up with a final product that is likely much better than whatever pre-made stuff you could otherwise purchase."

Pollack returned home to LA for summer break, hungrier for skills and knowledge. He interned at famed Chef Neal Fraser's Grace and recalls being somewhat clueless. "I wore pajama pants because I thought they looked like cook pants. I had New Balance running shoes instead of clogs," he remembers. "I didn't have any knife skills." But his good attitude and sincere eagerness made up for what he may have lacked. After a summer of straining stocks and peeling carrots, he earned a knife from Fraser and an invite to come back.

When he graduated from Brown, Pollack ultimately returned to Italy to hone his skills on the job rather than go to culinary school. After various stages at Michelin-rated restaurants in Italy including Ristorante Ambasciata and Il Duomo, Steve Samson, whom he met when they were both at Grace, was working at David Myers' Michelin-starred Sona. Samson invited Pollack to come on board as a line cook. When Samson and Myers opened Ortica in Orange County, Pollack followed and became sous-chef.

In 2011, the duo partnered with veteran restaurateur Bill Chait to open Sotto in Beverly Hills. Each ingredient from the house-cured *Mangalitsa guanciale* to the grassy Sicilian olive oil is carefully sourced. The pastas are all housemade. Dishes like cauliflower and almond zuppa offer layer upon layer of complexity. And curiously, even with the creaminess of the soup, it contains no cream or butter.

At Sotto, Neapolitan pizza is cooked in over 900 degree temperatures in an eight-ton artisan wood-burning oven built on site by Neapolitan craftsmen.

"A pizza is more or less 90 percent crust and 10 percent of what's on top," says Pollack. "You can have the greatest ingredients on top, but if the crust is garbage it's not going to be a great pizza." Diners can see most of the action in the open kitchen from one of the bar seats. The pendant lighting, chandeliers, glass, and rough-hewn wood tables add a rustic elegance.

In a short time, people took notice. In 2011, *Esquire* magazine dubbed Sotto one of the Best New Restaurants in America noting, "neither chef is full-blooded Italian-American, and for that they are doubly admirable for getting so close to the heart of southern Italian cooking." And when *Los Angeles* magazine came out with their pick of best new LA restaurants, Sotto was number one.

But Pollack, in his low-key, humble way, feels more comfortable focusing on what led him to the kitchen in the first place. "I still find the craft so exciting," says the chef. "Sourcing the raw ingredients, coordinating a harmony between them and then honing them into something new that is greater than the sum of its parts—that's what's most fulfilling for me."

....

Lucy Liu, Emmy-nominated actress

I love LA because there are so many things that are accessible. You can walk outside your door and go hiking. Or you can take a quick drive and can be skiing. Or take another quick drive and be at the beach. I love a place called Itacho. It's a beautiful Japanese restaurant that serves incredibly healthy, delicious foods. I love all the dishes that they have. It's Japanese tapas so you get to sample everything. Delicious.

Itacho Izakaya and Sushi, 7311 Beverly Boulevard, Los Angeles; (323) 938-9009; www.itachorestaurant.com

....

Eric McCormack, Emmy-winning actor

My favorite family restaurant that we go to every week is Patys. It's where we have our bacon and eggs. It's our place.

Patys, 10001 Riverside Drive, Toluca Lake; (818) 761-0041; http://patysrestaurant.com

. . . .

Tony Danza, Golden Globe– and Emmy-nominated actor and author

There's a place I like called Frankies on Melrose. It's Frankie Competelli's place. He's from the neighborhood on Mulberry Street. And it's good family style Italian cooking. There are a lot of great things Frankie makes. He does a blue claw crabs special with linguinie that is unbelievable. But you have to get ready to be a mess afterward. They have to hose you down after eating it.

Frankies on Melrose, 7228 Melrose Avenue, Los Angeles; (323) 937-2801; www.frankiesonmelrose.com

. . . .

Ken Howard, Tony- and Emmy-winning actor, and President of the Screen Actors Guild

My answer used to be play golf. But I really don't play much golf anymore. I played enough golf for several lifetimes and spent a lot of time at various courses.

My wife is very involved with a group called the Onyx & Breezy Foundation, which is centered back East but is nationwide. The organization helps provide financial assistance for animal rescue and spay and neuter programs. It's a problem across the country, but particularly in Los Angeles because of our sprawling urban area. The number of dogs in pounds getting put down and euthanized because they don't have homes is overwhelming. It's very much my wife's cause and I help her with it when I can.

So my answer now is really very simple stuff. We live north near Magic Mountain, so we drive into town, see a movie, and walk around. There are a few settings that I've always gotten a kick out of and they're mostly out by the water. We enjoy Point Dume, Malibu, the Marina, or the Santa Monica Pier.

And our favorite restaurant is Craig's.

Craig was a maître d' for years at Dan Tana's, and then he started this restaurant. He really knows what he's doing and it's just a wonderful place to hang out. So that's our new favorite hangout and then we may catch a movie or see friends.

The food is just great at Craig's. He knows his stuff. The ambiance is nice. They figured it out so it doesn't get too noisy, and the food's really good. It's comfortable. Very well done.

When I was in LA in the late '70s, the smog was so thick you could see and feel it. You could even feel it in your lungs when you played golf on a course. It was awful. Then they brought in all the emissions rules and it worked remarkably. At the time I thought, *Oh well, another regulation in emission. We'll see how much this does.* You wonder sometimes. But it really made a huge difference. It's amazing how much better it is. Even with all the traffic. We had a meeting at the top of the Sheraton Universal and it was clear as could be. There may still be some pollution, but it's wonderful how much they cleaned it up.

Craig's, an American Restaurant, 8826 Melrose Avenue, West Hollywood; (310) 276-1900; http://craigs.la

....

Jewel, Grammy-nominated songwriter, singer, and musician

I just ate at a great restaurant called Cook's County and it's all farm-to-table food and is really amazing. The radishes with Meyer lemon butter are awesome.

Cooks County Restaurant, 8009 Beverly Boulevard, Los Angeles; (323) 653-8009; www.cookscountyrestaurant.com

....

Kathryn Fiore, actress (*Wedding Band*) and **Gabriel Tigerman,** actor (*Supernatural*)

Gabe was born and raised here and I'm from New York. We went back and forth and sort of tied for his favorite and my favorite. So, we thought we'd tell you about both. The first place is Musso & Frank in Hollywood. It's just one of those great, old Hollywood joints where you can sit around and imagine Katharine Hepburn, Carole Lombard, and Cary Grant sitting around having Rob Roys.

My parents are both actors. My godfather is the film critic, Rex Reed. He and my dad are best friends. So when I was a little girl, one of my earliest memories was being in Los Angeles, sitting in the booth at Musso and Frank, and having seafood chiffonade and shrimp Louie. My dad always ate the seafood chiffonade which has lobster and crab. My uncle Rex would get the shrimp Louie. Somebody would always not have enough dressing and it would be all sorts of going back and forth with the waiters.

My dad's a character actor. He's pretty recognizable. Then pair him with Uncle Rex and they got the best table in the house. Waiters say, "I remember you on the *Mary Tyler Moore Show*, Bill. Rex, I remember your review of some movie from the 70s." It's just pretty funny.

I was raised on all the old movies. I thought that *Some Like It Hot* and *Seven Brides for Seven Brothers* were current movies. I thought Judy Garland was twenty-five. I had no idea about modern movies. It was sort of a weird little childhood. In fact, when I got to nursery school, someone told me that Cary Grant was very old or had passed away. I thought he was like Johnny Depp. I got hysterical and my mom had to pick me up from school. I was so devastated that I wasn't going to end up marrying Cary Grant.

So I remember being at Musso & Frank and hearing my parents talk about being on *The Ed Sullivan Show* and trading all these stories. It just felt very glamorous and cool. Shirley Temples were my signature drink. I didn't know it wasn't a real cocktail. I thought I am drinking too and I am drinking with the best of them. I'm so fancy.

Now it's our tradition that whenever Uncle Rex comes to LA, the whole family goes to Musso and Frank for the seafood chiffonade salad and the shrimp Louie. Now it's great to bring my husband there. It's a nice, Old Hollywood family tradition.
Gabriel Tigerman: And one of the few places where you can still get a Singapore Sling.
Kathryn Fiore: It feels very cool. Like I'm June Allyson and ordering a Manhattan. When I first came here I was so used to getting dressed. We always dressed for Musso and Frank. Our friend Heath Corson and Gabriel and I decided to start a "supper club" where we would get a group of friends together once a month and dress up and have a formal dinner and talk about art and literature. We have fantasies about being part of the Algonquin Round Table and so we thought a supper club would be the closest we would ever get. We hold the supper club at a different restaurant every time but Musso & Frank was the first place we went. We picked it for the Old Hollywood feel. We also appointed another friend, Austin Winsberg, as our "cultural liaison" and so he is in charge of what topics we discuss during dinner. We all wore formal wear.
Gabriel Tigerman: We were dressed to the nines.

Kathryn Fiore: All the boys wore fedoras. People thought we were crazy. Musso & Frank's is a good lunch place too. But I would go around 8:00, sit down, have a cocktail and get some of the sourdough bread. It's great and you wind up eating way too much of it. Just order any of those salads. Actually, there's nothing healthy on the menu. I mean everything is cream on toast with chicken liver on top of bread on top of eggs. And if you go when Bill Fiore and Uncle Rex Reed are there you'll hear a lot of complaining and asking for extra sauce. I look forward to having a kid and having him or her standing in the booth reaching into Uncle Rex's salad and pulling shrimp out the way that I used to.

Gabriel Tigerman: In LA, where everything is new, it's hard to find a place that has such a palpable sense of history. Our other favorite thing has much less historical relevance. It literally is my favorite day of the year and our New Year's Eve tradition.

Kathryn Fiore: This has now become sort of a trend. Our friends are all doing this and stealing our idea.

Gabriel Tigerman: They are, which I'm okay with. I guess. Instead of going anywhere fancy on New Year's Eve, we start our evening very early, usually around 5:00 or 6:00. We have an appetizer New Year's Eve. It's called Appeteaser Fest, which I wasn't going to mention because it sounds even lamer than what it is.

We drive all over LA and pick up all of our favorite appetizers from our favorite restaurants. We assemble them and then come back and lay them out in a massive smorgasbord and have them as our New Year's Eve treat. We really have to coordinate. We go downtown to Yang Chow just to get dumplings.

Kathryn Fiore: Yang Chow downtown has the best dumplings outside of Chinatown in New York.

Gabriel Tigerman: There's a bold statement, but I would back you up. I love Yang Chow dumplings. We go to the Capital Grille to pick up calamari with jalapeño peppers, which is amazing. We'll go to Mozza and grab chicken liver cristini. Spectacular. Then, if we're super classy, we'll go to Wingstop for hot wings and grab some of those. As our New Year's Eve cocktail, we may just go to the supermarket and pick up TGIFriday's mudslides to mix at home. Then we'll bring it all home and lay it out as a smorgasbord.

Kathryn Fiore: This year we're adding one place. There's an LA institution called Zankou Chicken, which is the best rotisserie chicken that you'll ever have. It's

Lebanese food and people go crazy for it here. It's this family-owned place. If you Google it you can actually read about the Zankou Chicken murder, which makes it seem strange.

Gabriel Tigerman: But the chicken is still great.

Kathryn Fiore: The chicken is fantastic. It has this creamy garlic sauce. The grandmother won't tell me what's in it. You get the chicken and you slather the garlic sauce on it and you stick it in a pita with hummus and tzatziki. And you just lose your mind with the deliciousness of it all.

Gabriel Tigerman: Really, throughout the year we'll have our list going of what's going to make the cut for this year's smorgasbord. So, we'll go somewhere and say, "this may be controversial, but I'm thinking about adding this to the list this year. I don't know. What do you think?" Sprinkles Cupcakes . . .

Kathryn Fiore: Oh, Sprinkles Cupcakes are totally on the menu. We've had people call us with suggestions of things we might want to add this year.

Gabriel Tigerman: We've tried them and sometimes we've been disappointed and then they get a call. We plan this out way ahead of time. So, we have to make sure our Netflix movies have arrived so we can have usually a double or triple screening. We give it a theme, whether it's 80s movies or 90s action films was last year. That's really how we welcome the New Year.

Kathryn Fiore: When you think about what young Hollywood is doing . . .

Gabriel Tigerman: We're just down the street from the Sunset Strip where people are having really exciting nights but so are we.

Kathryn Fiore: We have to be home at 8:00. You have to start gathering everything like 5:30.

Gabriel Tigerman: There's a lot of preordering. We strategize. We have the list and the GPS set up on the phone. We're good to go.

Kathryn Fiore: Some people go to the Soho House . . .

Gabriel Tigerman: One year, our neighbor dropped by on his way out to a big New Year's party. He knocked on the door and he looked like James Bond. The perfectly fitted tux. He came to the door to say, "Guys, I just wanted to invite you . . . if you wish." He stopped mid-sentence. He just looked at us. We're in our pajamas, 8:15 at night.

Kathryn Fiore: I'm covered in wing sauce.

Gabriel Tigerman: We looked like the last people you ever wanted to accompany you anywhere important. "We're busy. We've got plans. Thank you, though." It's a little different than classy Hollywood.

Musso and Frank Grill, 6667 Hollywood Boulevard, Los Angeles; (323) 467-7788; www.mussoandfrank.com

Yang Chow, 819 North Broadway, Los Angeles; (213) 625-0811; www.yangchow.com

The Capital Grille, 8614 Beverly Boulevard, Los Angeles; (310) 358-0650; www.thecapitalgrille.com

Pizzeria Mozza, 641 North Highland Avenue, Los Angeles; (323) 297-0101; www.pizzeriamozza.com

Wingstop, 2280 South Figueroa Street, Los Angeles; (213) 745-9464; www.wingstop.com

Zankou Chicken, 1716 South Sepulveda Boulevard, Los Angeles; (310) 444-0550; www.zankouchicken.com

Sprinkles Cupcakes, 9635 South Santa Monica Boulevard, Beverly Hills; (310) 274-8765; www.sprinkles.com

Soho House, 9200 Sunset Boulevard, West Hollywood; (310) 432-9200; www.sohohousewh.com

....

Richard Dreyfuss, Academy Award- and Golden Globe-winning actor

My favorite thing in LA would be to live somewhere in the Mulholland area and never leave my house.

Pink's has the best hot dogs. I like the spicy polish because I'm a spicy Polish. Actually, Pink's, it has been an institution in LA for seventy years. I discovered the place when I was about twelve and now it's more popular than ever. And now, you gotta wait for an hour to get a goddamn hot dog. In the old days you could walk right up.

Pink's Hot Dogs, 709 North La Brea Avenue, Los Angeles; (323) 931-7594; www.pinkshollywood.com

....

Marc Blucas, actor

We're foodies. But depending on what we're in the mood for, there's Baby Blues, which is fantastic. Have you been to that joint? Oh, God. The ribs. Go hungry.

Baby Blues BBQ, 444 Lincoln Boulevard, Venice; (310) 396-7675; www.babybluesvenice.com

....

Anna Kendrick, Academy Award– and Tony-nominated actress

It's funny. I trick myself into thinking that anything with the word "organic" doesn't have calories. But I love everything at M Café. They make all kinds of cookies and pastries. And I also love anything from Real Food Daily. It's another thing that I tell myself has no calories.

M Café, 7119 Melrose Avenue, Hollywood; (323) 525-0588; www.mcafedechaya.com

Real Food Daily (West Hollywood), 414 North La Cienega Boulevard, Los Angeles; (310) 289-9910; www.realfood.com

....

Michael Irby, actor

My wife eats raw vegan and I'm a carnivore. It's hard sometimes because the menu could be so limited for her. There are always seven choices for me. You know how there's always a protein and a couple of sides? She's usually just stuck eating a side everywhere we go.

But True Food on the promenade in Santa Monica hits both our palates. We can eat there and both be satisfied. The food is amazing. And the menu is very expansive. As far as vegetarians and meat eaters go, it's all very thoughtful. The edamame dumplings are off the hook. I think they serve them three to an order so you have to end up getting a couple of orders before the entrees come. They do a little truffle oil with them. Just a little bit, so it hits you in the nose. And we are both foodies so whenever we can eat like this together, it's so much fun.

True Food is all very thoughtful. The chef is thinking about pairings. They have a great wine list. They also do the whole muddling cocktail thing with a mix-ologist. You get to feel like a grown-up. In LA you are in such a hipster scene all of the time. But in Santa Monica it feels that people are over forty. It's just nice to feel like a grown-up. Also, coming from New York, it's nice to be outside, on the patio and in the city while it's all going on around you. The restaurant is in one of the new sections that they built. It's a nice place to go on a little date with your wife if you are into those kind of things.

The other place I love is the absolute polar opposite. My son is nine and I've created a carnivore there. It's our little sneak away place when mom is busy, and it's just the two of us hanging out doing our little Toys R Us run down in the Valley. There's a place called Dr. Hogly Wogly's BBQ in Van Nuys, it's just out on the flat lands of the Valley. And they've got about ten or fifteen tables and have been there for about twenty-five years. Sometimes working on a show, or in movies, catering brings food from there. They catered one of the shows I was working on. And it just became a little regular spot for my son and me to go out and eat without mom knowing.

They've got brisket. They've got hot wings. They've got beautiful beef ribs. Sweet tea. They've got a couple of barbecue sauces: hot and a sweet. It's just an old school throwback. You feel like you can be somewhere else. As soon as you walk inside you think, "Oh yeah, we could be in a little place off the side of the freeway in Texas somewhere." And it's very reasonable. My son says, "Oh Papa, this place is awesome." His palate is not as complex. So when he says something is awesome you think, "Oh, golden. Golden."

We were going to come out here for six months and give a shot. We still had our place up in Harlem before Bill Clinton was up there and before it became what it is now. And we kept our place and we thought we were going to be back in a second and then Susan got pregnant. And then I got a series. And then I got another series. I say, you've got to go where the fish are jumping. If you want to do the salmon run, you go to Alaska. You have to be where the fish are, and that's here. And on the flip side of it, it's 75 degrees and I love gardening. I have a little vegetable garden up on my hill, and I've got fruit trees up there. I couldn't do that in New York.

Here you've got to get the car and drive twenty minutes to go to Koreatown, or Thai Town, or you've got to go to that little spot down in LA that has the African restaurant. But we're ten minutes from the ocean. Also, being here in LA, I get to come home when I finish work, and I get to tuck everybody in. I get to say, "Hey, good morning. I'll see you guys tonight," rather than on the other side of that Skype saying, "Hey guys. I love you. I can't wait to see you."

True Food Kitchen, 395 Santa Monica Place #172, Santa Monica; (310) 593-8300; www.foxrc.com

Dr. Hogly Wogly's Tyler Texas BBQ, 8136 Sepulveda Boulevard, Van Nuys; (818) 782-2480; http://hoglywogly.com

....

Amy Ryan, Academy Award– and Golden Globe–nominated actress

Versailles has the best chicken with rice and beans you'll get. I've been going there for twenty years. It's been there forever and is just good solid home cooking.

Versailles, 1415 South La Cienega Boulevard, Los Angeles; (310) 289-0392; www.versaillescuban.com

....

Adrien Brody, actor

I really like a restaurant called Inaka. It's a macrobiotic little hole in the wall. The fish is so fresh and beautiful and needs no sauce. It's just good fish.

Inaka, 131 South La Brea Avenue, Los Angeles; (323) 936-9353; http://inaka.weebly.com

....

Ruth Vitale, founder and former co-president Paramount Classics, former president, Fine Line, and now CEO, The Film Collective, a consulting and theatrical distribution company

LA is not like New York City where on every corner you can look up and be astounded by cityscape, by the architecture. There is an abundance of beautiful buildings everywhere you look in New York City. But, here? Los Angeles? There is no there there, as Gertrude Stein would say. There is no center and that's what's difficult. In LA, you have to go looking. So when you're a city person and you come here, you lose your moorings.

One of the first times my mom came, we were sitting in the backyard. From my home, I have a lovely 180-degree view of downtown Los Angeles and the valley. I was pruning a rosebush. My mom burst out laughing. She said, "If you had told me that I was going to watch my daughter pruning a rosebush, I would have bet any amount of money that it was fiction." And I replied, "Well, you learn to adapt or you drown."

People say they stay because of the weather. I say, "The weather? Gee, that's fascinating. You get 110-degree weather and it's so dry I can't breathe." I feel like I'm swallowing dirt. I'll take moisture anytime. And there are earthquakes and fires. We're one step short of hell. They say, it never rains. What!? Are they high? When it rains, it is torrential. And it rains January, February, and part of March. AND NEVER STOPS.

People stay because they're in the entertainment business. Don't forget, it's a factory town, not unlike Detroit. Where people are in Detroit because of cars, people are here to be part of that elusive dream of fame, fortune, and creating "art." I use "art" in quotes because a lot of it, obviously, is not.

Don't get me wrong. I get a lot of comedy out of bitching, but there are a lot of lovely moments. And you get what you put in. I eat at a restaurant all the time called Caffe Roma in Beverly Hills. It's owned by a chef named Agostino Sciandri and he has another restaurant called Ago. I've been eating at Ago for fifteen years. It's co-owned by Meir Teper, Bobby De Niro, and others. And then they opened Caffe Roma and a few other places. Every time I go it's, "Hi, Ruth. There's your table. Sit down. We don't have your chocolate cake or we do have your chocolate cake." But that's anywhere where you treat other people as individuals and you establish a rapport. I don't think there's any city in the world that can be unfriendly if you have a desire to connect.

Caffe Roma was owned by someone else for years. It's in this little mall that contained a hair salon and a couple of stores. And before Ago bought it, it was the funniest place and it's still kind of funny. Sly Stallone, Mickey Rourke, Arnold Schwarzenegger frequent it when they are in town. And it looked and still does to some extent like a scene from OTB.

So I used to go to Caffe Roma on occasion if I happened to be in Beverly Hills and I would meet someone there for lunch. But when Ago took it over, I was walking by one day and his son-in-law said, "Ruth, why don't you eat here? You have to come because you always eat at Ago." So I started eating at Caffe Roma because it was a very central place for people to meet. Ago closed Caffe Roma for seven months and refurbished it, and it's beautiful. It has an indoor area where I always sit and there's a patio with umbrellas so you can stay out of the sun. But I stay inside in the corner in the back because it's my Sicilian heritage to always have my back to the wall.

They make a chocolate cake at Ago's. And so after throwing myself on the floor and turning blue for about two months, I showed up one day for lunch and they said, "We have your cake." I said, "How'd you have my cake?" He said, "We sent Salvatore to get it this morning. He went to Ago to get the cake." It's an amazing dark chocolate cake that they warm up for me and put fresh whipped cream on and they do that for me. It's a riot. I don't know why they put up with me, but they do. And, I love them for it!

Caffe Roma, 350 North Canon Drive, Beverly Hills; (310) 274-7834; www.cafferomabeverlyhills.com

....

Michael Shannon, Academy Award–nominated actor

I usually go to Jar for dinner. I like that place. The food is sensational. It's a beautiful room. The bartenders are real nice. I usually sit at the bar and they give me potato chips with horseradish cream sauce that they make. I just sit and eat those and drink red wine and catch up with whoever happens to be working that night.

Jar, 8225 Beverly Boulevard, Los Angeles; (323) 655-6566; www.thejar.com

....

Anthony Mackie, actor

My favorite place in LA is a restaurant called La Louisanne. It's way east, off of Normandie. My uncle used to live off 65th and Normandie, so I would always stay with him when I came to LA. He took me there one Father's Day and after that it became a tradition. So now I take my uncle there every Father's Day when I'm in Los Angeles. They have the best Louisiana-style soul food in all of LA.

La Louisanne Cajun Creole Restaurant, 5812 Overhill Drive, Los Angeles; (323) 293-5073; www.lalouisannela.com

....

Lisa Ling, host of *Our America* with Lisa Ling on OWN: The Oprah Winfrey Network

I like this little tiny place in Studio City called Daichan. It's a home-style Japanese restaurant. They have great fish soup and it's really healthy and very different.

Daichan, 11288 Ventura Boulevard, Studio City; (818) 980-8450

Robert Loggia, Academy Award– and Emmy-nominated actor and **Audrey Loggia,** producer

Robert Loggia: Our favorite restaurants, where we go frequently, are just across the street from each other in Brentwood.

Audrey Loggia: At Palmeri, the chef/owner, Ottavio, is Sicilian, as is Robert, so they are very compatible.

Robert Loggia: The food is really delicious, and always very fresh. The restaurant is very attractive, and always a pleasure to be there.

Audrey Loggia: Palmeri does a wonderful Branzino baked in a salt crust. Delicious! And one of our friends ALWAYS orders their grilled veal chop.

Robert Loggia: The other restaurant we like is Toscana. It has great atmosphere and wonderful food and is usually buzzing with industry people.

Audrey Loggia: It's always a fun place. The wait staff and hosts are always upbeat and gracious. We both love the pasta bolognese at both restaurants. They also both do a dish with grilled Santa Barbara prawns which are fabulous.

Robert Loggia: At Toscana, they also have a fabulous Dover sole, which is usually a special. Generally the meal begins with delicious grilled flatbread with a little olive oil and sprinkled herbs and a basket of crudités. The meal ends with an offering of a wonderful flaky pastry cookie.

Audrey Loggia: Other than that, unless we are in New York, or away on location, Robert spends a lot of time at Bel Air Country Club, trying to get his golf game to behave—a never ending challenge! It's a beautiful golf course, however, and a wonderful club. We've been members for over twenty years.

Palmeri Ristorante, 11650 San Vicente Boulevard, Los Angeles; (310) 442-8446; www.palmeriristorantespa.com

Toscana Restaurant, 11633 San Vicente Boulevard, Los Angeles; (310) 820-2448; www.toscanabrentwood.com

Josh Groban, Grammy-nominated singer, songwriter, musician, and actor

I grew up in Los Angeles. There are some great spots there. And I'm easy. I'm a cheap date. There's a great diner called Swingers that's really good. I've been going there since high school. For me, it's a nostalgia thing. I've been on many a high school awkward first date there. They're open all night. And I'm a late night guy. So generally, dinner for me is around midnight and they've got an excellent turkey burger. Basically, I'll just drive up, sit at the counter, order a milkshake and a turkey burger and it's my happy place.

Swingers Diner, Hollywood Swingers Diner, 8020 Beverly Boulevard, Los Angeles; (323) 653-5858

Santa Monica Swingers Diner, 802 Broadway, Santa Monica; (310) 393-9793; http://swingersdiner.com

....

Anjelica Huston, Academy Award—and Golden Globe— winning and Emmy— nominated actress

My husband brought me to Venice about twenty years ago, and it was still kind of rough. And it's gotten a lot more cultivated since then. But I think there's something about the freedom of expression in Venice. It's a place where the artists always went. It has such a great history in Los Angeles. It has the best beaches. Actually, it's the best kept secret but it has the best beaches in Los Angeles.

And I love Abbot Kinney. I like Gjelina a lot. That's a great restaurant. There's a lot of wonderful places to eat and be in Venice now.

Gjelina, 1429 Abbot Kinney Boulevard, Venice; (310) 450-1429; www.gjelina.com

....

Brooke Lyons, actress

When I moved to Los Angeles, I wanted to know where the center was. I quickly learned that there's no such thing. LA is a labyrinth of many hubs—each, in its unique way, the center of the action. I love getting coffee at Huckleberry in Santa Monica and then strolling down to the beach, looping back up to the Main Street Farmers' Market, and continuing on to Venice to browse the boutiques and galleries on Abbot Kinney before grabbing a mushroom and truffle oil pizza at Gjelina. I love the contrast between the sunny SoCal hues of LA's beach towns and the more muted, urban grays of its downtown area, where you can spend the day with Rauschenberg and Basquiat at MOCA, or admiring Frank Gehry's majestic Walt Disney Concert Hall, or enjoying the ballet at the Dorothy Chandler Pavilion.

Hike up into the hills at the right time of year, and you feel like you're in rural Vermont—that is, until you gaze down toward Vine, where Cactus Taqueria serves the best tacos in the city, or up at the Hollywood sign, which reminds you that this is the fabled land of Hepburn and Tracy and Bogie and Bacall. If you look closely, LA is anything you want it to be. What's more? It allows you to be anyone you want to be. The very fluidity that makes LA tough for some to love is, perhaps, its greatest asset.

Huckleberry Bakery and Cafe, 1014 Wilshire Boulevard, Santa Monica; (310) 451-2311; www.huckleberrycafe.com

Main Street Farmers' Market, www.smgov.net/portals/farmersmarket

Gjelina, 1429 Abbot Kinney Boulevard, Venice; (310) 450-1429; www.gjelina.com

The Museum of Contemporary Art, Los Angeles (MOCA), 250 South Grand Avenue, Los Angeles; (213) 626-6222; www.moca.org

Walt Disney Concert Hall, 111 South Grand Avenue, Los Angeles; www.laphil.com

Dorothy Chandler Pavilion, 135 North Grand Avenue, Los Angeles; www.musiccenter.org

Cactus Taqueria, 950 Vine Street, Los Angeles; (323) 464-5865

. . . .

Gene Simmons, rock bassist and co-founder of KISS, singer-songwriter, producer, entrepreneur, reality show star, and partner, Cool Springs Life and Stronach Group

Los Angeles is glamorous. It's Hollywood. Movie stars. Palm tree–lined streets. And millions of tourists in tour buses going up and down Sunset Boulevard.

It's also the city I discovered in 1979 and then made my home. We were on tour and the first thing that struck me was how the weather was perfect every day. And though it was a city, there were no skyscrapers. I later learned it was because of the possibility of earthquakes.

LA is a peculiar city. Unlike any other city, its main industry is show business itself. And because of that, the paparazzi are constantly on the prowl, looking for the next starlet coming out of a gym looking disheveled.

It also has a glorious history. Former semi-desert conditions that got turned into orange-bearing farms and then when the first generation of East Coast Jewish fur manufacturers, and nickelodeon owners—all had the same vision—moved to

Los Angeles, and the movie industry was born. Samuel Goldwyn (Sam Goldfish), Fox, the Warner Brothers, Carl Laemmle, and many others, created a city whose main purpose was to make movies. Unique. Unlike any other city in the world.

I was born in New York. Moved to Los Angeles. And I live here with my family. We film our reality show here. KISS is based here.

The Polo Lounge at the Beverly Hills Hotel, on Sunset Boulevard, has been my favorite breakfast location for thirty-five years. It has the best corned beef hash and waffles anywhere. But it's also the location of the "power brunch."

The who's who of the entertainment world eat there and make deals there and want to be seen there. And which table you get determines how high up on the pecking order you are.

In the old days, bellboys (young men, in semi-military-looking outfits), would walk through the Polo Lounge, ring a bell, and call out a producer's name or a star's name and loudly proclaim "Mr. Goldwyn, you have a phone call."

The industry elite would arrange to get phone calls there to announce to the assembled that they were in attendance. And while cell phones have taken over, and the bellboys no longer wander through the hotel, nothing much has changed.

Everyone wants to be seen. And everyone else wants to look to see who's there.

And I play the game, just like everyone else does. And the food is great. And you get treated like a VIP. And the Polo Lounge has a glamorous past. I actually lived at the hotel bungalows for a while. And every day, I would wander into the Polo Lounge, eat a great breakfast, and bask in the unique environment that is the Beverly Hills Hotel. Now celebrating its one hundredth year!

In fact, I just got hungry.

I'm getting up right now and heading over to the Polo Lounge.

The Polo Lounge, 9641 Sunset Boulevard, Beverly Hills; (310) 276-2251; www.beverlyhillshotel.com/the-polo-lounge

....

Jenny Wade, actress (*Wedding Band*)

El Conquistador is a Mexican restaurant in the heart of Silver Lake. It's just your typical Mexican fare but there's something about the energy of the place that I really like. It's decorated so gaudily that you might walk in and think, this is not going to be a tasty experience.

But when you arrive, you feel like you're walking into a party. Everyone who's working there seems to be genuinely happy. The margaritas in giant fishbowl glasses are pretty phenomenal. They're something like six dollars. There has to be three shots of tequila in each of those. One will knock you off your chair. Plan to sit and have your meal for at least a couple hours.

The restaurant is not too busy or too loud so it's a good place to go with one other person. But it's also fun to go with a whole party of people and make it loud. They play mariachi music. They barely speak English but the smiles are just ear to ear.

El Conquistador Mexican Restaurant, 3701 West Sunset Boulevard, Los Angeles; (323) 666-5136; www .elconquistadorrestaurant.com

....

Candy Spelling, author and producer

I love Madeo. They're always packed but the food is superb. As you can tell, I'm not one of these skinny minis. I like food. And I love their capellini arrabiata. Or if I'm really splurging, I love, love, love the veal milanese. They take a big veal chop and pound it down, bread and fry it in butter, and it's really good.

I was born in LA and I'm second generation. More and more, we're getting culture. We're a young town compared to New York. But our downtown, like LA Live, is becoming major. You can walk around the downtown area and there are great hotels and restaurants all close to the Staples Center.

Madeo Restaurant, 8897 Beverly Boulevard, West Hollywood; (310) 859-0242

....

Jennifer Morrison, actress

I love Madeo and I love Sushi Park. Whenever I'm in LA I have to go to both of those places. The food is just amazing, I mean, just amazing.

Madeo Restaurant, 8897 Beverly Boulevard, West Hollywood; (310) 859-0242

Sushi Park, 8539 West Sunset Boulevard, West Hollywood; (310) 652-0523

Meiko, singer/songwriter

I moved to L.A. from a tiny town called Roberta, Georgia when I was nineteen. I came here with my sister who was chasing a boy. I wanted an adventure, so I seized the opportunity to be the third wheel.

Growing up in a small town, you pretty much know who you're gonna see and what you're gonna do every day. Los Angeles makes me feel like anything's possible. I like not knowing what's around the corner, whether it's an adorable old Mexican lady selling tamales, or Justin Bieber driving by in that chrome car that could feed a small country for years.

I love it here. It excites me. And people who live here and complain about it drive me nuts! I'm like, "Go somewhere else then! More space on the 101 for the rest of us!" Also, I love sushi and LA has some of the best sushi spots. My favorites are: Chiba, Sugarfish, and Sushi Park.

Chiba Japanese Restaurant, 11713 Saticoy Street, North Hollywood; (818) 765-9119

Sugarfish by Sushi Nozawa, 11640 San Vicente Boulevard, Los Angeles; (310) 820-4477; www.sugarfishsushi.com

Sushi Park, 8539 West Sunset Boulevard, West Hollywood; (310) 652-0523

Scott Conant, chef, restaurateur, and owner of Scarpetta restaurants in Beverly Hills, New York, Miami, Toronto, and Las Vegas, and a guest judge on Food Network's *Chopped*

If you don't know what great sushi is, it's hard to explain until you have it. A great sushi chef holds the fish at reverence. And there's the quality of the product.

And Sushi Park is a great place that I go to often. I believe that it's owned by a Korean family trained in traditional sushi making. It's exactly what you're looking for and really spectacular. You don't need to add any sauce. The chef will normally take care of that for you at good sushi spots. It's not that it's cheap but it's not as expensive as Urasawa, which is really great but very expensive. Urasawa is probably one of the top three or four sushi places or Japanese restaurants in the country. So if you don't feel like dropping $2500 on dinner, Sushi Park is a great option.

It's always been a dream of mine to have restaurants in New York and Los Angeles. One of these days, I'd love to do another restaurant in LA. Living a bi-coastal life, back and forth between New York and Los Angeles is great. I always say I'm not so easygoing that I can live in LA full time. I need that New York edge.

A fun day is to walk up and down Abbot Kinney on a Saturday or Sunday, and stop at the different food trucks. There's so many food trucks on Abbot Kinney that you just walk up and down the street all day and stop in the different shops and grab something to eat or not. And it's Venice so there are always people watching.

The quality of the produce itself is really the big differentiator in LA and California in general. The quality of the product is spectacular. Certain produce from various farms is really great stuff. And there's something about being so close to Santa Barbara that you get the Santa Barbara spot prawns they're still alive, which is amazing.

The great part about dining in LA is that you can pull up to a random strip mall and you have a place like Sushi Park, which is a perfect example. Here's a great restaurant serving food with amazing integrity. Whether it be Sushi Park or another random restaurant that you'll find inside a strip mall. That doesn't happen to the extent anywhere that it happens in LA. What other city can you think of that has great restaurants in a strip mall?

It's one thing to say, okay, there are great restaurants in LA. Of course, there's Providence, what the guys at Animal are doing, Bouchon, and anything Wolfgang Puck. However, when you pull up to a strip mall and you have a bunch of Mexican guys making some of the best tacos and great Mexican food, and it's the best you've ever had in your life, at a strip mall, that's unexpected. That's the beauty of LA.

Sushi Park, 8539 Sunset Boulevard, West Hollywood; (310) 652-0523

. . . .

Wilmer Valderrama, actor

I'm South American, Venezuelan-Colombian, and I was born in Miami and raised in Venezuela. So being in LA, I love the Mexican culture and I love my Mexican friends, but I also miss my tropical rhythms and my tropical foods. El Floridita is a Cuban restaurant with a live salsa band. They have a great dish that we call *ropa vieja*, which is a combination of shredded beef and rice and beans and sweet plantains and yucca. So this is the only place where I can actually come in and fulfill some of that South American stuff. This is closest to Venezuela and Colombia as it can be. This little spot is the one place that kind of brings it back to me.

El Floridita Cuban Restaurant, 1253 Vine Street, Los Angeles; (323) 871-8612; www.elfloridita.com

....

Carrie Brownstein, actress and *Portlandia* co-creator and co-writer, and musician, vocalist, and member of the band, Wild Flag

I like a restaurant called Forage. This sounds ridiculous, but Forage is definitely in the Portland spirit. I'm one of those classic people who travels to different places and wants to re-create my home. Forage is in Silver Lake. It's the notion of every-thing we need is here in our community. So it's really fresh vegetables and food that's been gathered. But I have always wondered, are people collecting stuff from their backyard? It's actually the kind of place that makes me completely skeptical and sketched out and is sort of funny. But then I go and the food is really delicious. They change the menu, but usually I get fresh fish and a side of brussels sprouts or goat cheese salad.

Forage Restaurant, 3823 West Sunset Boulevard, Los Angeles; (323) 663-6885; www.foragela.com

....

Patrick J. Adams, actor

Silver Lake is a great neighborhood. You've got trees, families, and dogs. It's not the sprawl. Forage there is one of my favorite spots. They serve all locally grown produce and make really fresh delicious food that is locally sourced. I also like Little Dom's in Silver Lake, which has beautiful Italian food.

And I have a dog so we love hiking Griffith Park. You get to see all of LA from the valley to downtown to all of Silver Lake. You see the whole expanse.

Forage Restaurant, 3823 West Sunset Boulevard, Los Angeles; (323) 663-6885; www.foragela.com

Little Dom's, 2128 Hillhurst Avenue, Los Angeles; (323) 661-0055; www.littledoms.com

Bow Wow, rapper and actor

Bea Bea's is a breakfast spot in Burbank and they have the best pancakes in the world. I never had anything like them in my life. What makes them so good? That's a question for Bea Bea. She owns it. I ask her all the time what she puts in those pancakes but she won't even tell me.

Bea Bea's, 353 North Pass Avenue, Burbank; (818) 846-2327

Zach Pollack, chef/co-owner, Sotto Restaurant

It's a pity LA is sometimes (mis)labeled superficial or unsophisticated. There might be a small subculture here that warrants those harsh words (i.e., LA as portrayed in *Night at the Roxbury*), but it hardly represents the city as a whole. A more realistic picture of Los Angeles is the one that millions of immigrants from around the globe call home. It's not only the most human face of the city, it's also the most delicious.

New York has the upper hand when it comes to high-end dining, and San Francisco wins for rustic casual, but nowhere can compete with the spectrum and quality of ethnic food in Los Angeles. Thai, Chinese, Russian, Korean, Vietnamese, Japanese, Mexican, Armenian, Ethiopian . . . and so on. The multitude of ethnic eateries can be daunting, but there are three that I return to time after time.

The first is El Chato, a taco truck that occupies the corner of La Brea and Olympic by night. There's always a line, a fact I find more encouraging than deterring. Their burritos and quesadillas are great, but I go for the lengua tacos. I'll throw on a few habañero-pickled onions and tomatillo salsa and suddenly God looks like the woman inside slapping fresh tortillas on the plancha.

My other standby is Jitlada, a family-run restaurant in Thai Town, which, I've heard, boasts the largest Thai population outside of Thailand. Their acacia leaf omelet is a triumph of sweet, sour, salty, and spicy, and their southern Thai fish curries will bring tears to your eyes, first because they're incendiary and then because they are impossibly delicious.

But my number one ethnic food—if not my favorite cuisine altogether—is Japanese, and one of the best places to go for it is Torrance. The whole area is a mecca for authentic Japanese dining, but Torihei stands out as a favorite. I love their *odens* (dashi-based soups), but their *yakitori* is the real draw. Every part of the chicken, from wing to rump, is expertly prepared over white-hot binchotan charcoal. Throw in a pitcher of cold beer and a remarkably affordable tab, and the schlep down there on the sluggish 405 seems a small price to pay.

El Chato (Taco Truck), On southwest corner of Olympic and La Brea, Los Angeles; www.facebook.com/ElChato TacoTruck

Jitlada, 5233 West Sunset Boulevard, Los Angeles; (323) 663-3104; www.jitladala.com

Torihei, 1757 West Carson Street, Torrance; (310) 781-9407; www.torihei-usa.com

. . . .

Colin Egglesfield, actor

My favorite restaurant is called Gjelina. They have an amazing butterscotch salted caramel dessert that is to die for. It's amazing. In Los Angeles, I love that you can be in so close to the ocean. I love to run and mountain bike. I love the space. I love that my closet in my LA apartment is as big as my apartment in New York.

Gjelina, 1429 Abbot Kinney Boulevard, Venice; (310) 450-1429; www.gjelina.com

. . . .

Claude Kelly, Grammy-nominated songwriter and singer

I really love to visit LA and take in the air, the scenery, and get back to a good workout like climbing a mountain. For me it's spiritual. It's mental. So when I arrive, the first thing I do is wake up the next morning and go hiking.

I'm a studio rat. So I spend most of my time at the studio. But they have amazing food in LA. It's not super fancy, but my favorite restaurant is Hugo's. I'm a vegan, so it's the one restaurant that has amazing food for me and amazing food for the non-vegan. I can have meetings there. I can get two or three of my friends to meet there. It is yummy, home-style cooking and really healthy and organic.

Hugo's, 8401 Santa Monica Boulevard, Los Angeles; (323) 654-3993; http://hugosrestaurant.com

....

Michael Feinstein, Emmy- and Grammy-nominated entertainer and author

I have had a house in Los Angeles since 1977 and lived there since 1976.

There is a place called Flore in Sunset Junction that's fantastic and has a great vegan Reuben. And I believe it would go up against any real Reuben.

Being a collector of vinyl, I still love to go to Ameoba Records on Sunset, which is one of the places where you can actually find not only vinyl, but 78s and amazing treasures. So that is one of my fun pursuits as well.

As much as I love New York, I don't think I could live there full time. Also, I also have a house in Indiana because I'm an artistic director of a performing art center there [the Center for the Performing Arts] so I spend a lot of time in Indiana. But the thing about Los Angeles is that that's where my career started. It is where I met Ira Gershwin and Liza Minnelli and so many people who put me on the map. And I still have a lot of special friends there.

The day that I met Ira Gershwin changed my life. I never went to college, and I was self-educated musically. I worked for him for six years and he introduced me to all of his contemporaries. My association with him made it possible for me to have the career that I have. And it continues because I wrote a book on the Gershwins, the *Gershwins and Me.* The book is a chronicle of their lives and that period.

When I first met the Gershwins, I had just moved from Columbus, Ohio to LA. I had met a lady named June Levant who was the widow of a concert pianist named Oscar Levant who was a great interpreter of Gershwin music. We met through a series of coincidences. She invited me over to her house and one day she called me and said, "I just had lunch with Mrs. Gershwin and she wants to meet you."

A week later I was sitting in the Gershwins' living room and they asked me to start working for them to catalog their memorabilia. That was the life changing moment. It all happened through a series of coincidences that in retrospect appear to be absolutely as they were supposed to happen.

June Levant probably told Mrs. Gershwin that I was this twenty-year-old kid who knew so much about their work. I remember when Lee Gershwin called me she said, "June Levant says you're a treasure." I knew everything about their music and their work. So it was pretty amazing because I was unusual. I was a twenty-year-old kid. I had no friends. I was so focused on this music that it was as if I was subconsciously preparing for that experience. So it was a wonderful gift that June Levant gave to me.

To me, LA still has the real magic of show business. Also I tend to look at things through the past. I tend to look at Los Angeles as it used to be. Here's the apartment building that belonged to Ramon Navarro or here's Walt Disney's house. My neighborhood, Los Feliz, was the first movie star colony. My house is the former Russian consulate and Khrushchev slept there in the 50's. I love all the memories.

Flore Vegan, 3818 West Sunset Boulevard, Los Angeles; (323) 953-0611; florevegan.com

Amoeba Music, 6400 Sunset Boulevard, Los Angeles; (323) 245-6400; www.amoeba.com

....

David Alan Basche, actor, and Alysia Reiner, actor

David Alan Basche: I was shooting *The Exes* for TVLand in LA all summer and Michael Voltaggio did a cameo on our show as a celebrity chef. He said, "hey, come to Ink."

Alysia Reiner: It was the same episode that I actually did the cameo on David's show.

David Alan Basche: I think Michael might have had a little crush on my wife. He said, "hey, Alysia, come to Ink. and bring that guy . . . I guess." But really, we had one of the best dinners we ever had in LA.

Alysia Reiner: His food is amazing. If you haven't been there—

David Alan Basche: If you haven't been to Ink. on Melrose, go. What do they call it? The new gastronomy. It's so wildly inventive, yet the flavors are intense and pure. They're all new. He takes foods and just stands them on their head. You experience flavors with a little liquid nitrogen, a little puree, a little essence, a little foam. He's a culinary wizard.

Alysia Reiner: There should be a new word for the food creativity that Michael Voltaggio creates.

Ink., 8360 Melrose Avenue, Los Angeles; (323) 651-5866; http://mvink.com

Bonnie Raitt, Grammy-winning artist, guitarist, singer, songwriter, and activist who often partners with the Guacamole Fund

I like to eat really healthy, so the Sun Cafe is a great, great place. It's nice to find a health food restaurant that actually knows how to make stuff taste killer. They have really interesting sauces—without dairy, without cheese—that are just super healthy. And they have kale salads and vegan pizzas. Somebody just took me there because they said, "will you taste this?" I went back four days in a row.

I'm from LA, second generation on both sides. The traffic is nightmarish now. That's what happens when everybody wants to live there. But I love the diversity of it. I love the history. I love the fact that a half hour away you can be in the snow, at the beach. I love how spread out it is. There's a lot of great things about LA.

When you're an Angeleno you know how to get around the little back sides and find the little historic sections—the El Salvadorian parts of town, Koreatown, I love all that ethnicity of it. And I like the weather. I like to get outside in the day. I really appreciate being able to be outside every day and so close to the water and mountains.

You know one of the things that I love about LA—and he's just retiring—is Huell Howser and his show, *California's Gold*. It's one of the greatest TV shows and has been on for twenty-five years. You learn all this wonderful stuff about California not just LA. It made me appreciate my town so much more.

Sun Cafe, 3711 Cahuenga Boulevard, Studio City; (818) 308-7420; www.suncafe.com

Paige Morrow Kimball, filmmaker and actress

I love taking my two daughters ages six and nine to Zelda's Corner in Venice Beach, just off the boardwalk. It's a family owned take-out sandwich shop. They have the most delicious and fairly priced sandwiches, and they make mini-doughnuts fresh and in front of your eyes with an old-fashioned doughnut machine that my kids are fascinated by. (If you're too little to press your nose against the glass to see the doughnuts being made, they have a little foot stool under the counter, that you pull out, perfect for the vertically challenged/little munchkins!) They douse the doughnuts in cinnamon sugar, hand them to you in a white paper bag, and they're warm when you eat them. Pure heaven. We order three dozen at a time—sounds like a lot, but trust me, none go to waste! Then we wander down the eclectic Venice boardwalk a bit to one of our favorite little playgrounds where we enjoy our picnic feast (the sandwiches are the dessert), and watch the kids play with the shimmering ocean in the background.

Zelda's Corner Deli, 9 Westminster Avenue, Venice; (310) 314-6458; http://zeldascorner.com

....

Jonathan Cheban, TV personality on E!'s *Keeping Up with the Kardashians,* creator of JetSet Jewelry, and owner of Sushi Mikasa in Miami

I'll tell you all my places. The first thing that I do when I get to LA is get a chicken sandwich at Il Tramezzino in Beverly Hills. I don't even eat sandwiches, I actually hate sandwiches, and somebody talked me into trying this, and there's probably nothing better in the world than this sandwich. It's chicken with some special green sauce with cheese, and it's panini-style. I know it sounds generic and I'm so nongeneric, so you have to believe me how amazing this sandwich is. You dream about it for three days after. Oh, you have no idea. I mean, if you go there, I promise you, it's definitely a must.

For breakfast, I eat the matzo brei with strawberry jam on the side at Nate 'n Al. They call it the Larry King. Basically I go just to see Angela, the hostess, because she starts screaming when I walk in. Stop the presses. She's so funny and cute. People should go see Angela, she's a legend, literally. The waitresses have been there for so long—like thirty years, so they know everyone in town. They get invited to movie premieres, and they're just amazing. There's Gloria, Darlene, I know them all by name. And some have tags that say, they've been there since 1977, it's insane. They don't leave.

For lunch I often go to La Scala. Everyone goes there really for the chopped salad, that's their specialty, but they have probably the best bolognese in the entire country. You know, I'm a foodie. This is a mix between the pink sauce and the regular meat sauce, but it's literally one of the best things in the entire world.

When you're starving, you have to get fast food. I'll probably get killed for saying this, but I don't love In-N-Out. I go to Astro Burger, which has amazing crispy fries and the meat and bun are so great. I know everybody's obsessed with In-N-Out, but the fries are too soft and not crispy, so I go to Astro Burger late at night.

For dinner, one of my favorite spots is e.baldi in Beverly Hills. It's unreal. Sometimes, if you're lucky, they have wild strawberries for dessert and basically you can't get them anywhere in the country.

And the best, best, best shake—post workout, pre workout, during workout—is from BodyFactory and called the PB&V green. It's a meal in itself. I know Kim [Kardashian] loves it, too, I got everybody addicted. Actually Simon [Huck] got me into it. So I usually, when I work out, or I'm filming the show, I go there at 7:00 a.m. and get millions of parking tickets because I don't care. You start to go crazy if you need it. You crave it, so when you run to get it, it's, like, oh thank you. Oh yeah, that's definitely the best shake in LA for sure.

Il Tramezzino, 454 North Canon Drive, Beverly Hills; (310) 273-0501; www.iltram.net

Nate 'n Al, 414 North Beverly Drive, Beverly Hills; (310) 274-0101; www.natenal.com

La Scala, 434 North Canon Drive, Beverly Hills; (310) 275-0579; www.lascalabeverlyhills.com

Astro Burger, 5601 Melrose Avenue, Hollywood; (323) 469-1924; www.astroburger.com

e.baldi, 375 North Canon Drive, Beverly Hills; (310) 248-2633; www.ebaldi.com

BodyFactory, 6366 West Sunset Boulevard, Hollywood; (323) 469-2639; www.bodyfactory.com

. . . .

Jerry Springer, host of *The Jerry Springer Show*

I grew up in New York and I love delicatessens so I like Nate 'n Al's. They do a great bagel, cream cheese and lox.

Nate 'n Al, 414 North Beverly Drive, Beverly Hills; (310) 274-0101; www.natenal.com

....

Ken Paves, celebrity hairstylist and owner of Ken Paves Salons in Beverly Hills and Michigan

My favorite restaurant is an old, old, old Hollywood restaurant called La Scala in Beverly Hills. It's been around forever, since the 40s. Every time I go there, I get the same dish from 1956, spaghetti bolognese. It hasn't been overdone. There aren't too many bells and whistles in it. These days, every dish is so let's add this, let's add some nuts, let's add some of that. This is really just straight up spaghetti bolognese and it's insane. It's so good. I lick the bowl.

And the thing I love about Los Angeles is that it's cosmopolitan enough. But I actually live above a park called The Tree People, It's kind of living in the woods. So, I have the best of both worlds.

La Scala Beverly Hills, 434 N Canon Drive, Beverly Hills; (310) 275-0579; www.lascalabeverlyhills.com

....

Robert Wuhl, actor, comedian, and Emmy-winning writer

The Apple Pan is a West LA institution for hamburgers. It's been there since 1947 and is a little, retro art deco place. However, as good as the burgers are, they have the best egg salads. People in the know talk about the egg salad sandwich there. It is just dynamite.

There's nothing more subjective and personal than egg salad. There's no celery. It's purist. It's just a great and pure egg salad sandwich. Actually I've probably been going there about twenty-five years. But I always went for the burgers. Just in the last five or six years somebody turned me on to the egg salad sandwich and they were 100 percent right. I haven't had a burger there in years. They also have a great tuna salad

Langer's Deli is as good a pastrami sandwich as there is in America. It rivals anything in New York. Their pastrami sandwich can hold its own to Katz's, to the Carnegie Deli. It can hold its own against anybody.

They have the best rye bread you've ever tasted. That's first and foremost. The only thing that's different is that the water is not the same in New York. Larry King and I went recently. To Larry's credit he only nibbled because of his heart condition but I ate too much so I'll probably have a heart condition. I'd heard of all the hype and I didn't actually witness it myself until the last two years. But now I'm a total convert.

I love Osteria Mozza, Nancy Silverton's place. Interestingly enough, as good as the Italian food is there, and it's spectacular, for my money they've got the best steak in town. The *bistecca* is unbelievable. Ron Shelton, a writer/director friend of mine who did *Bull Durham,* and I go out for steaks every year. We usually go to Mastro's or the Pacific Dining Car. I said, "No, Ron, the best steak is at Osteria Mozza." And we went and he agreed with me.

Langer's Delicatessen-Restaurant, 704 South Alvarado Street, Los Angeles; (213) 483-8050; www.langersdeli.com

The Apple Pan, 10801 West Pico Boulevard, Los Angeles; (310) 475-3585

Osteria Mozza, 6602 Melrose Avenue, Hollywood; (323) 297-0100; www.osteriamozza.com

....

Doris Roberts, Emmy-winning actress

I like a little Italian place, Osteria Mamma. It's so loud, but you really get home cooking. It's like you're going to your aunt for dinner. It's terrific.

Osteria Mamma, 5732 Melrose Avenue, Hollywood, (323) 284-7060; www.osteriamamma.com

....

Constance Zimmer, actress

Having grown up in California, I find myself drawn to places that don't feel like California or LA, for the most part. So when we stumbled upon Trails Cafe in Griffith Park five years ago, it was like finding that great hidden cafe on a road trip. Picture a small menu, quality food, great outdoor dining in the middle of the woods (or so it seems until you see someone you recognize). It's great anytime of the year, but it's hard feeling the need to tell people about it. We wanted it all to ourselves. But in LA, it's hard to keep a great thing secret.

The Trails Cafe, 2333 Fern Dell Drive, Los Angeles; (323) 871-2102; www.thetrailslosfeliz.com

....

Denis O'Hare, Tony-winning and Emmy-nominated actor

I love M Café de Chaya, a little vegan restaurant on Melrose. They have really cool food like this amazing kale peanut salad. I love Silver Lake in general because it's so great. And I like a cafe called Café Tropical which is way out on Sunset. It's truly funky. It's truly, truly, truly funky. If you don't have a tattoo, you can't get in. I don't have a tattoo, but they let me in anyway. And it's truly funky in a way that only LA can do.

M Café de Chaya, 7119 Melrose Avenue, Los Angeles; (323) 525-0588; www.mcafedechaya.com

Café Tropical, 2900 W Sunset Boulevard, Los Angeles; (323) 661-8391; www.cafetropicalla.com

....

Ana Martinez, producer, the Hollywood Walk of Fame (aka "Star Girl")

We like to say that the star on the Walk of Fame is the only award that a celebrity can share with fans. The Oscar, Emmy, and Grammy go home with the celebrity. But the star stays. You can sit next to it. You can clean it up. Fans do that. You can go to the ceremony and actually see the person receive the star, which is free and open to the public. Or you can walk along the 2.5-mile boulevard and take photos of your favorite star.

My other favorite place is the Hollywood Roosevelt Hotel. Our offices are right next door. My boss, the late Johnny Grant, who was the chairman of the Walk of Fame and the mayor of Hollywood, lived in the penthouse at the Roosevelt. I worked with him for twenty years. We would eat together at the restaurant there every day and I'd hear the best stories about Hollywood. He knew everything and everybody.

When we first started, the restaurant was called Teddy's, after Theodore Roosevelt. In fact, the hotel is named after him. They closed the restaurant for a while, so we would go to the pool and have lunch instead. Johnny liked that because he could see who he called the "chicky poos."

Then they opened up a burger joint in the front of the Roosevelt called 25 Degrees, which has gorgeous burgers. They're delicious. There's also Public Kitchen, which looks like a British pub. They have an amazing healthy kale salad with pine nuts and breadcrumbs. They also serve all kinds of wonderful cheese. My daughter is a connoisseur of the cheese platter and learned about cheese from the restaurant.

The Hollywood Roosevelt Hotel is a beautiful place. The architecture is amazing. They remodeled it a couple times. It's the very first home of the Oscars. The awards were first held there in the 1920s in the Blossom Room.

At one point, the Chamber moved from Sunset Boulevard to the Hollywood Roosevelt Hotel in the cabanas by the pool. As grand as that may sound, that was when the hotel needed some repair. The offices were actual cabanas that were turned into temporary offices until the Chamber moved into its offices, a former Arthur Murray Dance Studio, adjacent to the hotel.

I've been to many parties at the Roosevelt for Walk of Famers and other events. Sometimes, I think if only these walls could talk about this beautiful place. Johnny's penthouse was way at the top. He had a 360 view of all of downtown LA. Marilyn Monroe often stayed at the hotel and Johnny said she would come up and visit him.

The Walk of Fame first began fifty-one years ago, but they didn't have ceremonies until the late 70s. People don't realize that there is a process to get a star. They think we just hand them out. I wish we could. We just don't say, "hey let's give one to _____ she deserves it." Basically it's a nomination process that is listed at walkoffame.com.

We accept applications from April through May 31 for the following year. And once a year in June, a committee meets. The criterion is longevity in the field of entertainment and there are five categories: recording, radio, TV, motion pictures, and live performance. And we request that people list awards and philanthropic work.

Also, the person receiving a star has to sign off on it. Anybody, including a fan, can nominate a celebrity. But the celebrity has to consent in writing. We average about twenty a year. We actually have a backlog of about forty selected people who haven't set a date yet. People have five years from selection date to get their star. We're now doing Neil Diamond and we've been waiting since 1992. We had to reinstate his star, because it expired.

Al Pacino and Denzel Washington haven't set a date. There are quite a few who just haven't had the availability. My main goal is to have Clint Eastwood get his star, but he's never done it. I've got one spot in front of the Chinese Theater and I'm saving it for him.

Hollywood Roosevelt Hotel, 7000 Hollywood Boulevard, Los Angeles; (323) 466-7000; www.thompsonhotels.com/hotels/la/hollywood-roosevelt

....

Loris Kramer Lunsford, producer

My favorite restaurant is Lucques. The food, the ambiance, the people that work there, everything about it is wonderful. The chef, Suzanne Goin, is a top chef. It's an understated, beautiful place, but it's not over the top. They change the menu seasonally, but one of their signature items is the short ribs, which are incredible. I've never had a bad meal there, ever.

I also go to the Geffen Playhouse. They consistently have great shows year after year. And the theater itself is really nice. It's right in Westwood so it's really convenient.

Lucques, 8474 Melrose Avenue, West Los Angeles; (323) 655-6277; www.lucques.com

....

Jeffrey Dean Morgan, actor

Village Gourmet is a little store that makes sandwiches and cheeses. It's a little secret that no one knows about in the whole Valley. The people who work there are great and knowledgeable. They only sell stuff that is magical and really delightful. If you like a foie gras, there's a truffle foie gras to die for. All the cheeses are beautiful. And they make a hell of a sandwich.

Village Gourmet Cheese and Wine, 4357 Tujunga Avenue, Studio City; (818) 487-3807; www.villagegourmet cheeseandwines.com

....

Janet Montgomery, actress

There's a sushi place that I love called Izaka-Ya. It's from the same people who have Katsu-Ya. They make a really great crab hand roll.

Izaka-Ya by Katsu-Ya, 8420 W 3rd Street, Los Angeles; (323) 782-9536; www.katsu-yagroup.com

....

Dan Angel, producer and writer

We're really boring. People have all these exciting things they love to do. Our big thing is our traditional Friday night movie night. We like to see the new movie that opened Friday night. That's a big part of our life.

And on the weekend, we do the food trifecta and see movies. We'll start on a Saturday and go to Bea Bea's, a fascinating breakfast place in a strip mall right near all the studios in Burbank. They're famous for their waffles and pancakes. It's this wonderful hole in the wall that is so popular, it's hard to get into on the weekend. They opened it a couple of years ago and it's just stayed hugely busy because the food is so great.

So that's step one. Usually we'll hit step two. In the middle of doing our crazy let's eat breakfast, then let's go to the movies, we've got to break up the day. We love step two, our frozen yogurt run at Menchie's. It's actually a running joke with many people in the business. We all have this Menchie's obsession.

And a lot of times dinners will consist of Patys, which we love. It's always about having breakfast for dinner: eggs, bacon, and toast and coffee. For some reason it just tastes so much better at dinnertime. I love it for breakfast, but dinner there is amazing. Also, Patys has a small town real diner feel.

We're in Bob Hope country. This is the town that Bob Hope built. We're surrounded by Universal Studios on one side, Disney, and Warner Bros. Most of the studios are right in the neighborhood and most people who live here work in the industry.

The reason we moved to the Burbank area is because it has a community feel. It might surprise people that those who live here are very committed to each other, to family and being together. When some people think of LA, sometimes they have an image of stuffiness and all the stereotypes. Every city has a stereotype, but it's not the reality.

The ArcLight Cinemas are beautiful movie theaters. There used to just be one in Hollywood, and now they opened in Sherman Oaks and in Pasadena. But what's unique is that they offer reserved seating. You might pay a couple of bucks more, but you don't ever have to wait in a line. You get to the movie five minutes before it starts and get in your seat. You can see first-run commercial big box office movies or art films.

In Hollywood, they have the Cinerama Dome, which is a famous landmark. When you're inside you feel like you're in a beehive. It's massive. The screen actually wraps around. So when you do all these fun eating adventures that we do, there's nothing better than going to the Cinerama Dome to cap off the experience.

Bea Bea's, 353 North Pass Avenue. Burbank; (818) 846-2327

Patys, 10001 Riverside Drive, Toluca Lake; (818) 761-0041; http://patysrestaurant.com

Menchie's, 13369 Ventura Boulevard, Sherman Oaks; (818) 788-9900; www.menchies.com

....

Angela Lansbury, Tony-winning, Academy Award–, Emmy-, Golden Globe–nominated actress

My favorite restaurant is my daughter's restaurant in West LA, Enzo & Angela. It's really the best Italian food in Los Angeles and a great spot on Wilshire Boulevard. I like all Italian food and everything they make. I'm very proud of her. My daughter's husband is the chef and she runs the place and she is also a very good chef herself. She learned how to cook from her husband and his mother. They have been in the restaurant business for many years. They had a restaurant called Positano. We cooked a lot when she was growing up, but everything she learned from him and his mother.

Enzo & Angela Restaurant, 11701 Wilshire Boulevard, Los Angeles; (310) 477-3880; www.enzoandangela.com

....

Nick Cannon, actor, entertainer, TV personality, rapper, musician, and CEO

I love a restaurant named Stevie's in the Valley. It's the food that I grew up on, which is soul food. And there are good people who work there.

Stevie's Creole Cafe and Bar, 16911 Ventura Boulevard, Encino; (818) 528-3500; www.steviescreolecafe-bar.com

....

Chris Nichols, "Ask Chris" columnist and editor at *Los Angeles* magazine

I've been an editor at *Los Angeles* magazine since 2001 and write the "Ask Chris" column for the magazine where I answer questions about the city's history and am always exploring quirky and hidden places. I try to explain how the city works and how to navigate around the secret places here. I've also been volunteering with the Los Angeles Conservancy since 1988 and have served as chairman of the Modern Committee of the Conservancy working to save midcentury architecture in Southern California.

How can I choose a favorite place when my entire life revolves around finding favorite places? People complain about Los Angeles's sprawl, but that only gives you more opportunities to find wonderful things hidden in far-off corners of our suburban metropolis. Of course you can go from beach to mountain to desert in a single afternoon, but you can also drive for an hour in any direction and the commercial strip never ends.

Sometimes if you're lucky, you'll come across some time machine place like the Covina Bowl or the North Woods Inn that can transport you to a midcentury fantasy involving Egyptian modernist bowling or dining on neon orange cheese bread on the Alaskan frontier. How could I not answer with Disneyland, the greatest fantasy of them all?

But I think that if I had to be locked inside a place for any length of time . . . if it was about being happy and inspired and having a great LA day, I'd say Pann's Coffee Shop in Ladera Heights. Yes, I like the homey comfort food, but what really inspires me is the architecture. Built in 1958, Pann's exemplifies the Googie style, with a magnificent roofline that jumps and plays and shelters and soars. It is built on an island of flowering plants and misshapen rocks all sunken below a sea of fast-moving cars. Tying this whole animated creation together is a flashing neon sign atop a spear piercing the roof at a jaunty angle.

Pann's is lush and comfortable, familiar and exotic. I first saw this magic place in a book called *Googie* when I was a teenager. I made my parents drive me there and called the author out of the phone book. Alan Hess became a friend and mentor and introduced me to the team that created this roadside wonder, and I became fast friends with architect Eldon Davis, designer Helen Fong, photographer Jack Laxer, and the Poulos family, who commissioned the restaurant and still run it.

Longtime staff knows everybody's name. They watch families grow and kids returning with their own children. After more than fifty years behind the counter, nonagenarian owner Rena Poulos still greets customers with a megawatt smile and escorts them to the red Naugahyde booths where they can sink in and enjoy a journey to a future that never was.

Covina Bowl, Covina, 1060 West San Bernardino Road, Covina; (626) 339-1286; www.bowlbrunswick.com/covina

North Woods Inn, Covina, 540 North Azusa Avenue, Covina; (626) 331-7444; www.clearmansrestaurants.com/northwoods/cv.php

Pann's Restaurant & Coffee Shop, 6710 La Tijera Boulevard, Los Angeles; (323) 776-3770; panns.com

....

Clark Gregg, actor, writer, and director

There's a place I really love called The Apple Pan which is a burger joint from the 30s. It's still there and has the most incredible burgers in LA. I'll go about once a month and order a steak burger with fries and a Diet Coke.

The Apple Pan, 10801 West Pico Boulevard, Los Angeles; (310) 475-3585

....

Ciara, Grammy-winning singer, songwriter, dancer, and actress

I love to eat at Hillstone, which is worldwide. However, I love the local crustaceans. And I love the garlic noodles. The cracked crab is the bomb dot com and when you get it, you'll want to go back for more and more. It's addictive.

Hillstone, 202 Wilshire Boulevard, Santa Monica; (310) 576-7558; www.hillstone.com/hillstone

....

Josh Charles, Emmy-nominated actor

I used to love to go to Dan Tana's when I lived in LA. It was always a fun hang and old Hollywood and you could get a nice meal and glass of red wine.

Dan Tana's, 9071 Santa Monica Boulevard, West Hollywood; (310) 275-9444; www.dantanasrestaurant.com

....

Jennifer Westfeldt, actress, writer, director

The Tower Bar is a great old school supper club. It has a lovely laid back vibe and is really stylish and private and we love the atmosphere. And we also love Griffith Park. Hiking with my dog in Griffith Park is pretty high up there.

Olga Garay, executive director of the Department of Cultural Affairs

A place that captures my imagination and feels quintessentially Hollywood is the very iconic Sunset Tower Hotel. It's very old school Hollywood and art deco. Marilyn Monroe lived there. And it has Hollywood built into its DNA. You feel like you're going to run into Carole Lombard there. The maitre d' knows everybody and is a complete charmer. It's a place to take your out-of-town guests if you want to show them what Hollywood is all about.

Jeff Skoll, founder and chairman of the Skoll Foundation, Participant Media, and the Skoll Global Threats Fund (and eBay's first president)

I live in LA, so I have many favorite places. One place that is so LA, and so nice, is the Sunset Tower. It's a great place to hang out. It's dignified and very old school. You can hear people talk. Anybody can get in. There are no crazy velvet ropes. There's no hoopla. And it's just a great environment for people to hang out and talk.

Eight years ago, I moved to LA to start Participant, my media company. For the film business, you have to be in LA or New York to some degree. For me, LA seemed to be the place. If you're going to meet writers, directors, talent and people in the business, that's the place to do it. So I moved down. I always expected I'd move back to Northern California, and now eight years later I really like it.

Bryan Batt, actor, author, and interior designer

Having been born and raised in New Orleans, I grew up with a definite passion for historical architecture and fine dining. A great combination if you ask me. Iconic restaurants like Antoine's and Galatoire's have been thriving for over a hundred years in the Vieux Carré. Also living and working in New York for many years just added to my devout love of columns and cuisine.

I don't want to offend anyone, however, upon arrival in Los Angeles, I was a little dismayed at the lack of a sense of history, both culinary and structural. But I am a firm believer in the adage "Seek and ye shall find." Although legendary haunts like The Brown Derby and Chasen's no longer exist to cater to industry luminaries, there are a few spots that satisfy my longing for Tinseltown elegance.

Chateau Marmont has a classic California old school feel and the lure of dark lore. The outdoor space is absolutely charming and the salon with its antiques and glossy Spanish tiled floors is reminiscent of those that Valentino once tangoed upon. This eternally "in" spot has been the setting for many martini-flowing outrageously fun Mad Men gatherings.

The Ivy in Santa Monica sports a decor that makes you feel like a relaxing visit on the Amalfi Coast and the perfect pink pigment on the walls for any palette. There is an old world charm that is unique to this wonderful oceanside eatery. But I have to say that the place I bring out-of-town guests and the spot I cling to for that sometimes needed dose of Old Hollywood glamour is the Tower Bar in the Sunset Tower Hotel. Upon entering, I am greeted by Dimitri, a world class maitre d', and a charmingly witty gentleman who always remembers my name (I can't help it, I like that), and whisked to a dimly lit clubby cozy banquet with cartoon drawings of stars of a bygone era.

After a refreshing adult libation . . . or two, I often have the feeling that Carole Lombard or Douglas Fairbanks could enter at any moment. Throughout the classic continental meal, the view of the twinkling lights of Los Angeles is breathtaking . . . as is the fashionably attired clientele. I realize we live in an ever growing casual society, and some people actually think a hoodie is a jacket, but every once in a while I love taking off the jeans, donning a smart suit, and enjoying a truly swanky evening amidst an elegant ambiance and space that existed long before myself.

Chateau Marmont, 8221 Sunset Boulevard, Hollywood; (323) 656-1010; www.chateaumarmont.com

Ivy at the Shore, 1535 Ocean Avenue, Santa Monica; (310) 393-3113; www.theivyrestaurant.com

....

Gulla Jonsdottir, critically acclaimed architect and designer and founder, G+ Gulla Jonsdottir Design

For dinner, I like the Tower Bar at the Sunset Tower Hotel. Movie industry people like that place. It's always buzzing, but quiet and elegant. And Dimitri, the maître d'hôtel, is quite charming, and just accommodating to everyone. They have a live piano player, and it's quite nice, like old school Hollywood.

And one of my other favorite restaurants is Red O. It's healthy Mexican cuisine by Rick Bayless, who's a famous chef. I designed the restaurant and put my heart and soul into it. It's nice to just go there for once in a while and have a margarita. And I love their goat cheese tamales and ceviches. It's like being in Mexico for a day on vacation.

Tower Bar, 8358 Sunset Boulevard, West Hollywood; (323) 848-6677; http://sunsettowerhotel.com

Sunset Tower Hotel, 8358 Sunset Boulevard, West Hollywood; (323) 654-7100; http://sunsettowerhotel.com

Red O, 8155 Melrose Avenue, Los Angeles; (323) 655-5009; www.redorestaurant.com

....

Donald De Line, film producer and studio executive

I love the vibe of old Los Angeles, which compared to New York of course is not very old. But I have old memories here. I live in Hancock Park, a historic neighborhood which is historically protected. So you can't screw with the original architecture or the intent of the feel of the neighborhood. It was all built in the 1920s and 1930s. It still retains that flavor very much.

To me, a classic LA day is first taking the dog out for a walk because it's always gorgeous and so mild. You start your day that way and kind of marvel at the consistency of the climate and the way we can use the outdoors year-round for the most part.

Then I would go to the Beverly Hills Hotel coffee shop with the counter downstairs. It's my favorite for breakfast. It's an old counter that was built in the 1940s in the Beverly Hills Hotel below the lobby. Of course, the Polo Lounge which is also in the hotel is glorious, especially sitting outside in a booth on the patio on a sunny day. But the secret is that it's all about the coffee shop, the Fountain Coffee Room, downstairs.

The hotel's coffee shop with its old kidney-shaped counter. is fantastic It looks just like you're back in the old Lucy show. There's the green and white palm frond wallpaper that they've always had. It's the classic green and white wallpaper of the Beverly Hills Hotel. So, it really feels like Old Hollywood, Beverly Hills in the 30s and 40s. The barstools are bolted to the floor. They're old, white, wrought iron and very classic. They ring around the counter. The same waitresses in little pink uniforms have been there forever. The place makes you feel like the world still makes sense.

They have big waffle irons and make fresh waffles, so I get pecan ones. They give you heated-up maple syrup with a side of bacon well done and make fresh orange juice to order. All the juice is made fresh to order. It's very old school, very homey. They have a great burger if you hit it at lunch. You can't beat the burger. But my favorite is to go in the morning there and talk to Ruth who's been there forever at the counter. The waitresses there are like broads. They don't take any guff. They do their job well. They're great.

LA is all about great Mexican food because that's so much a part of the culture. It's Southern California, we're on the border. Obviously, the Latin population is so big. It's mandatory Spanish in elementary school. It's part of your life. I like divey old school Mexican food—going to classic, old, mom-and-pop Mexican places with dark red booths, margaritas, chips and guacamole, enchiladas, and all the rest of that. One restaurant like that which I love is Casa Vega.

Again, it's straight out of the 50s. San Fernando Valley in the 50s. It's hilarious. It's very dark. They've got dark red booths. It's got the waitresses in the old Mexican dresses who are all kind of done up. It's very festive. It's always packed. There's always a wait. It's not expensive. It's consistently great. It's old school, unapologetic Mexican food. It's not trying to be fancy. This is down the center Mexican. It's best for an early Sunday dinner. A couple of great margaritas, a bunch of enchiladas and tacos in a big booth with your friends is the greatest. Serenata de Garibaldi is another place that is extraordinary and has been there forever. It's toward downtown by Dodger Stadium and specializes in Mexican seafood. It's fish tacos and very authentic.

The Fountain Coffee Room, 9641 Sunset Boulevard, Beverly Hills; (310) 276-2251; www.beverlyhillshotel.com

Casa Vega Restaurant, 13301 Ventura Boulevard, Sherman Oaks; (818) 788-4868; www.casavega.com

La Serenata de Garibaldi, 1842 East First Street, Los Angeles; (323) 265-2887; 10924 West Pico Boulevard, Los Angeles; (310) 441-9667; www.laserenataonline.com

....

David Hallberg, principal dancer with American Ballet Theatre and a premier dancer with the Bolshoi

We perform a lot at the Dorothy Chandler Pavilion, which is extraordinary. And nearby is a street called Figueroa. And you can find little shacks or little side carts that serve Mexican food really, really late. And it's very authentic with no pretense at all. They're just serving really great authentic Mexican food. It's the best Mexican food ever for tacos, burritos, and rice and beans. I'll go there after performances and order a huge burrito and Jarritos, which is a Mexican soft drink.

Dorothy Chandler Pavilion, 135 North Grand Avenue, Los Angeles; (213) 972-7211; www.musiccenter.org

....

Merle Ginsberg, fashion writer, television personality, senior writer, *Hollywood Reporter*

Ray's and Stark Bar is a great restaurant and bar at the LA County Museum. They have really good food, very nice wine, and it's just really cool. It's very near where I work and I live so I like hanging out there all the time. It's my home away from home. I just love that you can hang out at a museum.

I go to Ray's and Stark Bar for lunch a lot because it's across the street from my office and I'm always on deadline so I can't really travel very much. The bread is ridiculous. And they have this delicious chopped salad that gushes tart and salty And they have great vegetables. You just order a side of brussels sprouts and it's crisp, grilled, and delicious.

There are a number of sculptures around and you're in this courtyard between two buildings: the Eli Broad newer part of the LA County Museum and the established part. So there's always interesting people going through and walking around.

And very often, music plays on the patio. Then right in front of you is a Chris Burden light sculpture that is extraordinary. It's a landmark in Los Angeles.

I started my career in New York. When I came here, I went back and forth for a very long time but I realized, even when I was in New York, that my friends in LA had become my family. I just think it's funny that people always say to me, "you're from New York, right?" because I dressed in a much more New York way and move very quickly, I'm much more of a New York person. But there's something about the wide open spaces. You're living in a city but you still have mountains, sky, and stars and it's very, very easy to get away very quickly. You can really get a lot done here. You can run away from everybody and just write and listen to music, which I tend to do. Or you could be in the middle of the Hollywood craziness. You always have an option.

I also like a restaurant called Ammo in Santa Monica, which is out of my usual travel zone. But you always feel like you're going to visit a friend when you go there. It's dark, and it has little candles. It's utterly unpretentious, romantic and intimate.

The food is really nice. There's a sort of LA type of food that other cities like Sydney, Australia, come close to. It's always clean, always healthy, and usually has some sort of Asian influences. It's heavy on the salads, vegetables and the tofu. Of course, sushi is a huge, huge thing here. My entire diet is pretty much salads, sushi, and omelets. People are very self-conscious about the way they look and also everyone talks about health all the time so it's really hard to not think about it.

Ammo plays the best music I've ever heard. I'm a music person and I always hear something I haven't heard that I'm excited by. I would call it sort of the soundtrack of LA. I would describe it as KCRW music, which is a very, very well-known radio station here from Santa Monica College.

And this is my third reason why I love LA. KCRW is the greatest radio station in the world. The coolest people work there. They always have fascinating people on. They have authors. They have painters—all kinds of fascinating people. And they play amazing music. It's not lexactly rock and roll. Henry Rollins will play hard core punk. Other people will play something bluesy, other people will play something more alternative British. It's just always good. You can get it on the Internet, KCRW.com. And they have a twenty-four-hour Internet station that is really great as well. I know people listen to it all day long. They sponsor and produce a lot of concerts in Los Angeles. They're the center of culture in LA in so many ways.

I travel a lot. I have a lot of friends in Tel Aviv, Israel, which is a place I really, really love. I go to Europe and spend time in New York. But I think wow, LA is really great. When I'm here I bitch a lot. But that's true of everyone here.

Ray's and Stark Bar, 5905 Wilshire Boulevard, Los Angeles; (323) 857-6180; raysandstarkbar.com

Ammo, 1155 North Highland Avenue, Los Angeles; (323) 871-2666; www.ammocafe.com

KCRW radio, 89.9 FM, free Internet public radio station of Santa Monica College; http://kcrw.com

....

Ne-Yo, Grammy-winning singer-songwriter, record producer, actor, and dancer

I actually moved to LA right after high school with a group of friends in search of the music business. I lived there for about eight years. But I don't necessarily have a favorite restaurant unless you count Roscoe's Chicken and Waffles. Roscoe's was, at the time, the only thing that we could afford and it's great. I still eat at Roscoe's. I go and have the Jeanne Jones omelet with chicken and cheese and a waffle. And I have that pretty much every time.

Roscoe's House of Chicken and Waffles, 1514 North Gower Street, Los Angeles; (323) 466-7453; 5006 West Pico Boulevard, Los Angeles; (323) 934-4405; 106 West Manchester Boulevard, Los Angeles; (323) 752-6211; www.roscoes chickenandwaffles.com

....

Jack Black, Golden Globe–nominated actor, musician, and songwriter

There's this awesome vegan restaurant called Café Gratitude. They don't need the plug, they're always packed. But I like Café Gratitude. I like the way it tastes. And I like the dish that's just basic beans and rice.

Chris Riggi, actor

I love Café Gratitude. There are a lot of vegetarian and vegan choices. The pad thai and fake nachos are good. And they have dishes with "I am" names like "I am elated."

Francis Fisher, actor

I'm a vegan and there's a fabulous restaurant called Café Gratitude. It was started by a family up in San Francisco. And now, they came down and opened one here. I don't eat gluten and sugar. So, if I go to Café Gratitude, I can eat anything on the menu. I don't have to say can you take this out or take that out. At most restaurants, it can be a bit of a hassle to ask if something is organic or gluten-free. Here, the cheese is not real cheese. It's made from almonds and the food is so delicious. I have not had a bad meal there yet and it's so healthy.

All the dishes are affirmations: I Am Gracious. I Am Humble. I Am Awesome. I Am Calm. "Lox and a bagel" is a gluten-free kind of crackery thing. You would swear you're eating lox but it's made from nori. You get a tiny, little, fishy taste of lox and it's delicious. Of course, the cream cheese is not actual cream cheese. It's made from cashew butter.

Every morning, before they work with customers, the Café Gratitude staff has a powwow. They talk about what's been going on or anything bothering them. So they get that all cleared out so they can be there for the customers.

Also, there's always a question of the day. It could be, the thing I'm most grateful for is . . . Or I love . . . And then they ask customers to answer. It's also a great place to feel really good about what you're about to eat. And the vibe in there is wonderful too, because everybody's there keeping themselves healthy and thinking good thoughts.

And there are amazing farmers' markets in LA. You can go to one every day if you wanted to drive a little. I go to the farmers' market in Plummer Park in West Hollywood every week and get my fresh produce that's grown locally. It feels so good to help the local farmers and eat fresh food that doesn't have any pesticides or hasn't been genetically modified. I get Korean food there that is gluten-free and organic, like tofu, vegetables, and seaweed that isn't fishy tasting.

Café Gratitude, 639 North Larchmont Boulevard, Los Angeles; (323) 580-6383; www.cafegratitudela.com

West Hollywood Monday Farmers' Market, Plummer Park - N. Vista and Fountain Avenue, West Hollywood; (323)845-6535

Karen Schaler, Emmy-winning TV correspondent and host/author: *Travel Therapy*

There are so many restaurants I love in Los Angeles but hands down one of my favorite places to grab a quick bite to eat is Dan's Super Subs in Woodland Hills, not just because of the food but because this friendly deli is tied to so many great memories.

When I was seventeen, I moved from Washington State to California for my senior year of high school, leaving all my family and friends behind so I could work as a nanny in Los Angeles and gain residency for college. I attended Calabasas High School and I don't need to tell you that trying to make new friends your senior year of high school is tricky at best.

At Calabasas High a lot of seniors would go off campus for lunch and at first I really hated our lunch break because I didn't have anyone to hang out with, but one day one of the girls in my class, a popular California native, asked if I liked sub sandwiches because she knew a great place to go. I was game for anything so we hopped into her Volkswagen bug convertible and playing B-52s cruised down Ventura Boulevard to Dan's Super Subs, a small family-run deli that had just opened a few years earlier in 1980.

My new friend led the way and I got what she got, a mouthwatering extra lean pastrami sub with cheese and mustard only. That day I not only found a friendship that has lasted decades but I also found one of my all-time favorite sub sandwiches!

When we first started going to Dan's back in the 80s there were only about fourteen subs on the menu but today you'll find dozens. They come hot or cold and you can either get an eight- or thirteen-inch sub with signature favorites including the "My Cousin Elvis" loaded up with Dan's homemade BBQ brisket of beef, cheese, chilled caramelized onions, along with their homemade coleslaw, diced pickles, and Louisiana pepper sauce. Another cult favorite is the "Flying Dutchman" that's overflowing with lean roast beef, turkey, ham, provolone, cheddar, avocado slices, crispy bacon, herbal mayo, deli mustard, lettuce, tomatoes, diced pickles, mild peppers, black olives, onions, and Dan's Spicy Baja Sauce.

In all the subs Dan's staff prides itself in using the freshest, leanest, and highest quality of meats, natural cheeses, and fresh vegetables that are all sliced up daily right in their store, so if you don't find what you want on the extensive menu you can always create your own masterpiece. I also appreciate that even after three decades these years the subs are still affordable starting at around five and a half dollars a sub but note, Dan's is closed on Sundays so be sure to go Monday through Saturday between 8:00 a.m. and 7:00 p.m.

One of the things I love the most about Dan's subs is how they are served on this tasty bread that's made fresh from scratch every morning. Another secret to Dan's success is that they use high pressure steamers to steam up and warm up the subs. It's comfort food at its best!

I've also seen some pretty huge subs go out of Dan's because they also specialize in making these massive three- to six-foot party subs; now that's one party I wanted to be invited to!

Still, I have to admit that even after all these years, when I go to Dan's and see all these exciting new options on the menu I'll always order the same thing: an extra lean pastrami with cheese and mustard only because this is one tradition I'm holding on to.

Dan's Super Subs, 22446 Ventura Boulevard, Woodland Hills; (818) 225-8880; www.danssupersubs.com

....

Cindy Williams, Golden Globe–nominated actress

I grew up in Los Angeles, so my history is there. I live in the Valley now and I love going into Hollywood. This is the neighborhood where I used to live. If you go down Fairfax, you have the Grove and Farmers Market, and it's just such a great vibration of everything. And you have the museum next door, the La Brea Tar Pits. I love the part of the edge of West LA going toward old LA.

And I love to meet my friends at Greenblatt's. I would put Greenblatt's Delicatessen up against any New York deli. It is so fabulous, and it's right next door to the Laugh Factory. So you'll see Kathy Griffin and all kinds of comics in there.

The food at Greenblatt's is unbelievable. But the ambiance and energy in there are so wonderful, upbeat, and happy. And it smells so good. They are wine connoisseurs so it's also a very wonderful wine shop. It's perfect feng shui. You can't feel bad there, you just always feel good. Anything on the menu is great, but their hot pastrami sandwich is awfully good. It's incredibly good on their rye bread, unbelievable. I mean who doesn't like hot pastrami, unless you are a vegetarian. Which I should be, but I'm not.

If you are standing outside of Greenblatt's on Sunset Boulevard and you look to the right, you've got the Sunset Strip, which is absolutely so much fun. And then Sunset Boulevard goes all the way down to the beach. The light that shoots up through Sunset, through Wilshire Boulevard, through Olympic—is so beautiful. It's just incredible sky through the tall buildings. It's breathtaking. If you look to the left you are going down into Hollywood proper and Old Hollywood by the Roosevelt, by the Walk of Fame, by Grauman's Chinese Theatre and all of those just fabulous landmarks. And you keep going and you go all the way down and just keep following Sunset, you'll be in downtown LA and the Disney Center, and the cathedral are there. It's all just so intriguing. It's just fun, and there's so little of that in the world. So that's where I go to get my shot of happiness.

Greenblatt's Deli, 8017 Sunset Boulevard, Los Angeles; (323) 656-0606; www.greenblattsdeli.com

. . . .

Sacha Gervasi, director, writer, producer

There's a little taco place called Benito's that I absolutely love. They have a $2.99 chicken burrito. Fantastic.

When I first visited LA, in 1994, I was a freelance journalist for *Punch* magazine, the *Sunday Times,* the *Evening Standard,* and the *Observer* in England. I came to interview Guns N' Roses. At the time that they were breaking up.

I remember going to the studio to interview them and they were all out of their minds. Their publicist said we needed a binge window. We had to wait for what they call the binge window, which I never really understood. But I ended up spending a month and exploring LA, doing interviews, applying to UCLA Film School. And then, finally, I got the interview. But my first version of LA was really through the eyes of Guns N' Roses being completely stoned out of their minds.

The movie business keeps me in LA. *Hitchcock,* the movie I just made, would otherwise never have happened if I wasn't living there. Anthony Hopkins lives in LA and so does Helen Mirren. If you want access to those people, even though they are British, everyone is there. LA makes it easier to connect.

Benito's, 7912 Beverly Boulevard or 11614 Santa Monica Boulevard; Los Angeles; (323) 938-7427 or (310) 442-9924; www.benitos.com

....

Christopher Gorham, actor

One of my favorite places in LA is a restaurant called Terroni. It has my favorite pizza in the world. I get the San Giorgio, a spicy salami with mushrooms and cheese.

Terroni Restaurant, 7605 Beverly Boulevard, Los Angeles; (323) 954-0300; www.terroni.com

....

Da'Vine Joy Randolph, Tony-nominated actress

There's a restaurant called Joan's on Third in West Hollywood that is almost like a Dean & DeLuca. The food is very fresh. It's a low-key cafe where tons of celebrities go. It's an amazing lunch and brunch place. It's one of my favorite restaurants. I love the chicken Milanese sandwich. And it comes with homemade chips. Oh my God. It's to die for. So. So. So. Good.

Joan's on Third, 8350 West Third Street, Los Angeles; (323) 655-2285; www.joansonthird.com

....

Neal Fraser, *Iron Chef* winner, chef and owner of BLD Restaurant, and co-owner of Fritzi Dog, Strand House, and the Rectory at Vibiana

There are a lot of aspects of Los Angeles that I like. What I appreciate the most is the diversity. The other day my daughter and I went to a Korean shopping mall in Koreatown. In just a couple of minutes, it felt like we were in another country. And there are so many communities like that where you get immersed in another culture. It's pretty interesting.

As far as Korean food goes we mainly eat Korean barbecue because I have a seven-year-old daughter and she loves it. So it's not a hard sell. You get to grill it up. It's amazing living my life through the eyes of my child. My kid is just like every other kid. She's picky and she likes specific things. So when I can find something that I don't have to convince her to eat, it's more pleasurable for me as well. And then maybe every other time she will try a new dish. She'll have a new part of her that she will put into her repertoire of stuff.

Our favorite Korean barbecue place is Genwa. It's not super smokey, it's not super divey. But the flavors and side dishes are really great. They have things like little dried fish, glass noodles, broccoli. They have a couple different kinds of crepes. Their potato salad is interesting. They will have all certain kinds of kimchee and things that are kind of done in the same style as kimchee and not totally cabbage, but stuff that has chili and is marinated. It kind of pleases everybody.

Park's BBQ is also a great Korean barbecue restaurant. The first place I ever went is Soot Bull Jeep. maybe ten or twelve years ago. I want to say it's one of the first Korean barbecues, It's definitely the most authentic. You can barely see in the place and after an hour your lungs kind of hurt from the charcoal. It's definitely a great experience, but it's not where you go to impress people. Not to say the food isn't delicious and amazing, but it's down and dirty. I still love that place, And being a chef, I'm a food snob. I'm always looking for the finest of even the dives. As far as the Korean places that would probably be my top three.

Soot Bull Jeep, 3136 West 8th Street, Los Angeles; (213) 387-3865

Genwa, 5115 Wilshire Boulevard, Los Angeles; (323) 549-0760; www.genwakoreanbbq.com

Park's BBQ, 955 South Vermont Avenue, Los Angeles; (213) 380-1717; www.parksbbq.com

. . . .

Kristin Chenoweth, Tony- and Emmy-winning actress and singer

I love Mastro's. You have to try the butter cake. There's nothing better.

Mastro's, 246 North Canon Drive, Beverly Hills; (310) 888-8782; www.mastrosrestaurants.com

Fisher Stevens, Academy Award–winning filmmaker, producer, director, co-founder of Naked Angels Theater Company, and actor

When I want to really indulge, I love Du-par's pancakes in the Farmers Market. Nobody can make a pancake like Du-par's. I think they've been doing it for seventy years. I order a piece of raspberry pie, take out the filling, and put it on the pancake. It's the greatest thing in the world. And when I want to eat healthy, I love a place called M Café because it's really natural, healthy food.

My favorite thing about LA is listening to the radio station, KCRW. Now that I direct films, I've been turned on to a bunch of music. I just directed the movie *Stand Up Guys*. While I was editing, I heard a Gary Clark Jr. song, which I already knew but forgot about. Nobody plays Gary Clark Jr. but KCRW. So, I've got the song now in the movie. I like the show "Which Way LA" on there. Although it was strange that after the second presidential debate, they were very split, even though I thought Obama won. Very shocking. That just shows you they're very fair, I guess.

Du-par's, at the Farmers Market, 6333 West 3rd Street, Los Angeles; (323) 933-8446; www.du-pars.com

M Café, 7119 Melrose Avenue, Hollywood; (323) 525-0588; www.mcafedechaya.com

Eve Plumb, actress and artist

I like Du-par's in Studio City or any Du-par's. There's one in Farmers Market. I just love old coffee shops and diners. I love that 1950s feel, the style, the food, the simplicity. I like breakfast foods like scrambled or fried eggs, toast, coffee. I actually had a birthday breakfast at Du-par's once because it was just different and fun.

I was born in Burbank, raised in Van Nuys. You never have a sense of where you are when you grow up someplace. It's just where you grew up, where you lived. It's very familiar. I've always loved the history of LA. I've always mourned the loss of the history—the way that the city doesn't care at all for the history that it has. It created the movie industry. But a lot of that, like buildings, are lost.

But I think, finally, Hollywood itself is coming around after a long decline. When I was growing up and doing *Portrait of a Teenage Runaway*, Hollywood

Boulevard was so downtrodden. Fixing it up usually involved tearing things down and getting rid of cool neon signs. But I think it might finally be turning around.

Du-par's, at the Farmers Market, 6333 West 3rd Street, Los Angeles; (323) 933-8446; www.du-pars.com

....

Camila Alves, model and designer, MUXO handbags

I love going to Nobu Malibu. The sushi is so good. I love the yellow tail jalapeño and the crunchy spicy tuna roll there. The other Nobu restaurants do not make the crunchy spicy tuna roll like they make at the one in Malibu.

Nobu Restaurant, 22706 Pacific Coast Highway, Malibu; (310) 317-9140; www.noburestaurants.com/malibu

....

Lauren Miller, actress, screenwriter

I love LA. And in West Hollywood there are some great restaurants. I'm a big fan of Animal and Son of a Gun. The food at both places is so unique and they have flavor combinations I've never had before. The lobster roll and chicken sandwich at Son of a Gun is pretty outstanding.

Animal, 435 North Fairfax Avenue, Los Angeles; (323) 782-9225; www.animalrestaurant.com

Son of a Gun, 8370 West 3rd Street, Los Angeles; (323) 782-9033; www.sonofagunrestaurant.com

....

Tonya Pinkins, Tony-nominated actress

I really like Koi. I love sushi. I'm very into raw fish. I can live on raw fish every day of the week and am fond of halibut. Koi has good portions. The presentation is beautiful. And Koi's décor is very elegant. It reminds me of Hakkasan in London.

Koi, 730 North La Cienega Boulevard, Los Angeles; (310) 659-9449; www.koirestaurant.com

....

Lisa Lillien (aka Hungry Girl), *New York Times* best-selling author and the creator of the *Hungry Girl* brand

As a New Yorker, everybody warned me that I wouldn't love LA. And you know what? I fell madly in love with the place. I knew I always wanted to live here when I visited. The weather is perfect. The people are really nice. I think everything is easy and comfortable. I love everything about LA.

When I first arrived, I liked that there was always good hair weather. For the first six years I lived here, I felt like I was on vacation the whole time. I love the palm trees. And it feels like one long summer. I mean, I appreciate when the temperatures drop to fifty degrees and I can wear a jacket and some boots and a sweater. But I don't really miss the snow.

My favorite thing in LA is, without a doubt, to go to my favorite restaurant in the world, Kazu Sushi. I think it's the best-kept secret in the universe. I'm sure nobody's mentioned it, because it's like a private sushi club. But it's not private in any way.

Kazu Sushi is a little restaurant that has been open for more than twenty years. And I've been going there for probably ten. My husband has been eating there for probably twenty years. It is the place that made me fall madly in love with sushi. I eat there probably around three times a week and I used to hate and was very opposed to sushi. I was scared of raw fish. My husband would take me there when I first moved to LA. There was one cooked chicken dish and that's exactly what I would eat when I was there. Now it's no longer on the menu.

I didn't really want to go to Kazu Sushi. I would go just to be nice to my husband. And then one day, I turned the corner, fell madly in love and became sushi obsessed. What made me turn the corner was just my husband saying, "Just try it again." Or "try to not think about the fact that it's raw fish." I think I had issues with that. I grew up with a family who never ate sushi, and once I fell in love, that was it. I've eaten sushi in Tokyo. I've eaten sushi everywhere, and Kazu has the best sushi in the world. It's the freshness of his fish.

Kazu Sushi, 11440 Ventura Boulevard, Studio City; (818) 763-4836

Dylan Baker, Emmy-nominated actor

We love to go to the joint that the Rat Pack used to hang out in called Chez Jay. It's a little place that's still there. We went a couple of times recently. I love it. You see all these pictures on the wall. There's a story about the guy who originally owned it. There were a couple of ad guys who were looking at the pictures of him and they came up with the idea of the world's most fascinating man. He inspired that because this guy had been with everybody and everywhere.

Chez Jay, 1657 Ocean Avenue, Santa Monica; (310) 395-1741; www.chezjays.com

Tyler Perry, actor, director, screenwriter, playwright, studio owner, and producer

I go to BOA Steakhouse a lot on Sunset. It's not too far from my house. The food is good. I can get in and out despite the paparazzi. I'm really into grilled chicken and vegetables these days.

BOA Steakhouse, 9200 Sunset Boulevard, West Hollywood; (310) 278-2050; www.innovativedining.com/restaurants/boa

Scooter Braun, CEO SB Projects (his entertainment company represents Justin Bieber, Asher Roth, Carly Rae Jepsen, The Wanted, Cody Simpson, and others)

I love LA. It's an amazing city and the quality of life is incredible. But LA is like summer camp. If you have a great group of friends you'll want to stay forever, but if you don't . . . you want your mom to pick you up right away.

And the caesar salad at BOA is incredible. They make it fresh. It's a great caesar salad.

BOA Steakhouse, 9200 Sunset Boulevard, West Hollywood; (310) 278-2050; www.innovativedining.com/restaurants/boa

. . . .

NiRé All'Dai, singer, songwriter

If you ever want amazing authentic Mexican food and burritos, and you are in Koreatown there's a place called Marielas Taco, which is a little bit west of Vermont. Oh my gosh, the burritos are so good. I like carne asada burritos with cheese and they're only about $4.50 or something. They're huge. The nachos are good too, but I always just get the burrito.

Marielas Taco, 3662 West 3rd Street, Los Angeles; (213) 381-7356

. . . .

Thomas Matthews, actor

I like Figaro Bistrot in Los Feliz a lot. They have a steak tartare there that is really hard to find anywhere else. The Grill in Beverly Hills is also awesome. I love steak tartare. You can get steak tartare and creamed spinach as an entree. It's a big pile of uncooked beef. It's like sushi, but steak.

Figaro Bistrot, 1802 North Vermont Avenue, Los Angeles; (323) 662-1587; www.figarobistrot.com/bistrot

. . . .

Chad Greer, music industry executive, photographer and writer

I was raised in small town Louisiana. Well, truth be told, from my family's farm "going to town" required driving ten miles of blacktop before reaching the city limits. It was a drive that when made after dark meant switching headlights from bright to dim, bright to dim, while navigating the narrow two-lane roads.

Los Angeles has been home for fifteen years now, and with Mamaw's fried chicken only a memory these days, my comfort foods have adapted. I love East India Grill on La Brea for their spicy chicken korma, the original Loteria Grill in the old Farmers Market for their huge plate of salsa verde nachos, and NOTHING beats Piano Bar in Hollywood for their Sunday afternoon free blues and bbq!

For my own inspiration and escape, a nighttime drive along Mulholland never fails to do the trick. The infamous road runs the full stretch along the top of the Hollywood Hills, and rounding each curve, stunning views of the vast expanse of greater Los Angeles come to life. I see downtown to the southeast, ocean views to the southwest. The Valley, and mountains beyond to the north. There are a bazillion, I've counted, twinkling lights shining all at once down below, and it's just magical to me. And up there in the darkness, in my car, I feel like a teenager again as I get to use my brights.

Piano Bar, 6429 Selma Avenue, Hollywood; (323) 466-2750; www.pianobarhollywood.com

East India Grill, 345 North La Brea Avenue, Los Angeles; (323) 936-8844; www.eastindiagrillla.com

Loteria Grill, Farmers Market, 6333 West 3rd Street, Los Angeles; (323) 930-2211; www.loteriagrill.com

....

Giuliana Rancic, co-anchor of *E! News* and *E!'s Fashion Police,* producer, author, and reality show star

Bill [husband Bill Rancic] and I live near the water in Los Angeles. So, oftentimes, we take beautiful walks on Ocean Boulevard. You see the ocean, the Santa Monica Pier, the Ferris wheel, all the lights and all the kids playing and people walking their dogs. It's very relaxing. And we'll have dinner at the Ivy on the shore. Not the Ivy on Robertson where all the paparazzi are. But the Ivy at the Shore which is very chill. That's one of our favorite things to do. At the Ivy, there's a beautiful outdoor but enclosed patio. It has screens so you still feel the fresh air. You have a view of the ocean and the food's terrific. It's just a cool place. They make great gimlet martinis. You can find us there many times a week.

Ivy at the Shore, 1535 Ocean Avenue, Santa Monica; (310) 393-3113; www.theivyrestaurant.com

....

Gabourey Sidibe, Academy Award– and Golden Globe–nominated actress

One of my best friends lived in LA. She just moved to New Jersey so I have her back. But every time I went to LA, we would always go to Doughboys on 3rd. I like the beefy mac and cheese. When I'm there, it always reminds me of our friendship. She throws a hissy fit if anyone else wants to go with her. It's our special place.

Doughboys Cafe & Bakery, 8136 West 3rd Street, Los Angeles; (323) 852-1020; www.doughboyscafe.com

Debi Mazar and **Gabriele Corcos,** creators and hosts of the show *Extra Virgin* on the Cooking Channel

Gabriele Corcos: My favorite restaurant is Angelini Osteria on Beverly Boulevard. I spent a few months studying with Gino Angelini in his kitchen. He's a great master of great food and probably serves the most traditional food I have found in Los Angeles. It's fantastic.

Debi Mazar: I love Angelini Osteria. And my favorite hippy place is Café Gratitude. My mother was a hippy and I've always cooked very healthy, healthy foods. I like that the food doesn't taste like dust or cardboard. It has flavor and is super, super, super fresh. They have great juices. I love a dish called I am Fulfilled. I like it because it's fresh beans, avocado, quinoa, greens and salad.

Gabriele Corcos: The dish for me is the one with a little sour cream on top.

Debi Mazar: And I always get this drink with kale and lemon juice, It's just so tasty. My kids love going there. It's my one place to run to by myself, or with a girlfriend, or convince my husband. He'd always want to go to Angelini Osteria, but we left that to be our special date place. So Café Gratitude would be my pit stop when I'm rushing and running around town in LA. And I love Mozza. I'm friends with Nancy Silverton.

And in terms of walks I think one of my favorite walks with my husband is just walking around the Griffith Park area and looking at the Observatory with the old trees and walking through the trails. Also, my husband is a big motorcycle rider so he would go up to Angels Crest.

Gabriele Corcos: I love the mountain roads.

Angelini Osteria, 7313 Beverly Boulevard, Los Angeles; (323) 297-0070; www.angeliniosteria.com

Café Gratitude, 639 North Larchmont Boulevard, Los Angeles; (323) 580-6383; www.cafegratitudela.com

Tracee Chimo, actress

When I'm in LA, my all-time favorite thing to do is go to the beach. As soon as I land, I dump my junk off wherever I'm staying, get in my car, and drive to the Santa Monica Beach.

I grew up in Boston around the Atlantic Ocean near five different beaches on the North Shore. The beach was a big part of my life as a kid and all through my teenage years. So as soon as I get to a place where the ocean is accessible, that's the first thing I do. I never really go swimming. I'll put my legs in and I'll splash the water on my face. It feels cleansing. It relaxes and brings me back to myself. There's something meditative about it.

My favorite restaurant in LA is El Compadre. My buddy, Michael Urie, introduced me to that restaurant on my first trip ever to Los Angeles. And every time I'm in LA, I eat there weekly. Their beef burrito is my favorite. And they serve flaming margaritas, which they light on fire. The waiters are super fun but it's not a party scene. It's more of a family place. There are big, red booths. It's very dark. You can go with a big group of friends, sit in the back, be really comfortable, and eat really good food.

El Compadre Restaurant, 1449 West Sunset Boulevard, Los Angeles; (213) 250-4505; elcompadrerestaurant.com

....

Bill Borden, Emmy-winning TV and motion picture producer (*High School Musical, Kung Fu Hustle, Desperado*)

I was born in Santa Monica not far from the Pacific Ocean and in my soul I feel a great attachment to beach city, the water, the sand, and the surf.

I was raised about ten miles away in an LA suburb called Encino, or what my Italian grandmother called "the desert." After attending university in the San Fernando Valley and Italy, I returned to live within several hundred yards of the beach ever since. My house is in Rustic Canyon a few hundred yards from Pacific Coast Highway and the Will Rogers State Beach.

We live in a city with millions of people, but on almost any given day (excluding peak summer holidays) my wife and I can bike three minutes down to Will Rogers State Beach and be almost by ourselves. On the way to the beach and the beach bike path we can stop for breakfast at Patrick's Roadhouse, a classic roadside eatery, frequented by many of the Hollywood types coming into LA from Malibu.

There we can cross through the underpass and end up on Will Rogers beach with its massive expanse of "groomed" sand. Part of the tradition on Santa Monica and LA beaches is to groom the beaches which gives them a wonderful virgin look. There we can trudge the one hundred yards to the water and walk along the wide wet sand toward the Santa Monica Pier. Sometimes we stop at Back on the Beach Cafe, one of the only places in LA where you can dig your toes in the sand and watch the surf while you eat.

For breakfast and lunch we rotate hitting places like Sauce on Hampton, Rose Café, and if we circle back into Santa Monica, Interim Cafe on Wilshire. Also, when we are feeling like we have justified it with the bike ride we stop at Schulzies Bread Pudding right on the Venice boardwalk for home-cooked bread pudding, totally decadent. Great lunch spots are in the dozens, but the places we most frequent in Venice are Joe's Cafe, Abbot's Habit (great salad pizza), Lulu Cocina, Hal's, and three of our favorite places in northern Santa Monica, Babbalu Cafe, R&D Cafe on Montana, and Nawab on Wilshire, all consistently great. Also the lunch veggie Indian buffet at Chandni on Wilshire is hard to pass up. One other lunch spot we hit on our bike is Bay Cities Italian Deli—the best, unfortunately, it is always so crowded that in the peak times it means a long wait. One of my favorite restaurants for business lunches is also close to the beach, the Buffalo Club, a movie industry watering hole.

One of our nightspots close to the beach is the Reel Inn on PCH at Topanga Canyon. We have spent many evenings sitting around the wood-burning stove drinking wine and downing fresh fish and seafood. And then there is a staple, Caffé Delfini, amazing Roman Italian and fifty yards from PCH, so you can walk it off at the beach afterward. Over the years our family of three boys have celebrated many of their benchmark events in their lives by eating there.

One of my favorite spots to visit is the J. Paul Getty Villa. It is right off PCH. When I have a stack of scripts to read, I can go over there, sit in the gardens, read and when I want a lunch walk over to the museum cafe. One other beach-adjacent spot I wander about to think is Self Realization Fellowship Lakeside Shrine. It is just a few hundred yards off PCH on Sunset Boulevard; an oasis of serenity and a place that was founded by Paramahansa Yogananda in 1950. The spring-filled lake and gardens are a great spot to recharge one's soul. And for a cultural place, scarce on the west side, we subscribe to the Broad Stage, where we have seen many performances and enjoyed eating late at Rustic Canyon Cafe, a two-block walk from the theater.

Patrick's Roadhouse, 106 Entrada Drive, Santa Monica; (310) 459-4544; www.patricksroadhouse.info

Back on the Beach Cafe, 445 Pacific Coast Highway, Santa Monica; (310) 393-8282; www.backonthebeachcafe.com/cms

Sauce on Hampton, 259 Hampton Drive, Venice; (310) 399-5400

Rose Café & Market, 220 Rose Avenue, Venice; (310) 399-0711; http://rosecafe.com

Interim Cafe, 530 Wilshire Boulevard, Santa Monica; (310) 319-9100

Schulzies Bread Pudding, 1827 Ocean Front Walk, Venice; (510) 783-3464; www.schulziesbreadpudding.com

Abbot's Habit, 1401 Abbot Kinney Boulevard, Venice; (310) 399-1171

Lulu Cocina Mexicana, 2720 Main Street, Santa Monica; (310) 392-5711; http://mexicanfoodinlosangeles.com

Hal's Bar & Grill, 1349 Abbot Kinney Boulevard, Venice; (310) 396-3105; www.halsbarandgrill.com

Babalu Cafe, 1040 North Las Palmas Avenue, Los Angeles; (323) 860-8437; www.hollywoodcenter.com/ProductionServices/BabaluCafe.aspx

Nawab (of India), 1621 Wilshire Boulevard, Santa Monica; (310) 829-1106; www.nawabindia.com

Chandni Vegetarian Restaurant, 1909 Wilshire Boulevard, Santa Monica; (310) 828-7060; www.chandnivegrestaurant.com

Bay Cities Italian Deli & Bakery, 1517 Lincoln Boulevard, Santa Monica; (310) 395-8279; www.baycitiesitaliandeli.com

The Buffalo Club, 1520 West Olympic Boulevard, Santa Monica; (310) 450-8600; www.thebuffaloclub.com

Reel Inn, 18661 Pacific Coast Highway, Malibu; (310) 456-8221; http://reelinnmalibu.com

Caffé Delfini, 147 West Channel Road, Santa Monica; (310) 459-8823; www.caffedelfini.com

J. Paul Getty Villa, 17985 Pacific Coast Highway, Pacific Palisades; (310) 440-7300; www.getty.edu/visit

The Broad Stage, 1310 11th Street, Santa Monica; (310) 434-3200; http://thebroadstage.com

Rustic Canyon Winebar and Seasonal Kitchen, 1119 Wilshire Boulevard, Santa Monica; (310) 393-7050; www.rusticcanyonwinebar.com

....

Chloe Flower, concert pianist

Craig's is a new restaurant. The owner's name is Craig and he was maitre d' at Dantana's which is a very famous LA restaurant. It's my favorite restaurant in LA.

They treat me so well for no reason. I always get their dijon caesar salad with olive oil because they don't use any mayo. And I also like the meatballs. I love the atmosphere and energy. I just feel happy being there.

Craig's, an American Restaurant, 8826 Melrose Avenue, West Hollywood; (310) 276-1900; http://craigs.la

. . . .

La La Anthony, actress, disc jockey, and television personality

LA has great restaurants. I'm a fan of Katsuya and Katana. I like Beso, Eva's restaurant. But then I love Jerry's Deli simply because I have a five-year-old. We can get milkshakes or anything we want and just hang. Or he even loves Johnny Rockets on Melrose—spots just to have mom and son time.

Katana Restaurant, 8439 West Sunset Boulevard, West Hollywood; (323) 650-8585

Beso Hollywood, 6350 Hollywood Boulevard, Hollywood; (323) 467-7991; www.besohollywood.com

Jerry's Famous Deli, various locations; www.jerrysfamousdeli.com

Johnny Rockets, 7507 Melrose Avenue, Los Angeles; (323) 651-3361; www.johnnyrockets.com

. . . .

Craig Zadan, Academy Award–winning motion picture, television, and theater producer, director, and writer

The Ivy is a great restaurant on Robertson. I love the atmosphere and the food is fantastic. It's very country, beautiful and comfortable.

The Ivy, 113 North Robertson Boulevard, Los Angeles; (310) 274-8303; www.theivyla.com

. . . .

Illeana Douglas, Emmy-nominated actress, writer, producer

My favorite thing about LA is that you're in the center of where they're making movies. That always inspires me. I'm from the East Coast and I love the East Coast. But to me, this is where I love making movies. Also, I live in a historic district with a bunch of little California bungalows. I have a very old house that was built around 1916. It has the flavor of when the burgeoning silent movie era was starting. It's a small little bungalow and everybody on my street is in the movie business. I always try to think we're all in vaudeville. You know, an actor with a suitcase. I think of myself as a tourist here—probably what people thought in the 20s and the 30s.

I've gotten into a ritual where I go to the Farmers Market pretty much on Wednesdays or Fridays when I'm not working. I ride my bike there and I just love it. The one on Fairfax and 3rd is probably my single favorite place in LA. Fridays is the best day. Director Paul Mazursky has a table there on Fridays. So, it's kind of an eclectic mix of younger folks and a bunch of comedy writers, sort of headed by Paul. Different people come by: the artist Charlie Bragg, Richard Kind, Jeff Garland, Jo Anne Worley. It's a total blast to go there. And then, I'll bring friends that I'm working with like Laraine Newman. On Fridays, it gets to be a pretty astonishingly large group.

What I love about the Farmers Market is that it has been around for a long time. So it has some history to it. You can get pretty much anything, from a box of chocolates to a loaf of bread, to a whole chicken to a steak. There's amazing little food kiosks, but also, if you forget someone's birthday, you can grab a card, or you can grab fruit. There's a variety of different bakeries and you don't have to use a car. So you can just walk from place to place. The Coffee Corner has my favorite coffee. Across the way is Bob's doughnut shop which makes fresh doughnuts. I think it's the best doughnut place. I get what I call the classic Dick Tracy. I go for just the plain, the old-fashioned doughnut. They make the best doughnuts in California. They're just really, really fresh.

The other thing that's interesting about Farmers Market is that it changes throughout the day. So when we get there at say 9:00 in the morning, it's mainly older people and they're having their coffee and doughnuts and sitting around. They're talking about the day's events and it has a New York vibe early on.

Then, as the day gets into 11:00, 12:00, there's a different influx of people. There are people that have been rejected from *The Price Is Right.* That whole crowd wanders in. Then, you start to get the tourists. I usually try to get out of there by lunchtime because it is jammed with tourists. Then, in the afternoon, it gets quiet. At night, it becomes a singles place. You can get wine or beer. They've got karaoke, I mean, it's crazy. I've had birthday parties there. So for LA, for a place to change that much in a whole day, it's just amazing. It just caters to a whole different group of people.

I was always a huge Paul Mazursky fan and then, right after I had moved here, a friend of mine was at Farmers Market and I was doing a movie in Chicago. And he said, I see that Paul Mazursky is at the Farmers Market. And this table, boy I'd love to get into that table. I said, "well, I know Paul. When I get back, I'll stop back and say hi." So, I stopped by and said hi and then, before he knew it, we just were hanging out there. It's a nice, fun way to start your day by just sitting around drinking coffee, talking about movies and things like that. Then, it just slowly grew. More and more people started coming by. I mean, they have been going there for probably twenty years.

On Fridays, people come by who Paul has worked with over his career. One of the comedians, Ronnie Schell, is friends with a couple of the women from *Laugh-In*, Anne Elder and Jo Anne Worley. George Schlatter or Joseph Wambaugh comes by. It's an eclectic group. You hear jokes, or it's just people talking and it makes me not take things too seriously. We've all gone through different health scares and loved ones passing away and they were always very supportive. They have become a family.

Even if I'm away for a long time working, I get my coffee, sidle up to the table, and I'm back in business.

The Farmers' Market, 6333 West 3rd Street; (323) 933-9211; www.farmersmarketla.com

The Coffee Corner, 6333 West 3rd Street; (323) 938-0278; www.coffeecornerla.com

Bob's Coffee & Doughnuts, 6333 West 3rd Street; (323) 933-8929; www.farmersmarketla.com

....

Richard Kind, actor

I like going to the Farmers Market for breakfast or lunch with a lot of old guys who meet there every day Monday through Friday. They're funny. They talk about sports, politics, and movies and they look forward to it. It's fun to be there. There's an energy there—to see them young again when they get active. I call it the Algonquin Hotel roundtable of LA.

The Farmers Market, 6333 West 3rd Street; (323) 933-9211; www.farmersmarketla.com

....

Tena Clark, Grammy-winning composer, lyricist, and CEO/chief creative officer for DMI Music & Media Solutions

I love Pasadena. I've been in LA thirty years and for the first five or six years, I lived all over. I've lived in the Hollywood Hills, in Woodland Hills, in North Hollywood. And about twenty-five years ago, I ended up moving to Pasadena. I'm originally from Mississippi; Pasadena was the only place I had found in Los Angeles that really gave me that sense of community. It's very artsy, has a lot of culture, museums, great restaurants. And what drew me there at first was the very, very progressive walk your talk Episcopal church called All Saints Episcopal Church. And so I wanted to raise my daughter there in that church. It's still a pillar for me.

I know different people are passionate about different areas in Los Angeles. But to me there's nowhere else that's got this great architecture as far as homes are concerned. There's everything from the Huntington Gardens to Old Town Pasadena to the Rose Bowl. If I had to pick a place in LA that had the best restaurants, it would definitely be Pasadena.

My partner, Michelle, and I are foodies. We love the Arroyo Chop House. It opened about fifteen years ago. To me, hands down, it's the best steak and chop house in the US. I know that's saying a lot but it's fantastic. I pretty much get the same thing, the fillet. And Michelle has the crab legs. They have family-style vegetables which are very fresh and the wine selection is really good. The service is impeccable. The food is just very consistent. So many of my clients over the years who come into town always want me to take them there. So it's where I take everybody to eat.

My favorite breakfast place hands down is in this little bitty place in a house called Marston's restaurant. And I've been going there for twenty-five years. It's real homey and has great pancakes, french toast, and really reminds of the South. The multigrain blueberry pancakes are a must. They're thin, but a little bit thicker than crepes.

Huntington Library, Art Collections and Botanical Gardens, 1151 Oxford Road, San Marino; (626) 405-2100; http://huntington.org

Old Town Pasadena, 1 Colorado Boulevard, Pasadena; (626) 356-9725; www.oldpasadena.org

Rose Bowl, 1001 Rose Bowl Drive, Pasadena; (626) 577-3101; www.rosebowlstadium.com

Arroyo Chop House, 536 South Arroyo Parkway, Pasadena; (626) 577-7463; www.arroyochophouse.com

Marston's Restaurant, 151 East Walnut Street, Pasadena; (626) 796-2459; www.marstonsrestaurant.com

....

Kirsten Segal, of the Fred Segal boutique (and granddaughter of Fred)

I have lived in Los Angeles my entire life. There's so much that LA offers, But if I had one treasured place, I would say, my family's favorite restaurant is Divino in Brentwood. I've been going there since I was in elementary school.

I played soccer growing up. And after all of our elementary soccer games, a few families, we'd go over to Divino, have dinner, and that tradition continued to take place in high school. It evolved into it being my family's go-to restaurant for any and every celebration. For years, every birthday, anniversary, everything, we'd celebrate there. I actually turned twenty-five last week, and we celebrated there.

Goran Milic, who owns the restaurant, has become a very dear friend. He is so passionate about food, and service. His restaurant is his dream come true. He came from Montenegro with nothing, and his dream was to open a restaurant. It's been around for quite some time, and does very well. It's charming, and I always feel like I am in my dining room, and not in a fancy restaurant that's uncomfortable. It has a homey appeal. We actually have a joke because his second in line is also named Goran. So it's Goran number one, and Goran number two. And my dad has claimed that he is honorary Goran number three. Although, his name's Michael.

The food at Divino is unbelievable. I've tried almost everything on the menu. But now I have the same thing every time. The pasta e fagioli del mare soup, a bean soup with calamari, shrimp, and clams, is so fresh. I've never had anything like it, not anywhere else. The flavors mesh so well together. For a main course, I love pollo portofino, which is a moist and juicy chicken with tomato sauce and olives. It's making me hungry right now.

Even if we didn't know Goran, the restaurant would still be very special. The food is so delicious. The service is impeccable. The ambiance is so great. I've watched people leave there so happy.

Divino, 11714 Barrington Court, Brentwood; (310) 472-0886; www.divinobrentwood.com

Valentin Chmerkovskiy, dancer, *Dancing with the Stars*

I grew up in New York. I say people survive in New York, but they live in LA. That's the difference. Maybe it's the weather and the way the city is formatted, but everything in LA is designed for you to enjoy yourself.

My favorite spot is Fratelli Café. Fratelli means brothers in Italian and the restaurant was opened by two brothers. And it's a place that my brother, Maksim, and I visit. The owners are so friendly and it's so family oriented. The feeling you get there is like *Cheers*. Everybody knows your name and honestly the food is incredible, It's funny, the owner's name is Yaron and, I'll say, I'd like "the Yaron special" and that's what he makes—whatever he wants.

Fratelli Café, 7200 Melrose Avenue, Los Angeles; (323) 938-CAFE; www.fratellicafe.com

Cheryl Cecchetto, founder and president, Sequoia Productions, which produces the Academy and Emmy Awards Governors balls and many other events

I absolutely love Ray's and Stark Bar. It's actually named after the late filmmaker Ray Stark who did *Funny Girl*, *Steel Magnolias*, and many other films. It's been hailed by *Esquire* as one of the best new restaurants of 2011. You're sitting outside on a Friday afternoon having a glass of wine next door. One part is the restaurant, the other is the bar. Stark Bar has phenomenal cheeses and an incredible sommelier, Paul Sanguinetti. The executive chef is Kris Morningstar. The tastes are just overwhelming to one's senses.

The other place I love is—never go wrong, never go wrong—Spago Beverly Hills. I work with Wolfgang Puck [Spago's] and Joachim Splichal [Ray's and Stark Bar]. When I go in there, I see everybody. They're all my friends. I feel like I'm going home. You know when you go to a place and recognize people and they recognize you? That's awesome.

Ray's and Stark Bar, 5905 Wilshire Boulevard, Los Angeles; (323) 857-6180; www.patinagroup.com/restaurant. php?restaurants_id=133

Spago Beverly Hills, 176 North Canon Drive, Beverly Hills; (310) 385-0880; www.wolfgangpuck.com

....

Lisa Gilbar, ACSW, LMSW, a clinical therapist specializing in working with creative artists

When I was a kid growing up in LA, we lived just up the hill from Carney's, a hamburger/hot dog restaurant in a yellow train car. It was, hands down, my favorite place to eat. What kid wouldn't want to eat inside an actual train car on the side of the road? My parents always asked me if I wanted to go to "the train car" and they never once used the name "Carney's," so I thought it was actually called "The Train Car."

Coming back to LA as an adult, I asked some friends if they wanted to go to "The Train Car" and when they asked if I meant "Carney's," I had no idea what they were talking about. I was shocked to discover it had an actual name! And that other people knew about it! To me, The Train Car meant delicious hamburgers and french fries, a small root beer (because that's what my dad always ordered), and, the best part . . . a chocolate-dipped frozen banana. To this day, when I step into that yellow car, I still feel like that excited ten-year-old, preparing to enjoy my favorite meal in my favorite place. There are plenty of fancy restaurants around LA with exotic cuisine, but this inexpensive little hamburger place, my Train Car, will always be home to me.

Carney's, 8351 West Sunset Boulevard, Los Angeles; (323) 654-8300; www.carneytrain.com

....

Martin Papazian, actor, director, and writer (*Least Among Saints*)

Every Sunday for the last fifteen years, I go to my parents' house in Westchester. They have a backyard, so I get away from the city. My little brother is handicapped and has cerebral palsy. I have two German shepherds. We spend the day in the backyard and play, work and swim. I've trained the dogs to catch the ball that my brother throws to them and they put it back in his chair. That's my ritual and probably one of my most favorite things to do in LA.

Otherwise, my Saturday morning is all about boxing in Santa Monica, going to Axe for multigrain pancakes, and walking on the beach.

Joe Rivera at Focus Fitness has a great class on the promenade that's a killer workout and a great group of people. It's a workout via boxing, so it's a lot of fun. It's a serious class. The music is cranked up, you put on mitts and gloves and spar.

And religiously, I have to go to Axe and eat their multigrain pancakes because I'm addicted. Axe is a great restaurant on Abbot Kinney and very popular in Venice. The décor is so cool. It has concrete floors, wooden tables and open spaces. They have the back section where they have long wooden tables. The pancakes, I have to say, are incredible. And they only serve them on the weekends. They're great with an Americano. Once I was reading while I was eating and a person said "are you really going to read while you're eating that pancake," oh, sorry, I'll close my laptop and get to the business of why we're here.

I'm a screenwriter, so Axe is a great place to sit in the back and just get really focused on a piece and work, especially after a long week. And then I go walking the beach. After you've worked out really hard in the morning, it's a perfect day.

My brother is my grounding force and my favorite person in the world. It's such a treat to be able to do things with him. When my dog was really young, he was a wild German shepherd. I really wanted to take them all to the Getty Museum. And so I snuck my dog in with my brother. Because my brother is in a wheelchair and the dog is a German shepherd he had kind of a fancy harness. So we just cruised in, walked around, and saw great art. The dog got in line. We had an amazing day with this big hundred-pound part-wolf German shepherd and my little brother. Something about the idea of doing that was exciting and fun. It was just one of those days that I always revel in. My little caper.

Joe Rivera's Focus (Center) Fitness, (310) 499-4950; http://focuscenterfitness.com

Axe, 1009 Abbot Kinney Boulevard, Venice; (310) 664-9787; www.axerestaurant.com

. . . .

Stephen Schwartz, Academy Award–, Grammy-, Golden Globe–winning, and Tony-nominated lyricist and composer

I recently went to a really great restaurant called Bazaar in the SLS hotel. They do molecular gastronomy. It's fantastic. I had the tasting menu and tried a lot of things. They brought these frozen smoking drinks. It was wild and the food was great.

I also love to hike up in the canyons like Beachwood Canyon, where the Hollywood sign is, and Runyon Canyon. There are really nice walks there. There was a period of time in the 1990s when I had an apartment in LA and it was right below Runyon Canyon which is the big dog-walking canyon. And when I was writing, I used to go hiking up those trails in the morning to get inspired.

The Bazaar by José Andrés, SLS Hotel, 465 South La Cienega Boulevard, Los Angeles; (310) 246-5555; www.thebazaar.com

....

Jonathan Krisel, Emmy-nominated director and writer

Here's a place that no one knows about, the Beachwood Cafe. It's a secret restaurant hidden up in Beachwood Canyon. And it used to be a dump. It used to be the most depressing, nightmare zone. And a woman, a chef from Portland, took it over and they redid the wall paper. It's much friendlier and very kid friendly. It's really good now. They have oatmeal in the morning and it's really good. I hate oatmeal usually. They also have a great tofu dish.

Beachwood Cafe, 2695 North Beachwood Drive, Los Angeles; (323) 871-1717; http://beachwoodcafe.com

....

Sang Yoon, head chef and owner of the gastropubs, Father's Office, in Santa Monica and Los Angeles, and Lukshon by Sang Yoon

People always talk about New York being a great food city, which it is. I don't think LA gets credited as often because it's just so sprawled. To the outsider they think in any given neighborhood, we don't have the density of a New York City. So it doesn't look like we have as much. But believe me, it just takes longer to discover it because it's just so spread out. I know that our ethnic neighborhoods are where it's really at. If you took LA and gathered it, pushed it all together to a more dense area, it might be the best food city in the world.

There's so many great restaurants in the San Gabriel Valley. But one of my absolute favorite places that doesn't get a lot of hype is 101 Noodle there. They have this most amazing dish called a beef roll, which comes from northwestern

China. It's funny because when you grow up in LA, you eat a lot of burritos. This is almost like a Chinese burrito. It's magnificent, crisp, almost a cross between a crepe and a tortilla. It's flat, white, beautiful, flaky and delicious. Inside, it has amazing marinated brisket. It's a little spicy and just full of cilantro stems, lots of herbs, and it's cut into little, small sections like you're eating little burritos. It's magnificent.

It's sort of funny because this beef roll is Chinese food, but looks like a burrito. You know what? That's LA. That's who we are. We like handheld things. We live in our cars, so everything has to be handheld here. We're always on the run, we don't stop.

101 Noodle Express, 1408 East Valley Boulevard, Alhambra; (626) 300-8654

....

Ezra Doner, production, finance, and motion picture distribution attorney

Langer's Deli is the great Jewish deli of LA. It's on South Alvarado Street right near MacArthur Park, an area that is the furthest thing from being a Jewish neighborhood, much less a nondescript neighborhood with a corner shopping mall. Talk about an ethnic fish out of water.

The deli and food are fabulous. It is the ultimate Jewish deli food. I used to go there on my way to Dodger Stadium. I'd pick up sandwiches and smuggle them into the stadium, and they were so fantastic. I'd also just go there if I ever had an excuse to be around the area. It's the kind of place you pass through on a freeway, just west of downtown. The hours there are 8:00 a.m. to 4:00 p.m. now, so, it's not even open for dinner. You can't go downtown and go to the theater and say, we'll stop for a bite at Langer's afterward. But when you're craving corned beef brisket, pastrami, that's where you go. There are other Jewish delis in LA. But there's a kind of authenticity to the food at Langer's which is great.

Langer's Delicatessen-Restaurant, 704 South Alvarado Street, Los Angeles; (213) 483-8050; www.langersdeli.com

....

Max Jacobson, food, wine, and travel writer and journalist

My favorite places in L.A. are all food related. My first L.A. neighborhood, MacArthur Park, is still home to Langer's Delicatessen, which makes the best pastrami sandwich in the world. I also lived in the suburb of Monterey Park, a majority Asian city where the Sam Woo barbecue chain started. Their five spice chicken still draws raves.

Langer's Delicatessen-Restaurant, 704 South Alvarado Street, Los Angeles; (213) 483-8050; www.langersdeli.com

....

Matt Lanter, actor

I live in the Valley near Ventura Boulevard. So I'm always experimenting with new restaurants there. But one of my favorite spots is Aroma cafe. It's this nice quaint little place with amazing ambiance and the food is great. I get the turkey and hummus sandwich all the time. And their desserts are to die for.

Aroma Coffee & Tea Co., 4360 Tujunga Avenue, Studio City; (818) 508-0677; www.aromacoffeeandtea.com

....

Zane Buzby, comedy director of over 200 sitcoms and founder of The Survivor Mitzvah Project, a non-profit charity helping Holocaust Survivors in Eastern Europe

I came to LA from NYC with a rock 'n' roll band in the late 70s. At the old Columbia sound stages where Bette Milder and Alice Cooper were rehearsing during the day, we launched our band by setting up kick-ass midnight shows, not knowing that everyone in LA goes to sleep at 9:30 p.m. with their asses already kicked. After all, it's a film town, always in danger of losing the light. But the real surprise was that there was absolutely no real Chinese food here. The few Chinese restaurants that existed had a bottle of ketchup and a basket of white bread on the table. I was horrified.

Forget about pizza. Good pizza didn't exist. And if you just wanted a taste, you had to buy the whole lousy pie. The concept of selling "a slice" had yet to be invented in this new land. It became instantly apparent. This was no place for a New Yorker.

Then Genghis Cohen opened. Alan Rinde, another transplanted New Yorker in the music business desperate for Chinese food, opened his own restaurant. He got it right. Years later, this is still the only place in LA for real New York egg rolls. I've had the same meal there ever since: egg rolls, Queen Chicken, Crackerjack Shrimp, and Szechuan eggplant, dining with Conan Berkeley, Larry Brezner, or Rick Newman when he's in town. It's eat-the-plate good. And there's even a music space there now for up and coming performers.

And finally, a New York pizza joint, Two Boots, just opened downtown and in Echo Park. A fabulous mix of Italy and Louisiana (trust me on this one) has salivating New Yorkers coming out in droves, relieved that their "LA pizza nightmare" is finally over. After more than a quarter of a century, there is now great pizza by the slice in LA.

Genghis Cohen, 740 North Fairfax Avenue, Los Angeles; (323) 653-0640; www.genghiscohen.com

Two Boots, 826 Broadway and 1818 West Sunset Boulevard, Los Angeles; (213) 623-2100, (213) 413-2668; la.twoboots.com

....

Elizabeth Much, Much and House Public Relations

My favorite vegan restaurant in Los Angeles is Real Food Daily with locations in Santa Monica, West Hollywood, and Pasadena. My favorite location is on La Cienega since it's near my office—and the parking is easier during the day than the Santa Monica location. They have every kind of food imaginable to appease wary vegetarians to diehard raw foodies. The chef and owner, Ann Gentry, features weekly specials on salads and main courses so the menu is never stagnant. Also, the desserts and fresh smoothies and juices are delicious and nourishing. I love their macrobiotic dish, the Real Food Meal, since it's nature's perfect balance of foods, with their homemade peanut sauce. I always feel so good after I eat that. And I finally found a place that I could have a piece of chocolate cake and know that the ingredients are pure and healthy!

Real Food Daily (West Hollywood), 414 North La Cienega Boulevard, Los Angeles; (310) 289-9910; www.realfood.com

NOCTURNAL LOS ANGELES

 If you have an appetite and a curiosity for any kind of cultural desire it's an education to be in Los Angeles. Growing up here, we lived very close to UCLA, and so I saw every dance company that ever came through town. All the theater. at the Mark Taper Forum and the Dorothy Chandler Pavilion. I saw the Alvin Ailey Dance Company when Judith Jamison was a dancer with the company. It was a great place to grow up.

—Laraine Newman,
Emmy-nominated actress, comedian, and writer

"Merv says that he hired me because I turn the letters better than any of the two hundred other women who auditioned . . . And what's my secret? As I told *60 Minutes,* 'It must be in the wrist!'"

Some people might stumble upon this passage from Vanna White's auto-biography, *Vanna Speaks,* and merely laugh, turn the page, and move on. But for performer-writers Eugene Pack and Dayle Reyfel, this section and others were pure revelation.

Pack and Reyfel found the details utterly hilarious. They thought, what would it be like to actually read them to an audience? So when the owner of the Venice performance space, Creativity, asked Pack to do one of his one man shows there, Pack asked if he, Reyfel, and their performer friends could offer a night of celebrity memoir reading instead.

Armed with tomes from Mr. T, Elizabeth Taylor, and Neil Sedaka, Reyfel recalls the debut of *Celebrity Autobiography.* "It was more like a bunch of friends gathering together in this very cool artsy space." The first night was an instant hit and the owner asked them back on a weekly basis. Culling more and more material from libraries and used bookstores, they began to see how the "found" comedy worked its magic in front of an audience. "The goal wasn't, what are we going to turn this into," explains Reyfel. "We were just having fun."

It did not take long before a steady audience began to grow.

And then one day one hundred people showed up, filled up the space, and everything changed.

Celebrity Autobiography not only endured, but gained a fervent and devoted following. They began performing regularly at ROOM 5, a performance space in Amalfi restaurant (where Nat King Cole once performed). Steve Martin showed up and was wowed. *Star Trek*'s George Takei, whose memoir they read, sat in the audience and laughed along. Bravo turned *Celebrity Autobiography* into a TV special. The show made its way to New York City where it continues to play regularly at The Triad theater (now Stage 72). *Time* magazine anointed *Celebrity Autobiography,* "the funniest docu-theater stunt of the year." The show earned a Drama Desk award and has become an international sensation performed in theaters from Sydney Opera House to Edinburgh, Scotland, to London's West End.

Now a multitude of stars (Matthew Broderick, Kristen Wiig, Alec Baldwin, Nathan Lane, Brooke Shields, Rita Wilson, Ryan Reynolds) and countless others have joined the ranks of the rotating cast who can be found reading about what Sylvester Stallone stocks in his refrigerator or reciting the early love poetry of Suzanne Somers. Grocery lists, sexy escapades, and restaurant ordering rituals continue to be laid out in full detail. And they've added performances at LA's ACME Comedy Theater and music-themed readings at the legendary Grammy museum. "If you had been reading this out loud to someone you might say, 'can you believe they wrote this?'" says Reyfel. "But that's essentially what the show is. When we learned that the audience found it even more hilarious than we could ever imagine, that's when it started getting really exciting."

And that's what makes this LA night so exciting.

....

Susan Sarandon, Academy Award–winning and Golden Globe–nominated actress

I don't go to LA unless I really have to. But now I am opening a SPiN in downtown LA at the Standard. And my eldest son lives in LA and my daughter lives in LA.

SPiN is a great place to gather to philosophize, play, and get physical activity, because it cuts across age and gender and body type. Anybody can do it. There's music and food.

I would like to get Ping-Pong tables in all the underserved schools that don't have phys ed programs. We've already put them in forty schools in New York and if every franchise managed to take on that project, I'd be very happy and then we'll build a little Ping-Pong nation.

SPiN LA At The Standard (Downtown LA), 550 South Flower, Los Angeles; (213) 892-8080; standardhotels.com/ downtown-la/location

....

Michael Stuhlbarg, Golden Globe–nominated actor

I went to UCLA for two years and lived in Santa Monica. I loved going to the Nuart Theatre down the street from where I lived. They showed first-run foreign films.

Nuart Theatre, 11272 Santa Monica Boulevard, Los Angeles; (310) 473-8530; www.landmarktheatres.com

....

Corbin Bleu, actor, dancer, and singer

I like to go to a great salsa club called El Floridita. They have great food like rice and beans and good salsa dancing. On certain nights, they have live bands, but you have to check the schedule.

El Floridita Cuban Restaurant, 1253 North Vine Street, Hollywood; (323) 871-8612; www.elfloridita.com

....

Ilse Metchek, president, California Fashion Association

My favorite thing in the whole world is to go salsa dancing. I don't even know where they get the clothes they wear. People are well groomed, but flashy and always in the height of style. If pants are in, they wear pants. If shorts are in, they wear shorts on the dance floor. The only thing that's consistent is danceable shoes.

El Floridita is one of my favorite salsa dancing places. It's great food, a full dance floor, and a full band with a seven-piece orchestra in a little strip mall joint. You can't even imagine how they get all this stuff in there. I sometimes leave after one set and it's 11:30 at night on a Monday and there's a line around the block. I don't know what these people do. Where could they possibly be working?

El Floridita, 1253 North Vine Street, Hollywood; (323) 871-8612; www.elfloridita.com

....

Kellan Lutz, actor

One of my new favorite things to do in LA is to go to Sunday Night Jazz nights at the W Hollywood. It's special because I've never been one to go out and party or go to the LA scene. It's just not me. I love being outdoors.

But I just went to *Book of Mormon* at the Pantages, which was amazing. So I'm glad more stuff like that is coming. And this jazz night at the W has been going on for years. I just wasn't aware of it. And then I heard Brenna Whitaker there. I go all the time now, as much as I can when I'm in town, because it just feels so separated from LA and the industry. It's a more sophisticated, classy environment. There's so many more talented performers each and every week. Michael Bolton was there. My buddy Gavin DeGraw sang. A lot of great dancers show up. It's very classy.

W Hollywood presents Sunday Night Jazz nights, 6250 Hollywood Boulevard, Hollywood; (323) 798-1300; www.whollywoodhotel.com

....

Ruth Vitale, founder and former co-president of Paramount Classics, former
president of Fine Line, CEO of The Film Collective, a consulting and theatrical
distribution company

I came to LA because I had a job offer to be a production executive at United Artists. When I got the offer, I thought, I'd rather eat dirt. Okay? I'm not coming. And
Peter Guber, who had arranged the interview for the job said to me, "I think you'd
better come." So I ended up coming out here in 1988. And I remember thinking,
"Oh. Oh. I don't know." That was 1988. Need I say more?

The thing about Los Angeles is that it took me twenty-four years to get used
to it and embrace. When I first moved here from New York, I was so miserable.
A friend of mine said: "Don't worry, Ruth. You will get used to it." I looked at him
hopefully and asked: "How long will it take?" With a complete straight face, he said:
"About twenty years." And that's about how long it took.

The fantastic thing about Los Angeles is that it offers all different kinds of
activities within an hour to an hour and a half outside the city—which you can't
say about most places. I live at the top of Laurel Canyon. And from my home, it
doesn't matter where you're going; it always takes you twenty minutes minimum.
And so a lot of times an hour car ride doesn't seem very long, whereas when I lived
in New York an hour car ride seemed like an eternity. From my house to the snow
is an hour. Okay, maybe an hour and ten minutes. And I'm talking real snow. I'm
talking twelve feet of snow. And I can bring my godchildren out there and we can
go sledding and it's magical. Thirty minutes from my house is Middle Ranch where
I ride. One thousand acres of beautiful grounds with six hunter/jumper rings, two
dressage rings, a covered arena, an Olympic-sized swimming pool, and miles of
trails. Again, magical in its own right.

One of my favorite places is the Chateau Marmont. I've seen it change so
dramatically over the last twenty-four years. I remember when a friend of mine
used to live there when he was here from Germany. He'd say, "Come on over." And
I would be afraid to put my feet on the floor in his suite because it was just so dis-
gusting. It was so scary. He'd say, "Why are you looking so uncomfortable?" And I'd
say, "I don't know. It just seems like there might be rats on the floor here."

It was really questionable, really sketchy. And then they redid the place and now it's magnificent. And what's really fun is the lobby where you check in. You walk down a couple of steps and you're in a living room area and there's a piano. I've never actually seen anyone play the piano there in all the years I've gone. And there are big couches where you can sit and have dinner.

In LA you kind of get tired of eating out all the time—which I guess is the same in any city. So when you go to the Chateau, you make yourself comfortable in the living room on one of the sofas. It's like having dinner at your own home, only you don't have to cook. They have several groupings of sofas, club chairs, and tables where four or five people can hang around. It's still just lovely and a great kind of layabout for a night out. And then, outside of the living room area, there's a big garden with regular dining room tables, which is always lovely for dinner. I prefer inside only because I like collapsing on a sofa and curling up. The biggest problem about going to the Chateau, frankly, is parking. Since there's so little parking around there, they charge $12 to $20 to park around there. You've got to be kidding me!

Chateau Marmont, 8221 Sunset Boulevard, Hollywood; (323) 656-1010; www.chateaumarmont.com

....

Laraine Newman, Emmy-nominated actress, comedian, and writer

We would take our kids to see comedy around town. Then our kids got older and went off to college. But we kept up the tradition of going around town to see comedy with other couples. We go out to dinner and either go to the Groundlings, which is my alma mater and has amazing shows, or to the Largo at the Coronet Theatre. It would literally start out with a great meal somewhere like Mozza. And we would see something like Sarah Silverman and Friends and she would have people like Russell Brand, and all sorts of incredible stand-ups. You would never know who you'd get, but it was always a fantastic line-up.

In LA there are venues for people trying out new material, so you can see people like Maria Bamford, Eddie Pepitone, Danny Gold, Marc Maron, Greg Proops. You can go to the Upright Citizens Brigade (UCB) and see Paul F. Tompkins do shows that I've actually been in. I recently did his show called *Dead Authors* where he comes out as H. G. Wells, and through his time machine, he brings back a dead author to interview. I was Mary Shelley. I think he had Patton Oswalt with Shel Silverstein and Jen Kirkman with Dorothy Parker. He has amazing people.

Meltdown Comics, which is an amazing comic book store on Sunset, has a back room that is really not meant for the stage at all. I don't even know how they got any kind of zoning or anything like that. Incredible people do shows there—podcasts, you name it. Then there's MI Westside Comedy Theatre, which is in the alley in Santa Monica between Third and Fourth Street.

And when you live in Los Angeles, you have access to great music. I've always been a huge fan of rock and roll, ever since I was a kid. Where the Improv West stands now, used to be a club called the Ash Grove. Every single person you saw in that movie *Cadillac Records*—Eddie Taylor, Muddy Waters, Howlin' Wolf, Willie Dixon and the Chicago All-Stars, T-Bone Walker—I mean everybody. I've seen all those people playing at the Ash Grove.

I saw the Beatles at the Hollywood Bowl. When I was a teenager, I saw David Bowie at the Hollywood Palladium. And cut to 2012. Skrillex is now playing at the Hollywood Palladium. My almost but not quite eighteen-year-old wants to go but there's an age limit. Being the good mother that I am, I scored her a fake ID. I wasn't going to miss that show just because of some kid. Going there was such a time travel experience. I had been there once before because I do this animated series called *Metalocolypse*. The guy who writes it also writes the music, plays it, and tours. They had done a show at the Palladium. It was amazing. It's like Death Metal. It's so great.

These are the things that I love about LA. If you have an appetite and a curiosity for any kind of cultural desire it's an education to be in Los Angeles. Growing up here, we lived very close to UCLA, and so I saw every dance company that ever came through town. All the theater. I would go to the Mark Taper Forum and the Dorothy Chandler Pavilion. But there was great theater even at UCLA. I saw the Alvin Ailey Dance Company when Judith Jamison was a dancer with the company. It was a great place to grow up.

The Groundlings Theatre & School, 7307 Melrose Avenue, Los Angeles; (323) 934-4747; www.groundlings.com

Largo at the Cornet, 366 North La Cienega Boulevard, Los Angeles; (310) 855-0350; www.largo-la.com

Osteria Mozza, 6602 Melrose Avenue, Hollywood; (323) 297-0100; www.osteriamozza.com

The Upright Citizens Brigade Theatre, 5919 Franklin Avenue, Los Angeles; (323) 908-8702; http://losangeles.ucbtheatre.com

Meltdown Comics & Collectibles, 7522 West Sunset Boulevard, Los Angeles; (323) 851-7223; www.meltcomics.com

Ml Westside Comedy Theatre, Santa Monica, 1323 3rd Street; (310) 451-0850; http://westsidecomedy.com/index.cfm

Improv West/iO West Theatre & Training Center (formerly ImprovOlympic West), 6366 Hollywood Boulevard, Los Angeles; (323) 962-7560; http://ioimprov.com/west

Hollywood Palladium, 6215 West Sunset Boulevard, Los Angeles; (323) 962-7600

. . . .

Bobby Moynihan, actor and comedian

When I do get out to LA, I spend most of my time at the Upright Citizen's Brigade (UCB) Theatre and the Chinese restaurant around the corner. I don't even know the name of the Chinese restaurant, but I go there all the time when I'm in LA.

I was an acting major in college. I saw an Upright Citizens Brigade show and immediately thought this is something I want to do. I did UCB for about ten years and I'm still doing it now. That's kind of how I grew up. If you love comedy, it's a place for you and your friends to do it every day of the week. And you meet other people who like comedy and are like minded. Everyone who started with me there is now working in television in some capacity. I truly believe that I wouldn't be on *Saturday Night Live* if it wasn't for being there that long and meeting all these amazing comedians and working with them.

Upright Citizens Brigade Theatre, 5919 Franklin Avenue, Los Angeles; (323) 908-8702; http://losangeles.ucbtheatre.com

. . . .

Toni Trucks, actress (*The Twilight Saga: Breaking Dawn - Part 2*)

I love LA. I love Mozza. There are two sections—the osteria and the pizzeria. And I love the pizzeria side. The pizza has such wonderful fresh ingredients.

And then I have my guilty pleasures. KyoChon, which is Korean fried chicken, is just so good. The chicken is made with rice flour instead of regular flour. They have a way of cooking it so it just gets really, really crispy and tasty.

But what I really love about LA is the comedy. I go to so many comedy shows. The Meltdown comedy show is in the back of a comic book store called Meltdown Comics. And Wednesday nights at eight for something like five dollars all of these wonderful, giant comedians perform unannounced. They want to test out new material. They don't advertise it. I've seen Taj there—so many wonderful, great people.

KyoChon Chicken, 3833 West 6th Street, Los Angeles; (213) 739-9292

Meltdown Comics & Collectibles, 7522 West Sunset Boulevard, Los Angeles; (323) 851-7223; www.meltcomics.com

....

Justin Long, actor

I like going to the restaurant Animal. And then we walk over to the silent movie theater, called Cinefamily. I love it. It's not all silent movies, they show a lot of old cult movies and stuff that's been out of print for a while. It's a great, great night out in LA.

Animal, 435 North Fairfax Avenue, Los Angeles; (323) 782-9225; www.animalrestaurant.com

The Cinefamily, 611 North Fairfax Avenue, Los Angeles; (323) 655-2510; www.cinefamily.org

....

Merle Ginsberg, fashion writer, television personality, senior writer, *Hollywood Reporter*

One thing about LA that is very much part of my world, is the whole wine scenario. There's a lot of wine tasting and classes. People have gotten very serious about it. People don't go out drinking here to get drunk. Because first of all you can't get drunk because you're driving. And to me, that whole drunk thing is all about escapism anyway. We don't have that much to escape. People drink here in an "I want to learn" kind of way.

There is a restaurant and a bar called AOC which is the mark that goes on a wine bottle. I think it means Appellation d'Origine Contrôlée. AOC is kind of close to where I live and they serve wines by the glass but they let you taste all kinds of things and the staff is incredibly educated on all the wines. You could just learn so much and they also have little appetizers of food there that are exotic and delicious. They'll have a squid ink pasta but a little, small amount. They have a little cheese plate. They'll do interesting vegetable dishes and fish dishes but they're always small. It's like tapas. And there's just a really interesting crowd.

A.O.C., 8022 West 3rd Street, Los Angeles; (323) 653-6359; www.aocwinebar.com

....

Art Streiber, celebrity/portrait photographer

The first time I ever went to the Bel-Air hotel was for a Sunday dinner with my great-grandparents. They lived in Bel Air at the corner of Sunset and Copa De Oro. So for them, the Bel-Air hotel was kind of their local. But that place is just indisputably magic. You are two minutes off of Sunset Boulevard nestled into a canyon on a creek. It's out of the hustle and bustle, yet two minutes from Sunset Boulevard, one of the busiest streets. That's crazy. There's the flora, and the topiary, and the bridge, and the swan, and the lawn and the bungalows. It's historic, secluded, quiet, and gorgeous. It's an oasis. Two of my best friends were married there. And that's where I asked my wife to marry me so that's where we went on our engagement night.

I've done a couple of photo shoots at the Bel-Air hotel. I photographed Nancy Reagan and Betsy Bloomingdale having lunch on the patio. That was the other thing that really solidified it for me. I don't know if I'd be able to do that now, but the Bel-Air was so accommodating and helpful. We do a lot of work at very high-end restaurants and hotels. And my crew and I go out of our way not to disturb the other patrons. And the Bel-Air very, very nicely put up a little screen and let me photograph Mrs. Reagan and Mrs. Bloomingdale having lunch in the middle of lunch. Also, I photographed Elvis Costello interviewing Joni Mitchell there. So that place has been a magical place for me, probably for forty years.

If we were in Hollywood and coming back to the west side, it was a great place to stop and have a drink in the old bar. I love the house margarita with rocks and salt.

You know when you do something as a kid, and you may not do it again for a long time, but then you return, and all those memories come flashing back? When my wife and I were engaged in 1989, I may not have been back there for a decade or fifteen years. But I knew enough as a naive twenty-seven-year-old getting engaged, that the Bel-Air hotel was the ritziest place in town. I went there with my great-grandfather. And you go back and fall in love all over again.

Hotel Bel-Air, 701 Stone Canyon Road, Los Angeles; (310) 472-1211; http://hotelbelair.com

....

Adriano Goldschmied, founder and Creative Director of GOLDSIGN

One place that I really love is Sunset Junction in Silver Lake. There are a lot of cafes and vintage stores. In my opinion, it's the spirit of what I call "the real LA." The real LA is not about the Rodeo Drive. In some way that's for tourists. I would say this is the real LA. The people are generally young and creative.

The cafe I love is Intelligentsia. It's very slow placed in some ways. They decorate the cappuccino properly and do things with a lot of passion and love. Even small things, that normally you wouldn't give a lot of attention to, they do so well. You see people who really love what they do. They ask you how you like your cappuccino, in which kind of cup. In the end, a cappuccino is a very simple thing, but a simple thing can have a lot of details. Plus their location is very good. Another place I like is Cafe Stella, a restaurant in the spirit of a French brasserie. The food is very good and simple. It's typical French cuisine: steak, french fries, and good wine. But again, it's the people that make it special.

For me, California is a dream. LA, in particular, is a place where dreams are invented. It was my great passion to experience the innovation, the style, the life, and to live in California with European mentality. I thought, I'm going to be part of the future.

Intelligentsia Coffee & Tea, 3922 West Sunset Boulevard, Los Angeles; (323) 663-6173; www.intelligentsiacoffee.com

Cafe Stella, 3932 West Sunset Boulevard, Los Angeles; (323) 666-0265; www.cafestella.com

....

Tracie Thoms, actress

Rockwell is a restaurant with a stage. We do cabaret shows there and it's great for brunch and dinners. I go all the time, whether I'm working or not. I love it. They have an ongoing show called *For the Record* where they take soundtracks of movies from famous directors and put them together in a show.

They did John Hughes, Baz Lehrman, the Cohen Brothers, Paul Thomas Anderson, Martin Scorsese. It is incredible. It's the director's soundtrack with scenes from the movie and songs performed live. The performers are musical theater people who do that when they're not working on Broadway. It rotates so it's always a good cast. You're watching scenes from the movie and listening to the music while eating and drinking. It's a whole experience.

Rockwell, 1714 N Vermont Avenue; Los Angeles; (323) 669-1550; http://rockwell-la.com

....

Adrian Salamunovic, co-founder DNA 11/CanvasPop, the company creates DNA portraits for celebrities

Everybody likes a speakeasy—a little secret hidden spot. The whole idea of a speakeasy is people don't really know where it is. Roger Room is one of my favorite hidden gems that I take my friends to visit.

What's cool about Roger Room is that it's extremely hidden. From the outside, it look's like a fortune teller's place. But in fact, it's a really cool, underground drinking spot that makes very high end, very interesting, not your everyday variety drinks. As you walk into the room, you feel like you've gone back in time for fifty years to the prohibition era.

The most important thing there is the bartenders. They're not bartenders, they're mixologists who are cool, wearing suspenders, elegantly dressed. And boy, do they ever know what they're doing. I like them to surprise me. It's not the place where you want to order just a gin and tonic. You want to say, "Surprise me," and you will be surprised. They make some of the most unique drinks you'll ever have.

The most creative writers, artists, actors, and socialites in LA all hang out there, and it's very low-key. It's come-as-you-are, and it's a great place. Locals tend to go there, so it's a cool, cool spot.

Roger Room, 370 North La Cienega Boulevard, West Hollywood; (310) 854-1300

....

Tova Laiter, film producer and founder, Avida Entertainment

Yamashiro has the most fantastic view of LA at night. You drive up the hill and suddenly come to this incredible panorama. And no matter how many times I go, I'm still stunned by the view with all the lights. They have great strong drinks in the front room, and in the back, they have a Japanese garden restaurant where you eat sushi. And sometimes the restaurant is better than other times, but the drinks and the view never disappoint. And with the glass windows and you can actually see the view of all of Los Angeles in front of you. It's unique.

When young kids come to town, the children of friends of mine, and they all run to those fake clubs in Hollywood that are here today and gone tomorrow. It's all about flash. They all look the same everywhere in the world. But I feel it's my duty to take them to Yamashiro and show them how it's done. This is special.

Yamashiro, 1999 North Sycamore Avenue, Hollywood; (323) 466-5125; www.yamashirorestaurant.com

....

Laura Lane, entertainment journalist and television host

One of my favorite places in Los Angeles is Yamashiro, an incredible sushi restaurant hidden in the Hollywood Hills. To get there you have to drive up a long winding road, making it feel like a secret hideaway or the equivalent to a New York speakeasy. The restaurant is nestled on a cliff with a gorgeous view that looks out over all of Hollywood and Los Angeles—it's absolutely magnificent. There's a botanical garden in the front that has been the place of a few romantic walks and intimate conversations with friends after dinner, and usually after quite a bit of sake. The food is delicious and well priced. It's located near the Magic Castle, a membership-only place where magicians gather, and sometimes you'll find that the bartenders will do magic tricks.

On one trip, one of the bartenders told my friend and me that Yamashiro used to be an old haunted house. He had an entire intricate story to go along with it and asked if we wanted a tour. He took us down to the cellar, which was pitch black. We were terrified and held on close to each other. Little did we know he had devised a plan with another bartender who at some point in our tour—which wasn't much of a tour because we couldn't see anything but shadows—jumped out from behind a table. I think all of Hollywood probably heard our screams. I never did find out if the haunted house part was true or not. But if there is a ghost at Yamashiro, I've never seen it. And it's still my number one place to go every time I'm in Los Angeles.

Yamashiro, 1999 North Sycamore Avenue, Hollywood; (323) 466-5125; www.yamashirorestaurant.com

. . . .

Nick Karno, environmental prosecutor, city attorney's office

In Los Angeles going to an outdoor show and bringing a picnic is so great. The two venues I like offer the same concept but are so different.

The Hollywood Forever cemetery has outdoor screenings. When they first started they were basically showing old movies that were public domain so they didn't have to go through a whole lot to pay a lot for the movie rights. But I believe that was relaxed more and more. And when they became more established they were able to get more modern movies.

The people who select the movies are film buffs and very particular about what they choose. They have some that are crowd pleasers like *The Exorcist*. If they're going to do a horror film they want to do one that was particularly unique in its time and really broke new ground, like Albert Hitchcock's *Psycho*. They'll also show *Butch Cassidy and the Sundance Kid, Kramer vs. Kramer* or *Ordinary People*. I've seen a number of films there. You have to fight the crowd a little bit and it's a little tricky. Everybody has their own strategy because the key is getting in and staking your spot.

This is very hipster crowd. The people who put this on are a very trendy and cool group. So, at first they have a DJ playing really unique and cool music. They put giant speakers all around and there's a massive grass field where everybody lays down blankets. Some people become very elaborate and bring mini tables, mini tablecloths, wine, cheese, olives, and candles. But we just go to Whole Foods and grab a bunch of finger food.

The film is shown against the side of the mausoleum as a bunch of people sit on the grass. On one hand you're in a cemetery and you might be thinking, *how weird.* And yet, at the same time, it's so unbelievably peaceful and beautiful all around. You're in the middle of LA. This is the heart of Hollywood. Cars, trucks, and buses should be making all sorts of noise. Yet, you can't hear a thing. The Warner Bros. Studio is close by. So once in a while if they're filming at night with a helicopter, it may be circling around. That gets kind of annoying. But other than that, I've seen dozens of films there and it's really fun.

Theatricum Botanicum is in a completely different setting. You go deep into the woods in Topanga Canyon and down into this little creek. They put in a massive outdoor theater, almost like a shell. It's more like a proper outdoor theater where you walk up to your seat and look straight down to the stage.

There are canopy tarps overhead with a little area to the side where everybody picnics before the play goes on. They show Shakespeare. I saw *A Midsummer Night's Dream* there. I saw George Orwell's *Animal House* or they'll do Molière or some other classic plays. It's Shakespeare in the park but in Topanga and very special.

Both evenings offer the same concept: bring your food and go to see a show. But one's a very hipster movie thing in the middle of Hollywood. The other is much more refined. Let's go see a play. But it's also open to everybody and it's inexpensive.

Hollywood Forever, 6000 Santa Monica Boulevard, Hollywood; (323) 469-1181; www.cinespia.org/calendar or www .hollywoodforever.com

The Will Geer Theatricum Botanicum, 1419 North Topanga Canyon Boulevard, Topanga Canyon; (310) 455-2322; www .theatricum.com

....

Julia Gogosha, owner, Gogosha Optique

Here are a few places I love that exemplify LA life. Friday night wine tasting in the summer at Barnsdall Art Park. The Frank Lloyd Wright–designed Hollyhock House sits atop a hill with panoramic views in the middle of it all. In the summer, Silver Lake Wine puts on a wine tasting on Friday evenings. You bring a blanket, picnic, and a few friends and you sit on the lawn of a Frank Lloyd Wright masterpiece, watching the sky change hues and the lights of LA begin to twinkle. You're always bound to run into many familiar faces. It's a touchstone for the casual LA social scene, except, it's not a scene at all. In the fall they also do outdoor movie screenings! All proceeds from these events go to the restoration and preservation of the Hollyhock House.

I also love watching movies at the Hollywood Forever cemetery. On the weekends (summer and fall), Cinespia puts on cult classics from *The Warriors* to *Heathers* projected on the side of a building inside of one of LA's oldest cemeteries. We've been going for the last five years to see our favorite flicks. On some of the more quotable films, you almost get a *Rocky Horror Picture Show* vibe. Everyone is there just to have a great time.

Proceeds also go to restoring the cemetery to its old glory. Hollywood Forever cemetery is the final resting place for Fay Wray, Jayne Mansfield, Rudolph Valentino, and Bugsy Siegel. An only in LA experience.

Anytime is a great time to visit Little Tokyo. I love walking around the neighborhood, weaving through the street. The end destination is always Japanese Village. An outdoor plaza with shops, a wishing tree, and the best mochi (Mikawaya) and green tea doughnuts (Cafe Dulce) in the city.

Barnsdall Art Park, 4800 Hollywood Boulevard, Los Angeles; (323) 660-4254; www.barnsdallartpark.com

Hollywood Forever, 6000 Santa Monica Boulevard, Hollywood; (323) 469-1181; www.cinespia.org/calendar or www.hollywoodforever.com

Little Tokyo, 335 East 2nd Street, Los Angeles; (213) 617-1900; www.japanesevillageplaza.net

Cafe Dulce, 134 Japanese Village Plaza Mall, Los Angeles; (213) 346-9910

Mikawaya, 118 Japanese Village Plaza Mall, Los Angeles; (213) 624-1681; www.mikawayausa.com

....

Steve Walter, co-owner, The Cutting Room

The Apple Pan has the most amazing burgers. They serve water in paper cups that goes into holders. Remember them? French fries come in cones. Guys who work there wear paper hats. It's a tiny place. I love it.

Amoeba is an amazing record shop that is huge and they have CDs too. Now that Tower is gone, there are practically no record shops anymore. So Amoeba is great.

The Rainbow is such a throwback in time and an authentic rock and roll bar. It's where Zeppelin used to hang out and all the groupies. It hasn't changed. It's long haired rock and rollers and authentic. It's a good place to hang out. You feel the history there. And they have homemade soup.

Another good place is Dan Tana's for Caesar salad and great chicken parmesan. It ain't cheap, but it's fun. The bar is always packed.

Dan Tana's, 9071 Santa Monica Boulevard, West Hollywood; (310) 275-9444; www.dantanasrestaurant.com

Rainbow Bar & Grill, 9015 W Sunset Boulevard, West Hollywood; (310) 278-4232, www.rainbowbarandgrill.com

Amoeba Music, 6400 Sunset Boulevard, Los Angeles; (323) 245-6400; www.amoeba.com

The Apple Pan, 10801 West Pico Boulevard, Los Angeles; (310) 475-3585

. . . .

Barbara Fairchild, James Beard Award–winning journalist and former editor-in-chief of *Bon Appetit* magazine

You would think with my background, my career, and area of interest, it would be some place that was food related, but I have to say in all honesty, that my favorite place in LA for the LA experience, is the Hollywood Bowl.

There is a little bit of food-related stuff that goes on there because the food that you can eat there is very good. They have several venues for food. It's all run by the Patina Group, so the food is always very nice and you can get very nice wines by the glass or by the bottle.

But I think there is something about just sitting outside, enjoying a cultural event, and watching the sunset behind those hills. And what I really like about the Hollywood Bowl is that they really changed it up over the years. They are very intuitive about public tastes and popular tastes so that their programs have evolved over the years too.

Of course, they still offer classical music and things that people would expect stereotypically. But they also have some great popular culture–related events like the sing-along nights. And they just started something this past year doing songs from Broadway shows which is why they just did *The Producers*. It's a new concept for them and very pleasant to pack a picnic or eat there and see a great show.

I have a special place in my heart for the Hollywood Bowl because I saw the Beatles there when they came to LA in the 1960s. I was a little junior high student and it was their first visit to Los Angeles. It was 1964 and I was a huge fan, starting when I was about ten, and I still am. And it was great because the Bowl only holds eighteen thousand people. Even though I was way up in the cheap seats, the nose-bleed seats, I was still there with them. In 1966, they were at Dodger Stadium and it was a totally different experience. It was not as good because they were so far away and you felt it could be any four guys there singing.

I remember they sang "I Want To Hold Your Hand" and "She Loves You." But quite frankly, all of us were so busy screaming and singing along, I hardly have any recollection of what exactly they were singing. The screaming was so loud you couldn't really hear, especially up where I was. But that didn't matter, because it was really them.

That time seeing the Beatles would have been the first time I had ever gone to the Hollywood Bowl by myself. We used to go as a family with my mom and dad and my two sisters when we were growing up, we would occasionally go for a concert, taking a picnic dinner. My grandfather loved to go there when he was visiting from Maryland. So we would go a couple of times every summer. But the Beatles concert was the first time that I got to be there by myself. Although my dad drove and dropped me off with my friends. And then he, like all the other parents, basically waited until the concert was over so that they could pick us up and drive us home.

Chris Clark, event producer, Extraordinary Events

My quintessential LA experience is the summer season at the Hollywood Bowl. It really celebrates the summer experience in LA by being an amphitheater open to the sky and accessible for all.

The Hollywood Bowl is not just a pop concert venue. It's the summer home for the LA Philharmonic. Also, jazz plays, world music plays. They also make it very accessible for Angelenos to get there by having ticket pricing anywhere from a dollar up to big money. So high- and lowbrow are mixed in the same space.

I actually worked at the Hollywood Bowl as an usher for one or two summers when I was in high school. I think back to those concerts where I didn't know anything, but I got my early learning and appreciation for some great music.

Once everyone got seated and intermission was over, we were done for the night. I remember one night when the Bowl was sold out and there was an electricity to the amphitheater. I had no idea who was on the bill. But I knew that there was someone or something special. I happened to be working down in the boxes that week. After intermission, when all of the ushers got to leave, I decided to stay. I thought, I've got to see why all of these people are here. What's so magical?

And out strolled this gigantic man with a handkerchief around one of his pinky fingers, and he proceeded to reveal his amazing voice.

Pavarotti.

I thought, I'm seeing someone pretty great. I don't really know who it is, but I'm going to sit here. I think back to that concert. There I was, just sitting there on the stairs. A little ignorant usher, and thinking betcha I'm seeing greatness here. It was really an exciting time.

Anne Bartnett, head of business affairs, Gaumont International Television

One of my favorite places is the Hollywood Bowl. Summer does not officially start for me until I've gone there. It's an amphitheater in a canyon and such a beautiful and magical place. There are box seats in the front and also bleachers in the back. You can rent some cushions for the seats so it's more comfortable. Or if you're really lucky, you can get a box in the front. You can put out linens and pretty plates and have a wonderful picnic before the concert and sit outside under the sky and stars and listen to beautiful music. It's an ideal place and something that's very iconic of Los Angeles.

I've seen many people perform there, but also just listening to the Hollywood Bowl Orchestra or the LA Philharmonic is wonderful. Last year, they did a performance of all the music from *West Side Story*. You watched the movie without dialogue. The sound was being provided by the orchestra.

I also love Malibu. There's a beautiful beach, Wayward Beach, before you get to Zuma. It's not as crowded as some of the other beaches, so you can just take nice long walks there, and it's really pretty.

David R. Carpenter, former chairman and CEO, Transamerica Life Insurance, chairman and CEO, UniHealth Foundation, and co-founder, Cool Springs Life

One of the most unique experiences is to spend an evening at the Hollywood Bowl. It's outside. It's a beautiful area. It's sort of old LA, and I always liked being in those parts of Los Angeles. You really make a night of it. You leave home at around five, get there early, take a picnic with you and hopefully go with another couple. Usually you're in a boxed-in area where you can have a little picnic right in your box. You just enjoy getting ready for the sun to go down and the entertainment to start. The acoustics are great. The entertainment is top notch. It's just a wonderful experience. So, that would be my favorite memorable thing to do in Los Angeles.

I am always drawn to the functions around the 4th of July where they play the marches and have fireworks. It's just a thrill to be there at a time like that and hear all that percussion and all those big American sounds, the songs that we love about America. They usually have a very complex program.

The Hollywood Bowl, 2301 North Highland Avenue, Los Angeles; (323) 850-2000; www.hollywoodbowl.com

....

Debby Ryan, actress and singer

There's a venue in Anaheim called Chain Reaction. It's so dodgy, gross, and punk rock. It's a great place to see a show. The Troubadour is also one of my favorites, because it's small and it's intimate enough to see a good show and really connect. So I really like little venues.

There are times when you're an audience member and all you can see is spotlight. The performers don't know I'm here. They're just singing to a room. Then there are places like The Troubadour or The Roxy where you feel you're making eye contact with them.

I've been to an amazing show at The Roxy where the lead singer will grab a mike and walk through the crowd and you're there with them. And jazz night at the W Hotel on Sunday nights is unreal. The girl, Brenna, who performs, is just absolutely magical. She'll pull up Gladys Knight and people to just really sing jazz.

Troubadour, 9081 Santa Monica Boulevard, West Hollywood; (310) 276-1158; www.troubadour.com

Chain Reaction!, 1652 West Lincoln Avenue, Anaheim; (714) 635-6067; www.allages.com

W Hollywood presents Sunday Night Jazz nights, W Hollywood, 6250 Hollywood Boulevard, Hollywood; (323) 798-1300; www.whollywoodhotel.com

The Roxy, 9009 West Sunset Boulevard, West Hollywood; (310) 278-9457; http://theroxyonsunset.com

....

Thom Andersen, filmmaker (*Los Angeles Plays Itself*), film critic, and historian

For me, the Zanzabuku in Lakewood is the platonic ideal of a bar. I guess it must have opened just after the release of the 1956 film from which it takes its name, one of the last of the colonial "savage Africa" pseudo-documentary adventure films. A poster from the film hangs inside the front door. Once your eyes adjust to the light, you see a long room with a bar on one side and big red booths on the other. It's a neighborhood bar, and almost all the customers are locals. One regular told me, "I've been coming here all my life. When I was a kid, I would drag my mom and dad home." I wouldn't as a rule recommend a bar, especially a neighborhood bar, but the Zanzabuku seems far enough away from Hollywood to avoid being overrun by the crowd searching for the next big bar thing. If you must go, go in the afternoon when everything is mellow. It was also the last bar I know in Los Angeles County to allow smoking, which made it more convivial and encouraged concentrated conversation. It's been a while so I can't comment on their present policy.

Zanzabuku, 4835 Paramount Boulevard, Lakewood; (562) 423-9872

....

Offer Nissenbaum, managing director, The Peninsula Beverly Hills

I love to walk in Beverly Hills in what's called the Golden Triangle: on the streets of Rodeo, Camden, and Canon. The sidewalks are wide and there's great window shopping. You find little shops—ice cream places, chocolatiers, a cheese store, interesting unique boutiques. And there's parks all over around it. Usually people get into a car to get from point A to point B. But I love to walk in that particular area because it's fascinating, so pleasant and has great people-watching.

Also, outside at night on the roof of the Peninsula Hotel is one of my favorite spots. It's high up with beautiful 360-degree views. You see the lights of downtown, the lights of Century City with the tall buildings, the hills of Beverly Hills, and beautiful homes. And having a cocktail up on the roof is such a unique experience. It's calm, quiet, peaceful, and very open. It's my oasis up there.

And when I'm up on the roof, I really enjoy the Peninsula pinot. We have a winery in California, Keller Estates, that produces specialty red pinot made just for us under our label. The wine has a kick and is not completely mild, but is very easy to drink and comfortable. It's very smooth, not overbearing and goes with anything.

I also love going to the farmers' market on Sundays right next to City Hall. You find fresh fruits, vegetables, juice. People come from the farm country to set up their booths. I love to go around and taste different fruits and vegetables. I take my kids when I can on Sundays, so it's great.

Peninsula Beverly Hills, 9882 South Santa Monica Boulevard, Beverly Hills; (310) 551-2888; www.peninsula.com/ Beverly_Hills

....

Retta, actress

My favorite place in LA is the Red Rock on Sunset. I go there because they have good bar food and a great happy hour. They are very generous with the pour and a gang of my friends work there. It's the first bar I ever went to when I moved to LA and I have stayed a loyal patron since 1997.

Porta Via on Canon is another favorite spot. Again I have friends that work there. The once small Italian restaurant has expanded to include a larger dining room and a very sexy lounge. They also have a happy hour and phenomenal (I almost don't wanna call it it) bar food. It's got regulars who come for dinner three times a week. And as much as I go there for dinner and cocktails I JUST got hip to their brunch. The french toast is so good, it almost makes me angry. I have had a few birthday parties there and the management is very accommodating when it comes to throwing private events.

Red Rock Bar & Eatery, 8782 Sunset Boulevard, West Hollywood; (310) 854-0710

Porta Via, 424 North Canon Drive, Beverly Hills; (310) 274-6534; www.portaviabh.com

....

Peter Cambor, actor (*Wedding Band*)

I live on the west side. And I love going to the Santa Monica airport. There's a little observation deck up there by the tower. It is also attached to a restaurant. So you can get a glass of wine and sit out on the observation deck at dusk and watch planes land.

I know that sounds really silly, but it's just the coolest thing, because these little planes come in over the city. On the west side, the sunsets are just gorgeous so it's nice if you catch it right at dusk. And on a nice day, they usually take off going over the ocean so you can see the sun over that way. Oddly enough, I'm sort of terrified of flying. So it doesn't make a lot of sense, but there's just something about it that's very peaceful. It's just kind of neat seeing the most sort of primitive form of flight, with these really basic small planes. It seems so easy for them to land. And they come in so softly and quietly.

I can just sit there for hours watching planes land there.

I really love Venice a lot. Everyone always laughs or scoffs at the fact that I live in Venice because it adds so much toil and consternation to your daily life. So much of your life is spent in a car driving, so it adds kind of an hour to anything else you would really do.

So people who live here really choose it. If you were in Hollywood or closer everything would be much more accessible, but there's just a nice sense of community over here. Venice is its own little town. I don't think I could live in any other part of LA to be honest. I sort of landed here by accident.

A lot of New Yorkers live in Venice. And I think it's because of that sense of when I lived in New York, I knew the guy in my bodega and I knew the guy at my dry cleaning place and all the places in the neighborhood. There's a little bit of that sense there. It's one of the few places where you can walk or bike a lot.

I love all the cliché stuff about being close to the ocean, but there's just something about Venice that makes me have a strange love affair with it. It's kind of funky, and it sort of used to be bohemian in the same way the Village used to be in New York City. I lived in Alphabet City when I was there. I know it's all regentrified now. But the presence of the Craftsman houses—there's just something that's right up my alley. This kind of old seaside community.

Santa Monica Airport, 3233 Donald Douglas Loop South, Santa Monica; (310) 458-8591; www.smgov.net

....

Jonathan Cheban, TV personality on E!'s *Keeping Up with the Kardashians,* creator of JetSet Jewelry, and owner of Sushi Mikasa in Miami

Beacher's Madhouse is hidden in the Roosevelt Hotel. And you wouldn't believe what goes on behind those doors. First of all, it's star-studded, I mean, every celebrity. You name it. Johnny Depp, Miley Cyrus. Everybody goes there Wednesday and Saturday nights. But Wednesday is the big celebrity night, and it's insane.

Owner Jeff Beacher has people actually connected on a specially designed pulley system. When someone orders a bottle, the spotlight goes on, and there's a little person, maybe three foot five hanging on the ceiling with the bottle. They go across the room on a specially designed pulley system and get lowered down to a conveyor belt, and the person presents the bottle to your table. They have Ace of Spades champagne, which is my favorite, so I love that. The bottle is so beautiful. And the whole presentation is really gorgeous.

Jeff has performers like a ninety-year-old stripper grandmother, and a seven-foot-tall woman named Amazon Ashley. And he has people who impersonate Britney and Christina, I mean, it's crazy what goes on there. People don't even know.

Beacher's Madhouse, 7000 Hollywood Boulevard, Hollywood; (323) 785-3036; www.beachersmadhouse.com

....

Erica Moller-Islas, principal designer, EMI Interior Design

Dear John's is a weird little tiny restaurant which has a speakeasy vibe. It used to have a much older crowd, but has since become a little bit more hip. But it still brings in the older crowd, which is really, really charming. They come on Friday nights for the piano bar, which is really sweet.

I like to have just a regular dirty martini there. But what I love about their food is that it's very classic, hearty food. They'll have a black forest sandwich, which is prime rib and swiss on pumpernickel. My husband loves it because it comes with great dipping sauce and it's delicious. And it's rare to find Mexican soups in a restaurant like this, but on their specials sometimes they'll have *albondigas,* a meatball soup, and it's just so good. The restaurant is one of Culver City's best little secrets.

I also like La Fonda for their Mexican *folklorico* dancers. So, while you're having dinner there's a full-on show and it's very rich and entertaining. Their food is delicious. But I like it for the entertainment portion. And I think it's about a two-hour show, and then they kick you out. Then the next group comes in. It's still really fun.

Another place that a lot of people don't know about is the Culver Hotel, which is a historic little hotel in Culver City. During filming of *The Wizard of Oz,* the munchkins stayed there. What's charming is that it pretty much looks like what it looked like more than eighty years ago. It's sweet to go there for breakfast, or a quick lunch meeting. They have a small breakfast menu, with things like quiche or a continental breakfast. They have a really cute little lounge with big sofas. And the décor is really sweet. They just recently updated it, and it looks nice and cozy.

The Baldwin Hills scenic overlook is kind of new. And it overlooks LA, and Culver City, and a bunch of other little cities that you can see off in the distance, like Century City and the buildings in downtown. What's nice is that it's actually a state park. So they preserve a lot of plants and nature. You can do a quick little hike. It's been very popular for the steps too. They're big giant concrete steps that people like to climb up and down. When it's not smoggy, you see the buildings downtown.

Dear John's, 11208 Culver Boulevard, Culver City; (310) 397-0276; www.dearjohns.net

Culver Hotel, 9400 Culver Boulevard, Culver City; www.culverhotel.com

La Fonda Supper Club, 2501 Wilshire Boulevard, Los Angeles; (213) 380-5053; www.lafondasupperclub.com

Baldwin Hills Scenic Overlook, 6300 Hetzler Road, Culver City; www.parks.ca.gov

STORES, MARKETS & SPAS

✳ I love the energy of LA. I think it's a lot of fun and it's always glamorous.
There's a great little spa by my house. For $25, you can get an hour mas-
sage and they do your head and feet and you lay in these recliners and
my girlfriends and I tend to sneak in there a lot. I can't say the name.

—Jennifer Love Hewitt, Golden Globe–nominated actress

In 2010, when Patti Smith accepted the National Book Award for her memoir
Just Kids, she told the audience, "there is nothing more beautiful than the book:
the paper, the font, the cloth. Please, no matter how we advance technologi-
cally, please never abandon the book. There is nothing in our material world more
beautiful than the book."

Natalie Compagno always had a deep connection to books. Her mother was
a librarian. From the time she was little, her father always read to her and her sisters from *The Snowy Day* to Dr. Seuss. "He read the entire set of Little House on
the Prairie about three times," she recalls. But she especially loved travel books
that sent her to far away worlds. As an adult, before a trip, she cherished finding
a novel set in the place or written by an author from that locale.

So whenever Compagno visited Traveler's Bookcase in her beloved West
3rd Street neighborhood, she couldn't believe a store so devoted to travel like
that existed. The cozy bookstore was overflowing with novels and travel literature of every variety. "So many bookstores that are really stark, but this was like

going to someone's personal book collection," says Compagno. "The owner was so sweet and loved to travel, so going there was an experience. And when you love to travel so much, you want to be where other people have a similar passion."

But five years ago, she heard the news about her treasured bookstore.

"Traveler's Bookcase closing? I was just devastated," she recalls. "At that moment I knew that I was going to buy it because I couldn't let the store close. It's just too special. I wanted to save it."

Compagno contacted the owner, who was (natch) traveling in South Africa. When they finally met, they connected through their passion for books. The owner knew that the store would be in good hands. Compagno added chandeliers, painted travel quotes on the wall, updated the inventory, but more or less took the original owner's guidance of creating a community and ran with it.

Traveler's Bookcase continues to be a melting pot attracting people doing research for novels set in exotic locales to those traveling for the first time. "I think one of my favorite things that happens is when someone walks into the store is even if they don't buy anything," says Compagno, who with her husband has visited ninety-two countries. "They say I'm so happy I found you. It means they love books, other cultures, travel, discovery, and will share this with their friends."

As a hotbed for creativity and innovation, Los Angeles is filled with great markets, boutiques, and health spas. Look at these treasures.

Mandy Patinkin, Tony- and Emmy-winning, Golden Globe–nominated actor

My favorite place in LA is the Beverly Hot Springs.

To my understanding the Beverly Hot Springs is the only natural hot springs in a major metropolitan city. They were digging for oil in Los Angeles and they hit hot water. Then they closed it up.

A guy had a well in his basement that was capped, and he found hot water. So he said, "This is what we call natural hot springs." I think in America you're not allowed to use that phrase, but that's what it is. It's water with minerals in it. So they made a hot springs.

I love the woman who gives me a massage there that completely zones me out. And I love the hot water. I don't care what kind of day I'm having if I'm exhausted or wiped out, I can go to the Beverly Hot Springs. I sit in that hot water. I go into the cold water, back into the hot water, and I just feel renewed.

Beverly Hot Springs, 308 North Oxford Avenue, Los Angeles; (323) 734-7000; www.beverlyhotsprings.com

Heather Graham, actress

My favorite thing to do in LA is go to yoga. LA is where I deeply fell in love with yoga. The first teacher who really inspired me was Seane Corn who at that time taught at Yoga Works. I have so many good memories of taking her class. Her class is challenging. I loved getting so sweaty and doing something so intense that leaves you feeling completely calm and blissful. I feel like I'm floating after a class and it is not possible to think a stressful thought after yoga! There are so many great people who teach yoga and take yoga. Now I go to classes at Yoga Works with Vinny Marino, Jesse Schein, and Mia Togo. I also love Andrea Marcum at U Studio and Vytas at Brian Kest. I think some of the best yoga classes you can find anywhere in the world are in Los Angeles.

Yoga Works, various locations; www.yogaworks.com

U Studio Yoga, 5410 Wilshire Boulevard, #500, Los Angeles; (323) 488-6309; www.ustudioyoga.com

Bryan Kest's Power Yoga, Power Yoga Studio—West: 1410 2nd Street, 1st Floor, Santa Monica; Power Yoga Studio—East: 522 Santa Monica Boulevard, Santa Monica; www.poweryoga.com

Vanessa Hudgens, actress and singer

My favorite thing in LA is Soul Cycle. It's the most incredible workout ever in the world and I am stupidly obsessed. It's like a club but a workout.

Soul Cycle, 8570 West Sunset Boulevard; West Hollywood; (310) 657-7685; 11640 San Vicente Boulevard, Los Angeles; (310) 559-7685; www.soul-cycle.com

Kim Kardashian, star of E! *Entertainment's Keeping Up with the Kardashians*

Owning a store has been a dream of mine since I was a little girl working at my grandma's store. It's just really fun to be able to bounce ideas off my grandmother who has owned a store my whole life. I was talking to my grandma yesterday and offering her tips about whether she should put up a website for her store. That's really special.

I'm proud that my sisters and I started with one Dash store. That was a huge reach for us and we accomplished that goal. And now we're onto three stores and we're hoping to open up a lot more.

We have all our fragrances at Dash and fun Kardashian things. We have a whole bunch of stuff. And we just moved our Dash store to Melrose Place. That location is way more convenient than our Calabasas location. It's so fun.

I'm born and raised in LA, it's really all I know. To me it's home. It's very comfortable and warm and my whole family is there. When I'm in LA, I'm a stay at home kind of girl. When I'm out in different cities, I'm always out and about. But when I'm in LA, I love being home.

Dash Clothing LA, 8420 Melrose Avenue, Los Angeles; (323) 782-6822

....

Audra McDonald, Tony-winning and Emmy-nominated actress and singer

I like Korean Spa in Koreatown. I love those ladies. You go in there and soak and these Korean ladies in their black bras and underwear scrub the s*&t out of you and smack you and then say, TURN over. And then they scrub you and you come out glowing. You really come out glowing. I love that place.

Olympic Spa, a Korean Day Spa, 3915 West Olympic Boulevard, Los Angeles; (323) 857-0666; olympicspala.com

....

Ne-Yo, Grammy-winning singer-songwriter, record producer, actor, and dancer

I love Melrose near Hollywood Boulevard. Sometimes me and my friends just walk up and down the street a couple of times. It's fun. You see all walks of life. You know what I mean? You see the punk rock guys, you see the hipsters, you see the hip hop kids. You just see everybody there. There's great shopping. There are all kinds of restaurants up and down that strip. I just love going over there and just hanging out. I'll go over there and I'll go shopping for sneakers, or whatever.

....

Laraine Newman, Emmy-nominated actress, comedienne, and writer

The farmers' markets have splendid food. I mean, we are the nation's breadbasket. A great day is going to the farmers' market in Santa Monica or in Beverly Hills. It's every Sunday and spectacular. The one in Beverly Hills is right next to the Fire Department. It's organic poultry, meat, vegetables, fruit, goat cheese, coffee. There's stands that make crepes, tamales, and fajitas.

And because we are originally a Spanish land grant state, the Mexican influence in our cuisine is just wonderful. We get authentic tamales. There's a great place called The Corn Maiden. It doesn't actually have a restaurant but they make the best tamales you can get, and you can buy them frozen. They sell those at the farmers' market with frozen sauces.

There's the fish guy who is a complete grouch, who everybody is afraid of, but his stuff is really good. He is like the Soup Nazi. The market is from 9:00 till

1:00. I like to go early. so that I can avoid the rush, and sometimes they run out. There's a stand called Harry's Berries which sells strawberries that are unnaturally sweet. I don't know what magic voodoo they have, but these berries are just unbelievably sweet. There was a time when I started making ice cream at home, and I had a lost weekend with homemade ice cream. My daughter, the one who still lives at home, was saying, "mom snap out of it, come on back to me." My husband was just waiting out the illness. It was great. It just gives me such joy. Of course, there's flowers, but that's just another thing to keep alive.

Beverly Hills Farmers' Market, 9300 block of Civic Center Drive, Beverly Hills; 310-550-4796

Harry's Berries, 1600 Ivar Avenue, Hollywood; (323) 463-3171; www.harrysberries.com/Markets/Locations/HollywoodSun.html

....

Josh Lobis, writer, executive producer, co-creator, *Wedding Band*

Malibu Country Mart is a place that I love to visit with my family. There's a playground for the kids. That's always a pre-requisite. It's in the middle of a bunch of restaurants and fashionable shops and always a very peaceful place to visit. We go there on Saturdays a lot. And if you go across the street you can go to the beach.

And the farmers' market on Sundays in Pacific Palisades is great. The kids can eat as much really good free fruit as they want, you can bring your dog. There's good bread. It's just a good place to people-watch. It's not uncommon to see a ton of celebrities like Goldie Hawn and Kurt Russell or Jennifer Garner buying flowers or produce. We like to go to Cafe Vida for lunch. They have excellent turkey burgers. My friend, director Bryan Gordon, calls it "The Palisades Commissary." Or we head to Beech Street for pizza and pasta.

We live in the town and you can't go ten feet without bumping into somebody you know. So it's a good community place and great for families.

Pacific Palisades Farmers' Market, 1037 Swarthmore Avenue, Pacific Palisades; (818) 591-8161; www.ccfm.com

Cafe Vida, 15317 Antioch Street, Pacific Palisades; (301) 573-1335; www.cafevida.net

Beech Street Cafe, 863 Swarthmore Avenue, Pacific Palisades; (310) 573-1940; www.beechstreetcafe.com

Nicholas Jarecki, screenwriter, director, and filmmaker

LA places that are great? I love the Russian and Turkish baths on Pico. You get that old-school-conspiracy-back-room feeling there. And it has a wonderful heated Russian room where you can go. Also, I don't want to let the cat out of the bag but a lot of movie folks go there. You could be surprised. You might be casting your next film in the steam room. They even have co-ed days. I don't know how you want to interpret the innuendo on that one.

City Spa, 5325 West Pico Boulevard, Los Angeles; (323) 938-4800

Stephanie Austin, television and motion picture producer

As a longtime resident of the Hollywood Hills, I have immediate access to riding and walking trails, great music venues and clubs, delicious restaurants, sporting events, and fabulous shopping. But my treasured place is a chef's supply called Surfas and it's all the way across LA. They have a small cafe, with a limited but carefully curated menu, made with ingredients available in the main marketplace, which is a vast emporium of gourmet delights and professional kitchen equipment. Hundreds of varieties of oils, vinegars, mustards, sauces, pastas, crackers, liqueurs, condiments of every kind from all over the world, and a selection of unusual cheeses to die for. Despite the sign at the counter, FOOD IS NOT RETURNABLE, the staff is cordial, helpful, and knowledgeable—and you can wander for hours, checking out gadgets you never knew you simply had to have!

Surfas, Culver City, 8777 West Washington Boulevard, Los Angeles; (310) 559-4770; www.surfaslosangeles.com

Jesse Tyler Ferguson, Emmy-nominated actor

I am very drawn to the Silver Lake Junction area. It's a little corner where Sunset Boulevard and Santa Monica meet. It's just a great little area, there's a farmers' market. There's a wonderful restaurant called Cafe Stella. There's a great coffee shop called Intelligentsia Coffee, there's a tea shop, there's a little cheese shop, the

Cheese Store. It's really very European; it actually kind of reminds me of New York in a lot of ways, because you can walk from one place to another, and not have to get into your car. And you always see someone that you know in the area, so it feels very small town, and that's my favorite area of Los Angeles right now.

I like the Cheese Store because they're really savvy with their products. I try to just let them give me whatever they think I would like. The other day it was a cheese called Blue Moon Cheese that was really good. Cafe Stella has great mussels and is a very good place to feel like you're definitely not in LA when you're there. I usually like to go in the morning after the rush hour. If I don't have to work it's great to go for a coffee run and sort of beat the morning rush. So I would have breakfast at Cafe Stella and just start my day there.

I am very attached to the weather out here. I love seasons, but there's something very nice about being guaranteed a beautiful day, at least one to five times a week. I came out to LA kicking and screaming. I came out for work and felt like I was taken away from New York before I was ready to leave. But I have grown to love LA. I have a home with a garden with herbs and things. I certainly would never be able to do that in New York City, unless I had a very large windowsill. Also, instead of having your life on your back, to be able to use the trunk of a car. That's also fantastic.

Cafe Stella, 3932 West Sunset Boulevard, Los Angeles; (323) 666-0265; http://cafestella.com

Intelligentsia Coffee & Tea, 3922 West Sunset Boulevard, Los Angeles; (323) 663-6173; www.intelligentsiacoffee.com

The Cheese Store of Silver Lake, 3926-28 West Sunset Boulevard, Los Angeles; (323) 644-7511; www.cheesestoresl.com

....

Merle Ginsberg, fashion writer, television personality, senior writer, *Hollywood Reporter*

I grew up on the East Coast and was working for *Rolling Stone* as a writer. And I got sent to LA to interview somebody. It might have been Lindsey Buckingham but I'm not sure. I stayed at the Sunset Marquis which was the coolest, it's like a rock and roll hotel. Bruce Springsteen when he didn't have a house here used to be there. Sting and Rod Stewart hung out there. All the music people hung out there.

There's not a lot of gathering places in LA. Unless you are going to a party or somewhere where there's a cross section of lots of people, you don't see people.

If you want to see people dressed in an interesting way in LA, go to Barneys. Barneys in LA is much, much smaller than New York. It's only three floors, I know everyone who works there. They all know me. I walk through and I'm like the mayor of Beverly Hills or something. I like the way they curate, I like what they buy. They always have interesting fragrances and beauty products.

In Barneys, there are wealthy people and interesting artistic people. They all look completely different. And the way people wear clothes in LA, is so different than the way they do in New York or Europe. They may buy similar things, they may buy Azzedine Alaïa or Lanvin, they may buy Céline bags and Dries Van Noten shoes, but it's always much more sort of rock and roll boho here. There's always some element of kind of f##k you-ness, the way people dress here, which I've gotten very used to. And I like it because it's non-conformist. People can look amazing in New York, but they always look like they're trying to fit in. Here, people are not trying to fit in because there's no fitting in because there's no center. You're just who you are.

There is no Bill Cunningham. I wish there was an LA Bill Cunningham, if he were here he would be fascinated because he likes the unusual. You see interesting and unusual things. And that's what you would see here. Look, we've got skinny girls in tight black dresses and Louboutins too, but you know where to avoid them. It's a uniform. I hate uniforms, I really dislike them. It's a competition thing. I am of a certain group and I want to identify with them and I want you to think I'm in that group. Pretty is a big thing here. It's not about looking tough or sophisticated or edgy. It's about looking pretty, which I happen to like.

Sunset Marquis, 1200 Alta Loma Road, West Hollywood; (310) 657-1333; http://sunsetmarquis.com

Barneys New York, 9570 Wilshire Boulevard, Beverly Hills; (310) 276-4400; www.barneys.com

....

Gurmukh, co-founder, the Golden Bridge Yoga Center

I frequent the Farmers Market in Hollywood on Sundays. It's the best farmers' market I've been to in the entire world. They have organic food, plants, and fresh flowers. Tooty Fruity Farms has really good stuff. I always meet and greet friends when I'm there. It's divine. In truth that's about all I do when I'm in LA.

However, my favorite and most treasured place in Los Angeles is Golden Bridge Yoga, the home of Kundalini Yoga. Golden Bridge is where many of us teach Kundalini Yoga, which is a way of life. The Nite Moon Cafe in Golden Bridge serves good, healthful, vegetarian, organic food. Golden Bridge is a place where people of all ages, including pregnant women, children, and families, participate in yoga and meditation classes seven days a week. It's a live, heartfelt community in Hollywood.

Golden Bridge Yoga, 1357 North Highland Avenue, Los Angeles; (323) 936-4172; www.goldenbridgeyoga.com

. . . .

Kirsten Segal, of the famed Fred Segal boutique (and granddaughter of Fred)

Fred Segal has been around for over fifty years now. My grandfather started it because he had a dream to make fashion jeans. At the time, there were only Lee's and Levis, which were for working in. And they were selling for $2.99. He said, "why don't we make something fashionable, that's sexy, comfortable, that people will want to wear on an everyday basis. And lets sell them for $19.99." So he created the first ever fashion jeans.

No one believed in him, but he went ahead saying, "I'm doing it anyway." His initial jean line sold out in a day. Every major celebrity from Elvis to the Beatles wore them. Keeping that legacy alive, we evolved into a retail store. Then came individual ownership. Within Fred Segal Santa Monica, there are thirty-four individual stores under the Fred Segal umbrella. That concept allows for diversity and also creativity through different people coming together with the same mission— to offer the best fashion.

We don't do a lot of sales. But over the years, we've been known for the September sale. People used to line up around the block the night before to get the best merchandise which is 50 percent off. It's obviously come down to a new way of life, with the economy. But people still get excited for the sale and want to be the first ones there. I think it's been probably been going on for thirty years. It's always been at the end of September. I've seen a number of celebrities there who line up. Or you find people who have always wanted something from Fred Segal, but couldn't necessarily afford it at full price. They knew they could get that little treat during the sale. It's nice to see so many getting excited about it.

Fred Segal, 500 Broadway Street, Santa Monica; (310) 451-8080; www.fredsegal.com

....

Ilse Metchek, president, California Fashion Association

Every ten blocks in LA is virtually a new country. It's not homogenous at all. If you did a fashion show of LA style, you would have so much diversity. It's too hard to get a pastiche of one look.

You would have to do Pasadena style, which is very preppy. You would have to do the Korean world, which is very trendy almost like Japan. You would have to do Beverly Hills, which is high end, overdone. The hair and nails are perfect. It's about being at the right restaurant with the right handbag. And the complete reversal of that is Abbot Kinney where you are also in high style, but much more casual. There is the Pier, which is a mélange of everything. Then you have Westwood which is the college look, the college set. If you are a fashion editor here you would have a picnic because there is no set style. There are silos of energy here.

One of my favorite things is going to street fairs in the various neighborhoods. Abbot Kinney is near the beach in Venice and is in early October. It's a juried artisan fair where people show their wares. So it's not just cottage industry, it is juried cottage industry and you find the most amazing things. They have not only hand crafts, but plants, and artwork, and nothing that you would see at a normal commercial fair. It's nothing that's junk. It is once a year and I look forward to it.

The Gardens of Beverly Hills Art Fair is also once a year in May and takes up about ten blocks on Santa Monica Boulevard. It's beyond art, has all kinds of wonderful things and is great for people-watching. Those showing their wares do not want to be in galleries or stores. They want the freedom to go from fair, to fair, to fair. It's almost like a trade show.

Abbot Kinney Festival, Abbot Kinney Boulevard, between Main Street and Venice Boulevard, Venice; early October; (310) 396-3772; www.abbotkinney.org

The Beverly Hills Art Show, Beverly Gardens located along Santa Monica Boulevard, from Rodeo Drive to Rexford Drive; (310) 285-6836; www.beverlyhills.org/artshow

....

Retta, actress

The Grove has got everything: a Nordstrom, a movie theater, and great restaurants. It's a great place to shop and then sit down for some good food and some even better people watching. I have a membership to the Loyalty program so if you do enough shopping there you get some nice perks and free parking and ya can't beat free parking.

The Grove, 189 The Grove Drive, Los Angeles; (323) 900-8080; www.thegrovela.com

....

Allison Williams, actress (*Girls*)

I'm obsessed with the Brentwood Country Mart. Every time I go to LA, no matter how long I'm there, I make sure to go. And I'll stop by Pressed and get some juice. You can walk around all those cute stores. It makes me feel like I'm home in Connecticut again. Then you go back out on San Vicente and you're in the middle of Los Angeles.

   The Brentwood Country Mart is a little oasis. I really love it.

The Brentwood Country Mart, 225 26th Street, Los Angeles; (310) 451-9877; http://brentwoodcountrymart.com

Pressed Juicery, 13050 San Vicente Boulevard, Los Angeles; (310) 451-1010; www.pressedjuicery.com

....

Suzanne Goin, chef/owner Lucques, A.O.C., and Tavern

Without a doubt, the Santa Monica Farmers' Market is my go-to place and favorite experience in Los Angeles. And it's the first place I like to bring visiting guests and chefs to show off our city. I can spend hours there talking with the hardworking farmers who grow gorgeous produce, much of which you could never find in even the best markets. I get to sample the top of the season produce and make my selections. The market shapes my menus and has become the foundation for my weekly menu for Sunday Suppers at Lucques.

Santa Monica Farmers' Market, Arizona Avenue and 3rd Street; (310) 458-8712; www.smgov.net/portals/farmersmarket

....

Cheryl Cecchetto, founder and president, Sequoia Productions, which produces the Emmy and Academy Awards Governors Balls and many other events

I'm a yogi. Let me go to a yoga class. I pick them up wherever I can. My husband is a yoga teacher. It doesn't matter where we are, we go grab a yoga class.

Actually, Goda Yoga is right around the corner from my office. And I have a company Visa that I leave there. Any of my staff who wants to go to yoga, it's on me. You know why? If they're chill, then they're more productive. Not only that, we all need to go to yoga.

Goda Yoga offers a very peaceful kind of yoga. Cheryl, who owns the place, is really good. I'm fifty-four, and I feel she really caters to women who really need to keep their body flexible, open, and oiled. She has a way of making that hour and a half slip by.

And I'll pick up bikram classes too. I like Manhattan Beach Bikram Yoga. I grew up taking saunas all my life 'cause I'm from Sudbury, Ontario, and I grew up on a lake and I love the heat. I like Manhattan Beach itself because I grew up on water and like the beach community.

Hennessey + Ingalls is the largest art and architecture bookstore in the western United States. I get inspired to design my jobs there. I actually get inspired everywhere, but Hennessey + Ingalls provides a great location. They have these little stools which are used as stepping stools. And I just plunk myself down on one of them with a pile of books. I always leave with a couple hundred dollars worth of them. They have anything: architectural books, interior design, graphic design, art history, photography, landscaping. It's a great bookstore.

Goda Yoga, 9711 Washington Boulevard, Culver City; (310) 287-1255; www.godayoga.com

Manhattan Beach Bikram Yoga, 3618 North Highland Avenue, Manhattan Beach; (310) 802-0225; www.bikramyogamb.com

Hennessey + Ingalls, 1520 North Cahuenga Boulevard #8, Los Angeles; (323) 466-1256; and 214 Wilshire Boulevard, Santa Monica; (310) 458-9074; www.hennesseyingalls.com

Joachim Splichal, famed chef, restaurateur, and founder of Patina Restaurant Group

I love going to the flower market on Saturday morning. I love the flowers more than I love the ambiance of the place because it's so hustling and bustling. But it's something totally different. And I like to be surrounded by vendors, flowers, and people. It's a great way to start Saturday morning.

The market is basically three different buildings which have been there for years and years. There are a couple hundred flower vendors. One guy sells orchids. The other sells wreaths. Another sells cut flowers. There are some Dutch guys who control most of the market. They have the most exotic flowers. There are rose and tulip specialists. There are special guys for vases. There are a couple of decoration places upstairs where you can decorate for Halloween and Christmas. It's something that calms me down in the morning. It makes me think about other things than my day-to-day, which I enjoy.

Depending on what's in season, I tend to buy a lot of orchids or stem flowers or exotic things. I like my house to look perfect for the weekend. You find great stuff around Christmas time there. They have all different wreaths and new stuff that I haven't seen. And there are five or six suppliers and they have decorations you don't find anywhere else.

The Original Los Angeles Flower Market, 754 Wall Street, Los Angeles; (213) 627-3696; www.originallaflower market.com

Susan B. Landau, producer, manager, and photographer

Samy's is my favorite place in LA. In addition to being a manager and a producer, I'm a photographer. It's a great passion of mine. And Samy's is the largest camera store in California. It's probably the second largest camera store in the United States, second only to a place called B&H, which is in Manhattan and famous.

If you're a photographer in LA, then you know Samy's. It's four floors and crammed every inch with everything a photographer could want. So I would say I am there unfortunately three or four times a week.

Most camera stores even in LA are in a long room or on one floor. Samy's is four floors and the downstairs is just packed. In fact, I am beyond geeked out at Samy's. That word doesn't even hold a candle to what you can do in there. You can have a chat about anything. People go out of their way to try and be helpful.

Samy's Camera, 431 South Fairfax Avenue, Los Angeles; (323) 938-2420; www.samys.com

....

J Mascis, singer, guitarist, and songwriter for Dinosaur Jr.

I'm a guitar nerd. I like to go to Trutone Music in Santa Monica. It's a pretty cool local music store. They cater to musicians and can fix anything. I bought the Backwards Flying V there, which is pretty exciting. And a Martin 12 string. The people who work there have been around LA a long time. There are not too many music stores these days because everything's online, so it's more fun to go into a store. They sell used stuff and new stuff and a lot of boutique pedals.

Truetone, Music, 714 Santa Monica Boulevard, Santa Monica; (310) 393-8232

....

Elizabeth Stewart, celebrity stylist and former editor and stylist for the *New York Times Magazine*

I was a die-hard New Yorker when I moved to Los Angeles for my husband Rob. While house hunting, we kept driving up long canyon after long canyon, and I was dismayed at how isolated many of the homes were. We used to laugh that at our place in New York, we could walk in any direction and hit a movie theater in five minutes. So we added a caveat to our hunting, we wanted to be able to "walk to coffee," no small feat in Los Angeles. That's how I discovered Montana Avenue in Santa Monica. We now live a block and a half from it and walk to it every day, never failing to run into someone we know. We walk down and we hit the ocean, passing everything from a juice bar, to my eye doctor, to a million coffee shops. Walk up Montana and we pass another million coffee shops, to the best thing of all, the Aero Movie Theatre, recently renovated and there since my husband's parents lived in this neighborhood in the 40s. My kids were both born here and grew up walking to their preschool on the Avenue and now walk to meet their friends at

Yogurtland or Pinkberry. The funniest thing is we discovered many, many, ex–New Yorkers in the area, all of us re-creating our own very special LA-version of our days in New York.

Aero Movie Theatre, 1328 Montana Avenue, Santa Monica; (323) 466-3456; www.americancinematheque.com

Yogurtland, 1426 Montana Avenue, Suite 7, Santa Monica; (310) 395-8899; www.yogurt-land.com

Pinkberry, 1612 Montana Avenue, Santa Monica; (310) 264-4791; http://pinkberry.com/montana

....

Debi Dumas, Beverly Hills hair colorist who has worked with Chelsea Handler, Sharon Stone, Mischa Barton, and other celebrities

My most treasured place in Los Angeles just happens to be where I've spent the majority of the last eighteen years, my work neighborhood and Little Santa Monica Boulevard in Beverly Hills.

While Rodeo Drive is known for opulence and glitz, Little Santa Monica (or South Santa Monica Boulevard) is its smaller baby sister and filled with independently owned stores that give a unique twist to the city of Beverly Hills.

My favorite spot for coffee is Euro Caffe. They make the best cappuccino, hands down, which is validated by the many Italians sitting outside on any given day. I start my mornings there, grabbing something caffeinated before I start coloring hair. It's almost impossible to find a seat when there's a soccer game on TV. Patrons crowd both inside and out to cheer on their favorite team. The croissants and the pressed sandwiches make you feel like you are actually in Europe. The cafe is run by Vartan and his wife Mida, who know all the locals by name.

Another place I love is Kramers Pipe and Tobacco Shop, the oldest tobacco store in Los Angeles. It has been operating for over sixty years. They custom blend all their tobacco, and have sold their goods to everyone from Clark Gable to Steve Martin. One step inside transports you back in time, with its authentic relics, and photos of Beverly Hills back in the 50s. It's located two doors down from my salon, and I enjoy going over to visit with Marsha, who took over the store from her parents. Besides the many varieties of smoking items, she also stocks candy, pretzels, and other little snacks. She saves me when I need a quick sugar fix!

Euro Caffe, 9559 South Santa Monica Boulevard , Beverly Hills; (310) 274-9070

Kramers Pipe and Tobacco Shop, 9531 Santa Monica Boulevard, Beverly Hills; (310) 273-9777;
www.kramerstobaccoshop.com

....

Christopher Gartin, io/LA Founding Partner and actor

The farmers' markets are really fun, cool things to hit. During the summer every Thursday is Yamashiro's farmers' market. There's great food, music, food trucks, and a fantastic view. You bring your kids. And there's a taco stand there I really like.

Yamashiro Farmers Market (Thursdays 5 p.m. to 9 p.m., April through September),
1999 North Sycamore Avenue, Los Angeles; http://lacityfarm.org/yamashiro.cfm

....

Robert Wuhl, actor, comedian, and Emmy-winning writer

You can get anything at The Rose Bowl Flea Market in Pasadena. I've bought tables, chairs, you can get vintage clothes, shoes, food. Just about anything. You can get . . . my God, what can't you get? It's spectacular.

My wife would be upset if I didn't mention her favorite shop, Noodle Stories. It's a great boutique and a terrific collection which includes Issey Miyake, Comme des Garcons, Frank & Eileen. Caryl Kim, the owner, sells really eclectic stuff and her taste is impeccable.

The Rose Bowl Flea Market, 1001 Rose Bowl Drive, Pasadena; (323) 560-7469; http://rgcshows.com/rosebowl.aspx
Noodle Stories, 8323 West 3rd Street, Los Angeles; (323) 651-1782; www.noodlestories.com

....

Kimba Hills, interior designer and owner of the art, design, and décor boutique, Rumba

My favorite places in the LA area are the flea markets that occur every Sunday in different locations around the city and beyond. On the first Sunday of the month there is a small flea market held at the Santa Monica Airport, and a larger one at Pasadena City College. The second Sunday is the granddaddy of them all held at the Rose Bowl in Pasadena. The third Sunday is in Long Beach and the fourth again at the Santa Monica Airport. I usually get there just as the sun is coming up. This is when the shop owners and designers go in order to secure the best items. Each market location has its own uniqueness and cast of colorful characters. And for me I am always on the hunt for the "golden egg."

Pasadena City College Flea Market, 1570 East Colorado Boulevard, Pasadena; (626) 585-7906; www.pasadena.edu/fleamarket

Santa Monica Outdoor Antique & Collectable Market, 3050 Airport Avenue, Santa Monica; (323) 933-2511

Long Beach Antique Market, Long Beach Veterans Stadium, 4901 East Conant Street, Long Beach; (323) 655-5703; www.longbeachantiquemarket.com

The Rose Bowl Flea Market, 1001 Rose Bowl Drive, Pasadena; (323) 560-7469; http://rgcshows.com/rosebowl.aspx

....

Jacklyn Zeman, Emmy-nominated actress who played Nurse Bobbie Spencer on *General Hospital* for over thirty years

My family and I have lived in Malibu since my daughters were little girls. When they were young, we would go to Malibu Country Mart in Malibu. No matter what chapter of your life you're in, married, not married, little kids, grown kids, the Malibu Country Mart has something for everyone of every age.

There's a sand pit, swings, a slide. There are amazing restaurants, from little stands where you can get takeout and sit out on a picnic table. Or there are the fancier places where you could go on a date night. Or there's the in-between where if you have your bathing suit on and you've been at the beach, you could just throw a little cover-up on and have a sandwich or salad.

Taverna Tony, Tra di Noi and Guido's are upscale great restaurants. Marmalade or John's Garden are wonderful for a sandwich or a salad. I've been to Marmalade a lot, because when my daughters were young, they had a take-out and a sit-down section. But honestly, I love every restaurant. They're all so good. My daughters had their ballet lessons at a studio there all the time. They both danced with the Malibu Civic Ballet, and did all of the Nutcracker shows at Pepperdine Smothers Theater.

The other thing that's fabulous about Malibu Country Mart is shopping. You can browse around in high-end stores. They've started to get designer stores. There's also the neighborhood places that have been there. There's an at-home store, Room at the Beach, which has beautiful beach-y coastal things, like sea-shell napkin rings and chandeliers decorated with shells. They also have gorgeous white-and-linen-covered furniture, and jewelry. There's Madison. There's Planet Blue. There's a jewelry store, Traditional Jewelers. There's even a movie theater.

When I was twenty-four years old, I came out to LA to work on *General Hospital* from New York. Except for one time right before I moved here when I was in and out, I had never been to California before. I wasn't familiar with anything. I was staying at the Beverly Hills Hotel, which is fancy and very posh.

When they hired me to work on *General Hospital*, my agreement was that they'd put me up in a bungalow at the Beverly Hills Hotel for three months, give me a car, and driver. So my introduction to California was all of this luxury. I was a girl who grew up in the suburbs of New Jersey. To me, if you got in a limousine it meant that you were going to a wedding.

I remember standing outside of the Beverly Hills Hotel and seeing all the limos and the fancy cars come up. There were the Maseratis, Ferraris, Rolls Royces, and Bentleys. All these fancy cars.

And I remember saying to the doorman and the valet, "where are all the normal cars?" They started laughing. I said, "I'm from New Jersey where we don't see all of this." They said, "we don't get too many of those, but when we do, we hide them in the back, and put the most expensive ones in the front."

Room at the Beach, 3835 Cross Creek Road, Malibu; (310) 456-9777; www.roomatthebeachmalibu.com

Malibu Country Mart, 3835 Cross Creek Road #2, Malibu; (310) 456-7300; www.malibucountrymart.com

. . . .

Jerome Dahan, founder and CEO, Citizens of Humanity

My neighborhood, Santa Monica, is one of my favorite places because of its proximity to nature, the oceans, and the canyons. I race bikes, go fishing on my boat, travel, and spend time with my family so there is no better place to go and enjoy Los Angeles than the coast. On my way out, I often stop at ZJ Boarding House in

Santa Monica, a great surf shop that's been around for over twenty years. It's where local surfers pass on their expertise and great attitude for the ocean, mountains, and concrete. They are always welcoming and full of knowledge before spending a morning surfing at Zuma Beach.

From there, I ride up Pacific Coast Highway on my Ducati through the windy stretch of highway that carves through Topanga Canyon and Malibu. Malibu Canyon is probably the best hidden gem early on a Sunday morning to just ride and tell no one.

On the way back home, I stop at Vincenti Ristorante in Brentwood, where I can wear jeans and sneakers still enjoying the comfort of the cuisine. It's such a great Italian restaurant and the perfect way to end a day with some wine and pizza.

ZJ Boarding House, 2619 Main Street, Santa Monica; (310) 392-5646; www.zjboardinghouse.com

Vincenti Ristorante, 11930 San Vicente Boulevard, Los Angeles; (310) 207-0127; www.vincentiristorante.com

. . . .

Selma Blair, actress

My favorite places in LA:

Book Soup. I have been coming here since I first moved to Los Angeles. There is a great biography section and helpful staff who seem to be able to always recommend an amazing book. They know all the Bronte classics as well as the newest best sellers. It is small enough to not get overwhelmed and is warm and charming with a great newsstand outside. I could spend an entire evening here browsing art books and fiction and kids books too. Love it.

Favorite hotel. When I want to see a bunch of people I know or wish I knew, then the Chateau [Marmont] is my favorite hang. It feels like Hollywood home and I have spent many weekends and late nights. My late dog loved catching food off tables here and my baby is equally at home walking around in the garden. Beautiful.

Shutters is the place I go when I need to be near the beach. Heaven. Feels like a real vacation. Frette sheets and an ocean view with the most inviting lobby with fireplaces burning.

Hike: Fryman Canyon. It's shady and green. Right in town. Easy and beautiful. I can't wait to be able to share it with my son, Arthur.

Restaurant. The Ivy. It's old standard and I never leave hungry or disappointed. It still holds up. It was a hot spot for special occasions when I was younger and now it is just the place I go to enjoy a cozy meal in a sweet cottage. A great big cup of coffee is my poison now that I am a mom and it is delicious. But back in the day, I looked forward to those delicious gimlets. Fried chicken and banana splits are the deal. Or the grilled vegetable salad. Still. Good.

Baby clothes. Trico Field. Charming. Happy. Expensive. The baby always looks precious and cool in his Trico Field get ups.

Breakfast at the counter at Beverly Hills Hotel always cheers me up. Ruth feels like an old friend by now. The gift store is ideal for all your BHH needs. Baby pajamas even.

Book Soup, 8818 West Sunset Boulevard, Los Angeles; (310) 659-3110; www.booksoup.com

Trico Field, 9528 South Santa Monica Boulevard; Beverly Hills; (310) 786-8290; www.tricofield.net

....

Ruth Vitale, founder and former co-president of Paramount Classics, former president of Fine Line, CEO of The Film Collective, a consulting and theatrical distribution company

LA is a very curious place. You never know what to expect. I had a wolf hybrid dog. He was ninety-seven pounds of absolute energy and beauty. He went everywhere with me, and I'm talking everywhere. Cartier, Chanel. Saks. The women on the third floor at Saks knew him and loved him. I would take him there with me and he would go up in the elevator and I would take him off leash. Ninety-seven pounds of pure white fluff fur would bound down the aisles of the third floor and go straight to Evelyn in the fur department and Hilda in the Chanel boutique. Ev was terrified of him but loved him. Hilda always had cookies for him and loved him so very much. He would hang out there for a couple of hours, visiting with everyone and just delighted to be in the company of great women and beautiful fashion. I can't imagine doing that in New York or anywhere else for that matter. A pocketbook-size dog? Sure. But, a huge wolf hybrid? Not so much! These are the moments that I love.

Saks Fifth Avenue, 9634 Wilshire Boulevard, Beverly Hills; (310) 275-4211; www.saksfifthavenue.com

Chanel, 125 North Robertson Boulevard, Los Angeles; (310) 278-5505; www.chanel.com

....

Mohan Ismail, director of culinary, corporate executive chef, Rock Sugar Pan Asian Kitchen

I was born and raised in Singapore. So, visiting the Asian markets with all the smells and colors reminds me of home when I was growing up and going to the market with my mom.

The Asian markets are all over LA, but I really like 99 Ranch in Van Nuys which is really big. It has all kinds of different sections and offers lots of things that I could get in Singapore: seafood, meat, canned goods from home, Asian candies and dried fruit, produce, a bakery with Chinese breads. They even have a steam table area where you can get lunch.

I usually don't have an idea of what I am going to buy there. I just get a shopping cart and start from one end and go through every single aisle. I know the cashiers because they've seen me there for years. It's nice to see all the familiar faces.

I also love an Indian store called India Sweets & Spices which is also in the valley. I get all my Indian spices for my personal use there. They also have a great selection of Bollywood movies. I only usually watch the funny and happy ones and stay away from the serious films. But as long as there is music and somebody is dancing, it has my name all over it. They have all these remix versions of the songs and it's very pop and modern, but they have an Indian beat. In fact, I usually play Bollywood music in my car when I'm driving. It's so happy.

99 Ranch Market, 6450 Sepulveda Boulevard, Van Nuys; (818) 988-7899

India Sweets & Spices, 22011 Sherman Way, Canoga Park; (818) 887-1417

....

Melora Hardin, actress, director, and singer/songwriter who stars in *Wedding Band*

One of my very favorite places is the Beverly Hot Springs. It is so awesome. It's very earthy. What I think I love most is that there's nothing very glamorous about it. I believe it's the only natural hot springs in Los Angeles and it feels like I'm going somewhere else. I feel almost like I'm in a different country. They do these incredible body scrubs, where you lay yourself out on a slab and they scrub your whole body with these little mitts. If you ask them to show you the mitts after they scrub, they'll just show you like a handful of your dead skin. It just exfoliates your whole body.

The treatment I love is Body Scrub/Body Care. They rinse you off with warm water and massage your body with honey and milk and rinse it with milk and then massage with baby oil. And they wash your hair and place fresh cut cucumber all over your face and hands and you walk out of there and you feel your skin as soft as a baby's butt. You just feel so soft and it's such a sensual experience.

Also, I love that there are all these different kinds of women of all shapes and sizes. Nobody's really parading around. They're just being. They're just earthy. I leave there feeling so good, so babied.

Beverly Hot Springs, 308 North Oxford Avenue, Los Angeles; (323) 734-7000; www.beverlyhotsprings.com

....

Lainie Kazan, Tony-, Emmy-, and Golden Globe–nominated actress and singer

This is my favorite day. Take a yoga class at Bikram Choudhury's Yoga College of India. Go to the Beverly Hot Springs, and get a massage and sit in the natural spring waters. Then go for sushi with my daughter and granddaughter, at Teru Sushi in the San Fernando Valley in Studio City.

Yoga just revitalizes me and makes me able to move. It's a very strenuous yoga class. It's not an airy fairy class. It's Hatha yoga and about stretching the body to its full extent I have been doing it for thirty odd years. I am a yoga pioneer. Bikram Choudhury was the first yoga school in LA, and I just joined in 19 . . . I don't want to even tell you. If I stop for any length of time and come back to it, I find it very difficult. But it's so worthwhile. It's so worth it because when I come out of that yoga class, I'm high. I'm sailing and then to go into a massage and a sauna and a steam and a Jacuzzi . . . oh my God.

I have been going to the Beverly Hot Springs for thirty years too. It's not a frou-frou place. It's the real deal. It's clean. It's nice looking. But it's not a spa. It's not decked out. It's just for the purpose of getting healthy. The waters are natural spring waters. They come up from La Brea Tar Pits. They're in that arena, that area on Oxford near Weston. They have wonderful masseuses and masseurs and give a very deep and profound massage. I am a real hedonist in this arena.

Then I go out for sushi with my family. Teru Sushi has fresh fish, and it's beautifully served, and it's a good restaurant. It may not be the most expensive or the best in the city. I haven't eaten in all the sushi restaurants. But this restaurant has been wonderful to me and my family. So we go there about once a week and I love to get the seared albacore with garlic on top. It's so good.

Bikram's Yoga College of India, 11500 W. Olympic Boulevard, Suite 150, Los Angeles; (310) 854-5800; www.bikram yoga.com

Beverly Hot Springs, 308 North Oxford Avenue, Los Angeles; (323) 734-7000; www.beverlyhotsprings.com

Teru Sushi, 11940 Ventura Boulevard, Studio City; (818) 763-6201; www.terusushi.com

....

Suzanne Tracht, chef and owner of Jar and a contender on *Top Chef Masters*

One of my favorite butcher shops is Huntington Meats in the Farmers Market. I love Jim, the owner. He's a really great guy and a good friend. And I can walk over to the Farmers Market from my restaurant. I'll go there anyway because I'll have to pick up chicken legs from the poultry people to make my coq au vin. Or I'll have to pick up hamburger buns from somewhere else. But I always go to Huntington Meats, sit down and have a conversation with Jim.

We just talk about everything in life and new meats. Huntington Meats is amazing and makes beautiful meats. They make their own sausages. Sometimes we do cooking classes together where Jim will take a whole animal and butcher it. And I'll talk about recipes. It's immaculate. It's just one of those butchers that you visit and you say, "I want that, that, that, that."

I always have to pick up a piece of beef jerky. It's in these big, long strips and they have different types of flavors. It's just not like beef jerky that comes in a package and you have to tear it open with your teeth, or knife, or scissors. It's just piled up high and so beautiful looking. It's just so nice to walk away with a big piece of beef jerky.

The thing I love about LA is the diversity. If I feel like having some of the best Korean food in the world, I can get it at the drop of a pin. We have Koreatown. We have Vietnamese food. We have great Mexican food. Thai food. Chinese food. I could pick up these ingredients that I've never seen before in a Thai market. Or I could go to Chinatown or to a Hispanic market.

There's the diversity of people, food, and ingredients.

Huntington Meats, 6333 West 3rd Street # 350, Los Angeles; (323) 938-5383; www.huntingtonmeats.com

. . . .

Jonathan Cheban, TV personality on *E!'s Keeping Up with the Kardashians*, creator of JetSet Jewelry and owner of Sushi Mikasa in Miami

There's a store called American Rag where you can get custom jeans made.

It's really cool. So I'll bring my jeans in sometimes and have them redone.

They measure you and you pick the fabric.

The first time I came to LA, I had a disaster. Some girl invited me to stay with her, and she went completely cuckoo and threw me out. I left, and didn't know anything or where I was. And I got saved by Nicole Eggert, who was on *Baywatch,* and China Chow, Mr. Chow's daughter.

So I went to Nicole's house while she was filming in New York. And China Chow showed me around all of LA and drove me to a place called Mr. Chow's. I had no idea what that was. It was about thirteen years ago, and she said, my dad has a Chinese restaurant that everybody loves, and I said, really, what are you talking about?

That was my first experience at Mr. Chow's. And I dropped dead after I ate there because the food was something I've never experienced. It was the best thing I ever had, and then I realized why everybody was obsessed with Mr. Chow.

American Rag, 150 South La Brea Avenue, Los Angeles; (323) 935-3154; www.amrag.com

Mr. Chow, 344 North Camden Drive, Beverly Hills; (310) 278-9911; www.mrchow.com

....

Mary Vernieu, famed casting director and owner of the restaurant Primitivo

My favorite thing is to go to farmers' market in Mar Vista on Sundays. There's a bunch of different farmers' markets all around LA and they're all amazing. The one on Sunday in Mar Vista is wonderful because it's all farmers. There's another one that's on Main Street that has pony rides which is also very nice, but it's more of a festival environment rather than just a true farmers' market.

I own a restaurant on Abbot Kinney so I'm just very into seeing all the new fresh produce and sausages. All the farms come from up north and it's really in support of local in general.

At first, it took me a long time to get used to LA. It's just so different from coming from New York. I missed the seasons. I missed being able to stay out until four in the morning. In those days that was important to me. But then I found amazing people here.

There was that moment when it suddenly felt like home. It was really a function of time. It probably took about four years in. I just remember coming back from visiting my hometown in Albany and getting on the plane and thinking, "God. It's really nice to be coming home."

Primitivo, my restaurant, is a wine bar/tapas restaurant that has been around for ten years. My casting office used to be behind the restaurant so I was on Abbot Kinney fifteen years ago before anyone was there. I would travel all over the place and there were no wine bars in LA at all. The only one was a Broadway deli with three seats. I have a passion for wine. And I just really wanted to share that.

People started to appreciate Abbot Kinney. Primitivo was one of the first restaurants on the street. Then some great stores started to open and then another restaurant and it just grew to be a cool street. *GQ* called it the hippest street in America not that long ago. There's great shopping. There's great food. There's great furniture. It's a special place.

Mar Vista Farmers' Market, www.marvistafarmersmarket.org

Primitivo, 1025 Abbot Kinney Boulevard, Venice; (310) 396-5353; www.primitivowinebistro.com

....

Molly Shannon, Emmy-nominated actress and author

Flicka is a little neighborhood children's clothing store and they sell jewelry too. I know the owner and she's such a doll. Before I had kids, when I was living back and forth between LA and New York, I would always buy my nieces little dresses there. And now I had my own children. So I have gone to this store for almost seventeen years.

 Flicka is the kind of store that has a small town feeling. It's personal, you know the owners. They sell really cute dresses with original designs. They have all different kinds. Some are very fancy, some are old-fashioned, they have cute bathing suits. They have stuff that I don't ever see anywhere else. I buy gifts there for friends' kids. I love it.

 And I love the people who work at Landis' Labyrinth toy store and the owner, Devoney, is so lovely. The store reminds me of an old-timey, old-fashioned super personal little store. We could easily spend an hour there just looking at toys. And they're just so friendly to kids. They have very unique toys and are always finding out what the customer wants. If there's something they don't have, they'll say, "tell us what we should order!'" That's how personal and well run it is.

Flicka, 204 North Larchmont Boulevard, Los Angeles; (323) 466-5822

Landis' Labyrinth Toy Shop, 140 North Larchmont Boulevard, Los Angeles; (323) 465-7998; www.landislabyrinth .blogspot.com

....

Ryan Patterson, *Access Hollywood* supervising producer and fashion expert

My favorite place is called Larchmont Village. It's really not a village, it's really a street. It's a place that I first discovered when I came out to Los Angeles and within walking distance of my first apartment and my first job at Paramount Studios. So I've grown and it has grown. And it's one of those places I visit all the time. I was there when I was pregnant because it's easily walkable. My daughter's three years old and I take her there all the time. The people in the stores and who run the restaurants all know her name.

What I like about the street is all the mom and pop shops. There have been some chains, but it's kept its essence of being a small town place. Those who are anywhere else in the country might laugh because it's only about a block or so long. I know there are many places in the country that are entire little cities or villages that are this cute and adorable. But it's not something that we have a lot, because there's so much sprawl.

Because of the sidewalks, I can easily take my daughter to Larchmont Village. There are tons of families. At the toy store, Landis' Labyrinth, I sort of feel guilty that I have spent countless hours there. I've probably not purchased nearly enough. My daughter sees people from her preschool in there. It's just a little mom and pop shop; they have another one in Manhattan Beach. It's a cute, tiny little store and great for getting all the birthday presents we need without having to go to some big chain store. They offer good service. They wrap your presents. They have a little bit of everything. They have a couple of Barbies and those kinds of things but not so much. They have classic things like little Snoopy stuffed animals and lots of other stuffed animals. They also carry Jack-in-the-Boxes and things that are a little less common.

Chevalier's Books is another mom and pop shop on Larchmont that everyone loves. They have a sign that says, CATS WELCOME, DOGS WELCOME. You can bring in food. They have little trays of cookies they serve. They wrap your books for you. They'll get you anything you want, and they have an entire little kids' section. I can't tell you how many hours I've sat in there with my child at their little, tiny table while I'm sitting on a plastic chair six inches off the ground, just reading book after book after book to her. And they have readings on the weekends for kids. It's really all-inclusive, and they're part of the neighborhood. They make everybody feel welcome.

I'm from the East Coast so I'm not quite used to this much sprawl in Los Angeles. And Larchmont Village seems like a tiny, little pocket. For a minute, if you sort of block out the palm trees and the perfect shot of the Hollywood sign, you think that maybe you're somewhere else. You're reminded, okay I am here in a big city but in a place where I've found my niche. I see the same people and they know your name and they'll give my daughter a cookie. She doesn't live in a small town, but she's definitely picking up some small town flavor. This is going to sound so corny, but these places are creating memories that my daughter will remember forever.

Landis' Labyrinth Toy Shop, 140 North Larchmont Boulevard, Los Angeles; (323) 465-7998; www.landislabyrinth .blogspot.com

Chevalier's Books, 126 North Larchmont Boulevard, Los Angeles; (323) 465-1334; http://chevaliersbooks.blogspot.com

....

Mae Whitman, actress and singer

I almost even hate talking about it but I'll give it away because people deserve to know. There's a Korean spa called Olympic Spa and it is literally my favorite place on the planet. Here's the insider tip: If you get the scrub and mini massage, for $70 they scrub your entire body down, give you a facial, wash your hair, massage you in milk and honey. I mean it's the most luxurious. And it's so quiet. I have all my good thoughts in there.

Olympic Spa, a Korean Day Spa, 3915 West Olympic Boulevard; Los Angeles; (323) 857-0666; http://olympicspala.com

....

Natalie Compagno, owner, Traveler's Bookcase

My favorite place in Los Angeles is my neighborhood. It doesn't have a name, which I find hilarious. It's basically 3rd Street between La Cienega and Fairfax. We're right at the corner of Beverly Hills and West Hollywood, the Fairfax district and mid-Wilshire. But somehow they forgot to name our little neighborhood. And so I call it everything from "90048" to "3LAFA" to just "my hood."

So my favorite thing is spend the entire day walking up and down 3rd Street and experiencing one of the only small neighborhood community walking districts in Los Angeles. There is nothing like it anywhere else in the city. I can't step outside my house without running into people that I've known for years and years.

Another reason this is such a special place is because we are at a juxtaposition next to Beverly Hills and West Hollywood. You see all kinds of people in the neighborhood. There are apartment buildings that I lived in when I first moved to LA that are really inexpensive. Then there are million-dollar homes next to them.

And so people on 3rd Street come from all backgrounds, all ethnicities, all personalities, and we all convene here.

So my perfect day would start by having breakfast at Joan's on Third. I've eaten there so much, I could probably recite the entire menu to you. I'll eat the soft boiled egg with *pain de mie* and also order bagels and lox. Yes, I have both with a soy latte. Breakfast is nice because it's usually not as crowded. It's so delicious and they have really cool foods from all over that you can purchase. My dad loves food from around the world so I'll get him canned sardines or tomato sauce from Palermo or salt from Slovenia. Joan's on Third has all of that stuff. So I like to stock up on goodies.

Then I would saunter along 3rd Street. There are so many amazing places. Fran has owned New Stone Age for a million years. She has such exquisite taste, and I always find a unique something there. Entre Nous is a resale shop with name designers for less money. A lot of celebrities drop off their Gucci and Prada at Entre Nous and we get to reap the spoils.

Polkadots & Moonbeams has been there forever. There's a vintage side along with a regular clothing section. The women who work there are so sweet. Larry Schaffer has owned the amazing store, OK, forever. He travels the world finding wonderful and unique things, especially design items from Finland and Italy. He carries jewelry but mainly has vases and glassware. He finds these incredible art books. Next door is Area, a linen store. I always pop in there for pillows.

I have furnished my store and home from Floor Plan. Also if you need some pampering, have a hair cut from Erik at Taboo. Or for color, try Roy at L & R salon. They're both on 3rd Street and not pricey at all.

I would definitely get a coffee and a latte at Toast. They have the best red velvet cupcake. At one point during the day, I'll hit Swerve, a very special dance studio. They have a little mini-gym. And I always find some fun class like Bollywood Bhangra Beats where you pretend you're in a Bollywood movie. The women who own Swerve are so nurturing. I go there every day. They also mix in meditation and positive reinforcement with exercise.

Simple Things has amazing salads and soups. I go there sometimes when Joan's is crowded or when I'm craving their organic chicken salad. I also like Little Next Door for a glass of wine. I'll sit on the patio and pretend I'm in France, which basically is how you feel sitting there. Actually, The Little Door is a super high-end French-Mediterranean restaurant and they opened Little Next Door next to it. So you can sit on the Little Next Door patio and have wine and a cheese plate. I've had many meetings there. El Carmen is a really cool tequila bar. Also, Haru Sushi on San Vicente is a total must.

A lot of Angelenos do not leave their area. If they live in Venice and there's an art show in Eagle Rock, forget it. You might as well be asking them to fly to Vegas. It does not happen. My neighborhood is great, because it's right in the center of everything. I can get nearly anywhere in LA in about twenty minutes. I can be in Venice. I can be in Eagle Rock. I can be in the Valley. I can be downtown. My neighborhood rocks.

Taboo Hair Care, 8446 West 3rd Street, Los Angeles; (323) 655 3770; taboohaircare.com

Joan's on Third, 8350 West 3rd Street, Los Angeles; (323) 655-2285; www.joansonthird.com

Polkadots & Moonbeams, 8381 West 3rd Street, Los Angeles; (323) 651-1746; polkadotsandmoonbeams.com

Entre Nous, 8430 West 3rd Street, Los Angeles; (323) 655-9096; www.entrenousonline.com

Area, 8307 West 3rd Street, Los Angeles; (323) 951-0133; www.arealinenshop.com

Floor Plan, 8115 West 3rd Street, Los Angeles; (323) 951-9103; www.floorplanla.com

L & R Salon, 302 South Edinburgh Avenue, Los Angeles; (323) 653-6600; www.landrsalon.com

Simple Things Sandwich and Pie Shop, 8310 West 3rd Street, Los Angeles; (323) 592-3390; www.simplethings restaurant.com

OK, 8303 West 3rd Street, Los Angeles; (323) 653-3501; okthestore.com

New Stone Age, 8407 West 3rd Street, Los Angeles; (323) 658-5969; www.newstoneagela.com

Swerve, 8250 West 3rd Street #205, Los Angeles; (323) 782-0741; www.swervestudio.com

Little Next Door, 8142 West 3rd Street, Los Angeles; (323) 951-1010; www.thelittledoor.com/lndhome.html

Toast Bakery Cafe, 8221 West 3rd Street, Los Angeles; (323) 655-5018; www.toastbakerycafe.net

El Carmen, 8138 West 3rd Street, Los Angeles; (323) 852-1552; www.elcarmenrestaurant.com

....

S. Irene Virbila, *Los Angeles Times* restaurant critic

For me, the farmers' markets, especially the long running Santa Monica market, which celebrated its 31st birthday in July, make southern California a cook's paradise. A short stroll from the beach, every Wednesday and Saturday dozens of farmers set up their stands along Arizona and the Third Street Promenade in Santa Monica. The biggest collection is on Wednesday morning. That's when the chefs go to shop and hang out, writing up their menus as soon as they get back to the kitchen. Alain Giraud of Maison Giraud is a regular. So are Spago pastry chef Sherry Yard, Ink's chef/owner Michael Voltaggio, and Pizzeria Mozza's Nancy Silverton. The competition can be fierce for the first Royal Blenheim apricots, Queen Anne cherries, and fat spring asparagus. Follow the chefs to the best purveyors of eggs with deep gold yolks, tiny local clams, heirloom tomatoes in a rainbow of colors, and deliciously obscure vegetables. Even if you're not a cook, you can enjoy the scene and the cast of characters, from serious cooks and famous faces to raw food adherents dressed in hemp, lithe runners and athletes, surfer dudes, and hustlers. I wouldn't miss it for the world.

Santa Monica Farmers' Market, Arizona Avenue and 3rd Street; (310) 458-8712; www.smgov.net/portals/farmersmarket

....

Glynis Costin, west coast bureau chief, *InStyle* magazine

One of my favorite places in LA is the Brentwood Country Mart. It's a cool, low key hang out with shops and restaurants but has infinitely more character than a mall.

For one thing it still looks like it did back when it was built in 1948—a series of connected old red barns, which is a miracle in this city with a "tear it down and build a new one" mentality.

Its "heart" is a central patio with a fire pit surrounded by communal wooden tables and benches, where everyone always seems to see someone they know.

I have spent many a Saturday afternoon with my family there, surrounded by locals who gather and dine on the perfectly roasted chicken from Reddi Chick (there since 1979— they have the best fries on the Westside), a burger from Barney's, tostadas from Frida Taqueria, or a gourmet BLT from Farmshop.

Over the years, the place has become more and more gentrified with chic stores such as Intermix, Calypso, James Perse, and Union Made, but there's still an old-fashioned candy shop, a toy store, a post office, a shoe repair, a barbershop, and mechanical kiddie rides for 50 cents. On weekends there are even pony rides in the parking lot!

But my favorite thing about this place is the people watching. Back in the day it was a respite for local stars such as Joan Crawford, Elizabeth Taylor, and Shirley Temple, and today it's a mix of chic soccer moms with their little league and ballerina tots in tow, and dads fueling up with a java from Café Luxxe, mingling with the likes of Cindy Crawford, Steven Spielberg, Tom Hanks, Helen Hunt, Jennifer Garner, Ewan McGregor, Harrison Ford, and Dennis Quaid. (These are all people I have actually seen there.)

I like to sit there and savor a salted caramel ice cream cone from Sweet Rose while I read a book from Diesel, one of the few non-big chain bookstores left in town.

It's definitely a cozy neighborhood hangout.

The Brentwood Country Mart, 225 26th Street, Los Angeles; (310) 451-9877; http://brentwoodcountrymart.com

....

Zane Buzby, comedy director of over 200 sitcoms and founder of The Survivor Mitzvah Project, a non-profit charity helping Holocaust Survivors in Eastern Europe

For shopping on the very cheap, there is no place like a walk to Santee Alley and the hundreds of storefronts in the new Apparel Mart, which stretches for more than a ten-block grid downtown below Main. It's got to be seen to be believed. You can buy anything there, from the latest styles to vintage stuff, from piñatas to restaurant supply, from fabrics to notions, from handbags to shoes, all for a fraction of the costs at a retail store. You can have a seamstress bead a wedding gown or find incredible designer sample sales year round. Or try the bustling Chinatown mall on Broadway, where you can buy just about anything for a few dollars, especially a good suitcase. Everything there is highly negotiable.

Santee Alley, located between Santee Street, Maple Avenue, Olympic Boulevard, and 12th Street; www.thesantee alley.com

SUPERSTAR STRUCTURES, SEXY SPACES, BEATIFIC BRIDGES & POCKETS WITH PANACHE

 I remember going to see a filming of *The Brady Bunch*. My mom was doing a TV series for a summer out there and I stayed with her. And they were shooting *The Brady Bunch* on the lot where she was shooting. I met William Shatner and I was a big *Star Trek* fan. He was doing a show called *The Barbary Coast*. I remember the back lot of Paramount. It was just very exciting because I loved movies.

—*Ben Stiller, Emmy-winning actor*

If the Bradbury Building on 3rd and Broadway was an actor, it would have had a very, very eclectic career. It's not every day that you encounter birdcage art nouveau elevators, ornate wrought iron balustrades, oak paneling, Belgian marble staircases, and a dramatic five-story glass atrium skylight roof radiating natural light. So no wonder the place makes its way into popular culture.

According to Thom Andersen's masterpiece documentary, *Los Angeles Plays Itself*, the landmark had its first closeup in the 1943 Gene Tierney and George Montgomery film *China Girl,* when it doubled for a fancy hotel in Burma. However, it's also been depicted as a seedy hotel, a London military hospital, and an office building (but one containing bad guy thugs and killers). Most famously, the Bradbury had a key role in Ridley Scott's 1982 science fiction classic *Blade Runner.*

Even more recently, the place became the Kinograph Studios staircase in the silent film and Oscar hit, *The Artist.* (Remember the spot where Peppy Miller blew George Valentin a kiss?) The building also appears in *500 Days of Summer.* Commercials and music videos were also wise to the Bradbury. Heart, Genesis, and Janet Jackson (Rhythm Nation 1814) shot videos there too.

It all started with real estate developer and mining tycoon Lewis Bradbury. Bradbury lived nearby in a fifty-room manse in tony Bunker Hill. He envisioned a design-forward wonder of an office building that he could walk to. When seasoned architect Summer Hunt's designs seemed uninspired, Bradbury turned to an unknown draftsman, thirty-two-year-old George Wyman, to create his masterpiece of light and wrought iron.

It has been said Wyman, feeling that he wasn't up for the gig, first turned down Bradbury's design offer. However, as legend has it, he found inspiration from a Ouija board. According to the story, his late brother, Mark, sent a message: Take the commission. It will make you famous.

The late architectural historian, Esther McCoy, who interviewed Wyman's daughters, discovered that Wyman found some of his design inspiration from Edward Bellamy's 1887 novel, *Looking Backward.* The book described a utopian society set in the future where the office building was a "vast hall full of light, received not alone from the windows on all sides, but from the dome, the point of which was a hundred feet above. . . . The walls were frescoed in mellow tints, to soften without absorbing the light which flooded the interior."

The original estimated cost was $175,000, but the bill for 288 radiators, water-powered elevators that ran like delicate clocks, giant plate-glass windows, fifty fireplaces, and all that marble added up. The final price tag came closer to $500,000.

In a sad twist of fate, Bradbury passed away before the building opened. And while Wyman rose to prominence, it is said that none of his other projects could ever match the Bradbury, which remains the oldest commercial building in Los Angeles.

Perhaps *Arts and Architecture Magazine* described the Bradbury best: "It is a forever young building, out of a youthful and vigorous imagination. But it has left nothing to chance. Stairways leap into space because of endless calculations. The skylight is a fairy tale of mathematics."

LA is chock full of fairy tale buildings, monuments, and structures. Just look at these finds.

....

Dustin Hoffman, Academy Award–, Tony-, Emmy-, and Golden Globe–winning actor, director, and producer

I just love The Broad Stage. If you are in Los Angeles, that decadent city, it's in Santa Monica and it's a beautiful theater. The theater has modern, beautiful architecture. It's very intimate with 550 seats. I'm the so-called chair of the acting part, Mikhail Baryshnikov is chair of the dance part, and Placido Domingo is the chair of the opera.

The Broad Stage, 1310 11th Street, Santa Monica; (310) 434-3200; http://thebroadstage.com

....

Antonio R. Villaraigosa, 41st mayor of Los Angeles

No place in Los Angeles embodies the spirit of the city quite like the Watts Towers.

The Towers were built over three decades by Simon Rodia, working alone in his free time, with no predetermined design. It is decorated with found objects picked up from Watts to Wilmington, like old pop bottles, scrap metal, seashells, and broken tiles—pieces of the city itself. Rodia referred to the project as Nuestro Pueblo, "our town" in Spanish.

Like our town the structure has faced hard times, almost being torn down in the late 50s after being mischaracterized as blight. But it remains standing—a testament to the City's strength and vibrant character. I go there sometimes to absorb its energy and marvel at the monument that in my eyes stands as the truest example of the beauty of LA, my hometown.

Watts Towers Arts Center, 1727 East 107th Street, Los Angeles; (213) 847-4646; www.wattstowers.us

....

Ben Stiller, Emmy-winning actor

I moved back to New York almost two years ago. But I went out to Los Angeles because I never really lived away from New York. I went to UCLA for a little while and then I came back home. I didn't have a good experience.

So I came back to Los Angeles and was there for a few years. And we were developing *The Ben Stiller Show* for about two years before it got to the point where we did the pilot. So, over that time I was going back and forth. It just seemed like everything was going on out there. I think more than anything it was a chance for me to live somewhere else and have an experience away from home that I never had. Then I ended up staying for twenty years. I liked the weather. That's a cliché. But I met friends and was twenty-five. I had my youth, in those years, twenty-five to forty-five. It's fun to be young out there.

Also, as a kid, I always wanted to go out there too. I was sort of fascinated. I remember going to see a filming of *The Brady Bunch*. My mom was doing a TV series for a summer out there and I stayed with her. And they were shooting *The Brady Bunch* on the lot where she was shooting. I met William Shatner and I was a big *Star Trek* fan. He was doing a show called *The Barbary Coast*. I remember the back lot of Paramount. It was just very exciting because I loved movies.

Paramount Pictures (Paramount Studios Tour), 5555 Melrose Avenue, Hollywood; (323) 956-1777; www.paramount studiotour.com

....

Candace Nelson, founder and pastry chef of Sprinkles Cupcakes and Sprinkles Ice Cream and a judge on the *Food Network's Cupcake Wars*

The Hammer Museum is definitely one of my favorite spots in LA. It's right in Westwood Village and a world class museum. But it also has a very manageable and neighborhood feel to it.

The exhibits are so rich. They have constant programming that I wish I had more time to support. They constantly have guest authors and a theater where they show kids' movies. I took my son there to watch the original *Muppet Movie*. It was his first time in a movie theater. Every week they use that theater for Mindful Awareness which is a program out of UCLA where you basically go and meditate. It's set up so beautifully. You walk in off the city street from the bustle of Westwood and go into a very serene setting. It's built around a courtyard. It's just so beautiful because you're in the middle of this city, yet you're in open air outside and surrounded by all this great art.

The Hammer Museum has a great cafe and an amazing gift shop with wonderful art books. They also have a whole section for kids' art books and beautiful jewelry made by local artists. It's my special go-to secret spot for buying birthday presents. I also love their exhibit of rotating wall murals right when you come in and you walk up the stairs. They are stunning showstoppers that stay in your memory. And they really introduce new artists to the community. I've learned about so many new artists by seeing these jaw-dropping murals and inquiring about the artist who produced it.

Hammer Museum, 10899 Wilshire Boulevard, Los Angeles; (310) 443-7000; http://hammer.ucla.edu

....

Matthew Rolston, photographer, director, and creative director

A perfect day in LA (if I was going to show off the city to a visitor) would be to focus on my love of all things Old Hollywood. It would begin with breakfast at the Fountain Coffee Shop at the Beverly Hills Hotel. This hotel has literally been a part of my life since before I was born. How? My parents were married in the Beverly Hills Hotel's Crystal Ballroom.

One way or another I've been going to the Fountain Coffee Shop at the Beverly Hills Hotel since I was a little kid. I'd usually get to go with my father on a Saturday. It would be a special treat and I'd always order a "Grilled Russian" sandwich for breakfast or lunch, and a glass of fresh-squeezed orange juice, and that's still my habit to this day.

The Fountain Coffee Shop is a perfect time capsule of the late 40s, early 50s. The original Don Loper palm-frond wallpaper remains. It's a kind of shrine, and people who have grown up in LA know and love it. When the hotel was recently updated the only thing that was done to upgrade the Fountain Coffee Shop was that the old black Formica counter was replaced with black granite. In every other way it's exactly as it's always been.

My next stop would be a private tour of Paramount Studios (which I would arrange through friends who work there) because it's the most historic lot of all the old Hollywood studios that are actually in Hollywood.

It's unforgettable to pass through the original wrought iron gates—those famous iron gates that Gloria Swanson (as Norma Desmond) drove through in the film *Sunset Boulevard*, in her quarter-mile-long custom built Isotta Fraschini.

There's a powerful film noir quality about Paramount, even today. And when you explore the streets on the lot (those small streets between the soundstages) and you look in at an empty soundstage—well you can just feel and smell the history of the place. If you do go on a studio tour, you will learn what famous productions were shot on which stages, which is fascinating.

From there, I would take my guest to see the corniest thing on earth (but it's so great), the famous "forecourt" of Grauman's Chinese Theatre on Hollywood Boulevard. You can stand there and imagine all those fabulous movie premieres as you take in the footprints and the ornate kitsch Chinese décor of the place. I don't really have a favorite foot or handprint, I love them all.

And from there, since it would now be time for lunch, I'd have another counter meal, this time at the Musso and Frank Grill, which is the oldest restaurant on Hollywood Boulevard. Again, it was a special treat as a kid growing up and I used to get to go with my dad when I was little. I always enjoyed watching the grill chef prepare the food. I liked the feeling of camaraderie and warmth. My dad would always chat up the chef. It was fun to listen to. We always sat in a special spot right in front of the grill. If it was wintertime, it would feel warm and cozy—you could see the coals, and the grill chef making steaks and lobster. And the waiters have been there for millennia. It's a place unchanged—it's so atmospheric . . . it's like being in Hollywood in the 1940s.

After the world's most perfect vodka martini (not something I indulged in as a youngster), I would order the beef tenderloin medallions with béarnaise sauce, and shoestring potatoes. The sauce is delicious (although completely old-fashioned), and it's a taste of my childhood, a memory.

I was recently at a Hollywood event on my own. Sometimes I have to attend Industry events and I go alone, it's just easier. Anyway, it was some huge movie premiere and I had no intention of going to the after-party, but I was starving. So I slipped into Musso and Frank at 10:30 p.m. right before they closed. I hadn't been in there in maybe twenty years. Everything was the same. The food was the same.

How can you make the food the same for twenty years? The same staff. It's unbelievable. We used to call it "Mussolini and Franco's"—that's an Old Hollywood joke.

Now, where would we go? We'd go to the Los Angeles Observatory, high up in the hills above Griffith Park, for the sunset view, and to look at the place where *Rebel Without a Cause* was filmed, and to tour the inside of the old part of the museum, which is very historic (at least by Los Angeles standards). The original building was put up in the late 1920s—it's art deco, and there are some wonderfully eccentric displays. My favorite is the Tesla coil—you push a button and a giant bolt of electricity shoots out. I went as a schoolchild (taken there on field trips from elementary school) and I will never forget the Tesla coil.

I would end my evening after the sunset hour by going to a new place that evokes Old Hollywood, Cleo Restaurant, in the Redbury Hotel at the corner of Hollywood and Vine. I actually designed this hotel brand. Brand design is different from interior design, because it encompasses all elements of the brand, from architecture to lighting, even to the "scent experience."

At the Redbury I attempted to conjure up a very Hollywood-inflected place. It features enormous backlit historic Hollywood portraits throughout. For example, when you enter the Cleo restaurant from the lobby, you pass through an ornate Moroccan doorway that evokes a film set (the archway frames a twelve-by-fourteen-foot backlit enlargement of Theda Bara as Cleopatra). It makes a big impression (and she is, after all, the namesake of the restaurant).

Guests stare at that image—it looks so exotic (it's the famous photograph of Theda Bara wearing a metallic snake bra, with kohl-lined eyes, and a very intense expression). Anyway, people tend to look at that image and they think it's something foreign—they can't imagine that the picture was taken in 1917 only four blocks away in "Gower Gulch" (where many of the Old Hollywood studios were back then). People forget how American Old Hollywood was. They think it's someplace far away and exotic, and Old Hollywood was nothing if not exotic.

I was born and raised in Los Angeles. My work has always revolved around celebrities—extraordinarily beautiful, talented, and intelligent women. Actresses and singers have become my subject matter. Not models. So Los Angeles is very important for me because that's where my subjects are. And if they're not here, they're in New York, which is like my second home—so I flit back and forth between Los Angeles and New York every three to four weeks.

I think my first discovery of Old Hollywood glamour was as a kid going with my mom to visit her father. My maternal grandfather was a well-known doctor in Los Angeles. He had been the chief-of-staff of the Cedars Hospital, and in later years he was in private practice. Most of his private patients were Metro stars, and Metro (or MGM) was the number one studio. So he had very famous patients whom he treated privately. When my mom and I would visit him, we'd go into his private consulting office, which was covered with beige shantung wallpaper, and had huge limed oak furniture, really heavy, 1940s Streamline Deco. The desk and side tables had crystal and silver art deco framed photographs of affectionately signed and autographed images of some of Metro's most important stars.

I didn't know who the photographers were at the time. But this was my first chance ever to see black and white Hollywood photography, by masters like George Hurrell and Laszlo Willinger (who were the MGM photographers). And I just fell in love with that style of photography—that Old Hollywood quality— the velvet shadows and the satin skin and the star-lit sheen. These movie stars looked so unreal, so powerful. I didn't know that these photographs were by Hurrell then— but I know now of course.

Later, as a teenager, I simply hated Los Angeles. And what teenager doesn't hate the town they grew up in? I wanted to get to anywhere but there. It was the 1970s—not in my mind a very stylish period. At that age I had imbued myself with images from movies of the 1930s. I was more than a little obsessed with the 1930s films of Josef von Sternberg, the ones he made at Paramount that featured Marlene Dietrich. *The Devil Is a Woman*, *Shanghai Express*, *Blonde Venus*, *The Scarlet Empress*—these were my favorites.

I've always been fascinated with a certain dark glamour. And LA in the 1970s was all about blond highlights, and suntans, and "tennis court estates," and *Shampoo*—I couldn't relate to any of that. What I wanted was to go to live in New York or Paris, where I imagined there was the real dark glamour, not all this LA peachy sunshine and blondness.

And I escaped—I did go to work in New York and Paris quite a bit (because in the early part of my career, my first ten years, I shot a lot of fashion photography for *Harper's Bazaar*). I was in Europe at least six times a year for the collections, between Milan and Paris, and I left LA as a home base, but I never left it behind in my heart.

Then my career shifted towards advertising, and back towards Hollywood, back to talented, beautiful women and away from models and fashion (although I still use fashion as a way to express myself in my photographs). And at that point, I began to appreciate LA in a whole new way.

When you are constantly on the move between big cities (New York comes to mind, or Paris) you're always with other people. The moment you go out of your hotel or apartment, you're in an elevator with people, you're on the street with people, you're in the car with a taxi driver, or maybe a limo with a driver. But there's always people, people, people. And you really have no privacy of any kind.

But in Los Angeles, the greatest luxury in the world is privacy. Here I can live in a nice house. I'm not a billionaire. I have a garden, I walk through my house to my garage, I have a gate around my front yard. I go out of my private garage out of my private gated home. I drive in my car, my bubble of a car, down a beautiful pine tree–lined hilltop street. Not to make it sound too grand, but it is what it is, and to me that is the greatest luxury in the world—to have that quiet, that privacy.

Where I live, up in the hills, it's pretty much surrounded by greenery. I live in an area of Beverly Hills called Trousdale Estates (it's the former hunting lands of Greystone, the Doheny mansion). I live in a house that has a Hollywood history. It was originally the home of Freddie de Cordova. Freddie was the longtime producer of Johnny Carson's *Tonight Show*. His wife Janet was a prominent Hollywood socialite. They threw a lot of parties in that house. Johnny, Doc Severinsen, Ed McMahon, even Frank and Barbara Sinatra—they were all frequent guests. I'm not a party person, but it is a famous Hollywood house. And it's a lovely house, made of redwood, stone, and glass. It looks out onto pine trees and greenery on all sides. It's so peaceful to be able to live like that in the middle of a major urban center.

Trousdale Estates is enjoying something of a revival at the moment. Some of my well-known neighbors include the artist Ed Ruscha, the photographer Steven Meisel, the Saint Laurent designer Hedi Slimane, and actors and personalities such as Jennifer Aniston, Ellen DeGeneres, and Kelly Wearstler. They are drawn, as I was, to the mid-twentieth-century modern architecture, the space, the city views, the quiet, and the proximity to Beverly Hills.

I can't imagine anywhere else where you could live exactly like this. Certainly you could live behind walls with an incredible private park in Paris, or Milano, or London, but you'd have to be a gazillionaire (or a member of the aristocracy) to live like that. There are of course private homes behind walls in these cities—think of the whole embassy section in Paris. But it's hard to think of any modern, new world city except Los Angeles with that privacy and that greenery and to be up in the hills above the city. I can drive down about ten minutes and be in the thick of things. Then I can go home and it's so quiet and serene. So if you ask me why I love Los Angeles the most, it's for this reason.

The Fountain Coffee Room at the Beverly Hills Hotel, 9641 Sunset Boulevard, Beverly Hills; (310) 276-2251; www .beverlyhillshotel.com/the-fountain-coffee-room

Paramount Pictures (Paramount Studios Tour), 5555 Melrose Avenue, Hollywood; (323) 956-1777; www.paramount studiotour.com

Grauman's Chinese Theatre, 6925 Hollywood Boulevard, Los Angeles; (323) 465-4847; www.chinesetheatres.com

Musso and Frank Grill, 6667 Hollywood Boulevard, Los Angeles; (323) 467-7788; www.mussoandfrankgrill.com

Cleo Restaurant, 1717 Vine Street, Los Angeles; (323) 962-1711; www.cleorestaurant.com

....

Constantine Maroulis, Tony-nominated actor and singer

I love the Hollywood Roosevelt. It's just a classic great place and it's always on trend and hip. You can get a quiet room. You can hang by the pool and there can be a scene there or there could not be. You can get a spare room. It's a decent location to get everywhere else. I've had friends who worked there. it's always good.

Hollywood Roosevelt Hotel, 7000 Hollywood Boulevard, Los Angeles; (323) 466-7000; www.thompsonhotels.com/ hotels/la/hollywood-roosevelt

....

Adrian Salamunovic, co-founder DNA 11/CanvasPop, the company creates DNA portraits for celebrities

The Eames house is so cool. It's a sixty-five-year-old house, and yet it looks like it could have been designed last week. When you look at pictures of the house on the Internet, it's very, very modern. It's even modern by today's standards.

The house is a piece of architectural history. The exterior is open to the public. You can make an appointment to access the grounds, walk around outside the house. And when you look inside, you see one of the first and original Eames chairs right in the living room. You can imagine how Ray and Charles lived in their house with all their original furniture just sitting there. There's a curator who is usually there on a volunteer basis. If you're into architecture design, this is the mecca. Honestly. I've talked to a lot of people in LA and they don't even know about it.

The whole idea is to see this very design-forward house from the outside. They often open the doors and put a little chain across the entrance, so it's almost like you're in the house. You don't seem like you're locked outside. It's all right in front of you and a very open concept. There's lots of glass.

There's a swing that Ray and Charles used to swing on and gorgeous views of Pacific Palisades and the ocean. The neighboring houses are tens-of-millions-of-dollar homes. It's a great place to go on a date or just to go by yourself if you want to experience a piece of architectural history. Not just LA history but worldwide architectural history. This is untouched.

Speaking of architectural history, the place on the other side of the spectrum is the Getty Villa. J. Paul Getty, a rich, rich oil man, created a museum, based on an Italian villa. He spent millions of dollars building this Italian villa in the hills, that was designed to emulate this ancient villa in Italy from the first century. You can see Getty's private collection of statues and other works of art.

It's free to visit the Getty Villa but you have to register online to schedule a visit. The collection of original Egyptian and Greek-era items in that house are extraordinary. There's millions of dollars worth of historical, original pieces, but also the garden itself is striking. Mr. Getty never even got to see the completion of the Getty Villa. [He was living in England when he died.] It's a neat piece of LA history.

The Eames House, 203 Chautauqua Boulevard, Pacific Palisades; advance reservations required by calling; (310) 459-9663; http://eamesfoundation.org

J. Paul Getty Villa, 17985 Pacific Coast Highway, Pacific Palisades; (310) 440-7300; www.getty.edu

....

Dan Mazeau, screenwriter (*Wrath of the Titans*)

I really like the Getty Museum. It's beautiful and amazing up there, like a shining city on the hill. When my wife and I first started dating, it's one of the first places that we visited. There's a garden that overlooks all of Los Angeles. You can see the coast. I was new to Los Angeles. when I first visited the Getty. I came from Northern California to pursue a dream to be a writer. I was scared about what was going to happen but excited about the future.

The J. Paul Getty Museum, 1200 Getty Center Drive, Los Angeles; (310) 440-7330; www.getty.edu

....

Paige Morrow Kimball, filmmaker and actress

I tend to love everything that's old about Los Angeles because I'm a New York transplant. So I love the Farmers' Market. It has so much character.

Also, because I'm a jack-of-all-trades, I love the fact that you don't have to choose what to eat. You can sample a little bit of everything. I'll buy a bag of wonderful dark chocolate almonds and just have a little bit of a taste. And I get lost in the rows of food stands.

The other place that I love is the carousel at the Santa Monica Pier. It feels like you're stepping back in time, into early 1920's. I imagine ladies in long dresses sitting sidesaddle on those horses. I love that old image and they run it really well. They put in a soda fountain, Soda Jerks, so you can sit at an old fashioned-looking soda fountain and order ice cream with the carousel behind you. And the carousel is not expensive. It's not a rip off.

When I was growing up, I loved the movie, *The Sting.* I watched it probably 25 times. Maybe one hundred times. They shot the carousel sequence at the Santa Monica pier. Also, my dad used to take me to Coney Island and the carousel there all the time. I would try to grab the golden ring. So the carousel pulls me back to my childhood. And they've really preserved it well. It's just a piece of old Los Angeles.

We had a birthday party for my older daughter at the carousel when she was three. It was so much fun. The sun streams in through the huge windows. It's very spacious. You're by ocean. And on one of those beautiful Los Angeles days, that's really one of my favorite places to be.

Soda Jerks, Santa Monica Pier, 200 Santa Monica Pier, Santa Monica; (310) 393-7632; www.sodajerksusa.com and www.santamonicapier.org

Richard Bloom, mayor of Santa Monica

My favorite place in Santa Monica is none other than the world-famous Santa Monica Pier; an iconic, historic and rare wooden pier that the City has carefully preserved at the insistence of local residents. The Pier has changed over the one-hundred-plus years of its existence but retains it essential character as a gathering place where locals and visitors (six million in 2011) can enjoy and feel connected to a community and to the beautiful ecology of Santa Monica Bay. The Pier provides us with a visceral connection to our environment, to our historic past, and to our very vibrant present. I love to walk the length of the Pier at different times of the day and in different seasons. There are times of quiet serenity and there are times when the Pier teems with people from every corner of the world . . . and from just around the corner. There are grand vistas to enjoy, particularly from the end of the Pier and the top of the well known "Pacific Wheel" Ferris wheel. But, mostly, it is the parade of people of every age, background, and ethnicity that make this place so special for so many, including me.

Santa Monica Pier, 100 Santa Monica Pier, Santa Monica; (310) 458-8900; www.santamonicapier.org

Jenica Bergere, actress, comedian, and creator of her one woman show *You Can Eat Me*

I was born and raised in Van Nuys, California, by two artists, one a jazz drummer from the 40s and a burlesque dancer from the 50s. I used to refer to my home as the barrio, because it was. Every weekend my pop would scrape up some money for some change for the meter, we would jump in the VW Bug, head down the impossibly crowded 405 South, and line up on the yellow brick road aka Venice Boulevard towards the great OZ—Venice Beach. If my mom was in tow we had blankets, boogie boards, chairs, towels, a radio, an umbrella, and sandwiches. If it was just me and my dad? Nothing, but change for the meter and our swimsuits.

We stopped by Muscle Beach to visit his friends he may or may not have been in prison with for dope crimes. We would sometimes slip by Woody's apartment (a saxophonist who loved my dad like a brother). If we had day-old bread we would feed the ducks in the Venice Canals. But ultimately we would body surf the waves right at the Venice breakwater. After our skin would turn a deep shade of brown and we couldn't laugh anymore and sand crabs became a thing of the past, we would head home. This was my favorite part; we would stop by the liquor store on the way back to the freeway on Lincoln Boulevard and Venice and buy Alta Dena chocolate milk.

Today, I live in Venice Beach with my husband who was sensitive enough to buy me a chocolate milk from that liquor store in honor of my dad and propose marriage by the very same breakwater my childhood memories are made of. My husband is a chef, a different kind of migrant artist, who has been the executive chef of an exclusive west side restaurant, who once owned a little groovy cafe on Abbot Kinney and is currently running a successful catering company while we raise our beautiful daughter True.

We reside in our nine hundred square foot apartment that was architecturally designed to be at the center of the street, angled just right to view the entire street down to the beach, to the breakwater. I can look across the street to Abbot Kinney's ancestors' quarters and know that his visionary Venice Canals are a stone's throw away and my best friend Mary and her dogs like to meet my dogs there for a walk over the bridges to gander at the gondolas.

On July 4, 1905 Abbot Kinney built "Venice of America" for thousands of tourists to enjoy his theme park. He transformed the sand dunes and marsh into beautiful canals and a pier for an expected tourist crowd. In order to shepherd these tourists to all the sights, a railroad was originally installed with a mini trolley like train (which also incidentally failed to attract tourists).

The alley behind my apartment, which runs parallel to Abbot Kinney Boulevard, served as the railway. The street is actually named Irving Tabor Court (named after Kinney's chauffeur.) Along Irving Tabor Court ran trolley tracks that intersected with a Chinese looking ticket booth of a house. This gorgeous piece of history is out of view, next to dumpsters and has been many businesses. The dichotomy is that by 1912 not enough people enjoyed Abbot's vision and so by 2012, the tracks are now paved over and long forgotten but tread by thousands every week.

Years ago our building's original owner was standing in my backyard with his granddaughter and a video camera; he had overalls on and looked like a character in an Alexander Payne movie. I invited them in; over coffee he shared about his Venice and growing up in our very own apartment, which was a house at the time and the bottom served as the general store. Even though our drywall was different from years of leased office spaces and now a residence on top of a store, the frame remained the same. Our front room, the room with the view down the street, was the lookout point for the neighbors and the safe harbor for some through fires and floods and yes, he could indeed look straight down to the breakwater. We are living in the hub!

People trolling the streets of Abbot Kinney looking for a kobe beef souffle off a food truck under my window or a Steven Allen shirt have no idea that my little apartment has been through so much in just MY lifetime. Marriage, death, birth, death, three cats, three dogs, a bunny rabbit, a nest of raccoons, a restaurant opening and closing, even the sale of my own pilot *You Can Eat Me* about my chef husband who caters to celebrities and his wife Jenica (me) who wants to be one, living in super-hip Venice on a trendy street.

I'm not a homeowner. I have made enough money to own a home and spent it all on fun, because I want to remain in Venice. Instead of beating myself up about the mortgage I don't have, I get to live on the street that's in the center of it all. Yes our little charming home is now loud and dirtier from exhaust filling our windows, because what once was a residential street is now a mecca of art, food, fun, and shopping. It's filled with tourists, but I'm glad my daughter gets to be this close to my history and we get to be a part of historical Venice.

Abbot Kinney had the idea that people from all over the world would come see his little island by the sea—Venice—and not too many came. It took people awhile, but that's the charm. It's mysterious, beautiful, dirty, sometimes dangerous, hip, artsy, eclectic, historical, aloof, ever changing, never uprising, but always a retreat and always a memory. I feel so lucky and grateful to rent my apartment on Abbot Kinney in Venice, an island right in Los Angeles. Because everything I crave in life lives right here with me.

Muscle Beach, 1800 Ocean Front Walk, Venice; (310) 399-2775; www.musclebeach.net

....

Carol Martinez, former associate vice president, Los Angeles Tourism & Convention Board

I love LA because it's a place that's so creative, unique and quirky. LA is pretty much able to be whatever you want it to be. There's a lot of creative people here and we have a lot of unusual art and food. You can do something out of the ordinary that in other places people might say, "oh, that's kind of crazy." But in LA people say "'oh, that's interesting. That's good."

We have kosher burritos. Where else could people come up with a kosher burrito? And we have a convent in Hollywood, Monastery of the Angels. It's a cloistered nunnery where the nuns have a little gift store and sell bread and candy and religious objects.

Oftentimes my favorite thing to do in LA is whatever is new. And the great thing about Los Angeles is there are always new attractions, new restaurants, new theater. I like to do what's next now.

The Endeavour space shuttle just came to LA. It's going to be here forever.

I'm not a big space fan. I didn't think that I'd really care. But after seeing it and visiting the exhibit a couple times, I find it really intriguing and interesting.

The shuttle is such a big huge vessel and I think about how it went into space. From afar it looks like papier-mâché. Then you see the toilet that the astronauts had to use. You learn a little bit about their life in space. You have to get a timed ticket, but anyone can see it at the California Science Center. Right now it's horizontal and eventually, in a couple of years, it will be vertical.

I had the opportunity to see the Endeavour with a friend who worked at the Kennedy Space Center. So I feel that I got a total insider's look at how it worked.

And one of the most surprising things is that the section of the huge space shuttle where the astronauts lived was really small because a lot of the aircraft was taken up with experiments.

When the Endeavour arrived, it was such an exciting time for Los Angeles. It flew into LA on top of an airplane. And it was great to look out the windows of downtown LA and see it fly over the Hollywood sign. Then it landed at LAX and had this amazing journey to the California Science Center. It had to travel very slowly on the ground. It was a great moment for LA to welcome this piece of history into the city.

Sometimes when you don't expect to really like something and you see it and like it, that makes it a little bit better.

California Science Center, Space Shuttle Endeavour, 700 State Drive, Los Angeles; (213) 744-7400; www.california sciencecenter.org

Monastery of the Angels Cloistered Dominican Nuns, 1977 Carmen Avenue, Los Angeles; (323) 466-2186; http://monasteryoftheangels.com

. . . .

NiRé All'Dai, singer, songwriter

I like the vibe in Los Angeles. I'm spoiled. When I travel and go to all these different places, I think, these places are cool. But everything isn't so convenient and the weather isn't like this. I love the fact that people can just be themselves and dress how they want and it's acceptable. Where some places, people are like "What are you doing, you're crazy?"

In LA, if you have the confidence to pull off whatever your mood is for the day, you could get away with it. Nobody would question you. Nobody would look at you twice. They're like "Oh, whatever, that's just being original." If you do the same thing in a different city, it's kind of like "Oh my gosh, she's wearing THAT!"

LA is a cool mixing pot of whatever your style is. There's the hipsters. There's definitely going to be the Emo kids that rock all black and have the big combat boots. You're going to see the trendy chicks that are on the Kim K status—where the hair is flowing, with the nice jewels on. There's the skater crowd and you have the stoners who haven't figured out what they want to do yet, other than play guitar. They're everywhere in Hollywood.

The Lake Shrine is actually a legendary place. An Indian yogi, Paramahansa Yogananda, had a dream that he was supposed to come to California and get a piece of land that would be dedicated to a devotion of God. He was actually said to be the person to bring yoga to the West. And this man, who owned all this property in Pacific Palisades, just happened to have a dream that he saw a platform in a middle of a lake and ministers of all different religions were speaking to a congregation of thousands. They got in contact; Paramahansa got the land.

They brought in plants and flowers from all over the world, and created this amazing garden. And they had all these holy people come and pray over everything, and made it really, really holy ground.

People come there every day and just walk around and meditate. They have all these different meditation waterfalls and there's actually pieces of Gandhi's ashes on the property. It's an amazing place to go if you're stressed. Or if you just want to be at peace and you need to clear your mind. Or you just want to feel good overall. Everything is gorgeous. They say, if you walk around the place three times you start erasing or burning off negative karma. I was introduced to it as a kid. If I need to pray or write a song or just clear my head, it's a beautiful place to be. It's peace.

Marco Reed, celebrity trainer, Get Beyond Fit with Marco Reed

My favorite place in LA is the Self Realization Fellowship in Pacific Palisades.

It has an amazing shrine, lake, and spiritual center welcome to all. My family loves going on Sunday mornings. We get to meditate and hear an inspiring message. Then we walk around the beautiful lake and feed the koi fish. And if the weather is nice we are only two minutes from the beach.

The fellowship also has sentimental value since it is where I met my lovely wife. One day I saw her meditating and I thought, damn, a girl that looks like that and takes time to meditate. I'm sold. For those reasons, I place the Lake Shrine in the Pacific Palisades as my favorite place.

Sam Russell, TV and celebrity wardrobe stylist and founder of the nonprofit organization, The Giving Closet, which provides clothing to women in need

When I have a free day off, I love going to the beach or Topanga on the weekday. So I found Lake Shrine by accident coming home from the beach. With the all hustle and bustle and chaos in Los Angeles, it's a complete surprise to find someplace so serene and full of nature. It's completely unexpected. So now, whenever I have a free moment, I drive out there.

The place is very spiritual and it's all inclusive of all religions No one feels alienated. There's a walkway around a body of water. It has swans and fish and turtles. It's really quite magical. It's so nice to find something that gives back to you.

The Self-Realization Fellowship, Lake Shrine Temple, 17190 Sunset Boulevard, Los Angeles; (310) 454-4114; www .lakeshrine.org

....

Olga Garay, executive director of the City of Los Angeles Department of Cultural Affairs

Many people in Los Angeles are passionate about Barnsdall Art Park and see it as an urban oasis within the city. And then there's a whole cadre of people who have never heard of it.

Aline Barnsdall was an oil heiress. She was an artist herself, and she commissioned Frank Lloyd Wright in the 30s to build a house there, called Hollyhock House, which is now a house museum. It's being bundled with ten or twelve other Frank Lloyd Wright properties to become a World Heritage Site. The Great Wall of China, the Eiffel Tower, and the Egyptian pyramids are all World Heritage Sites.

On this art park is the Hollyhock House, Frank Lloyd Wright's first commission in California, which is historic in itself. There's the Municipal Art Gallery, which is a ten-thousand-square-foot gallery dedicated to showcasing mostly Southern California works. It was the site where the first Van Gogh exhibition ever shown in California took place. It has a small theater, which is used by community groups. There's an outdoor garden where countless festivals and performances have taken place. It's a mix of cultural venues in a very bucolic setting right in the middle of the city.

A lot of people do tai-chi or yoga, or you can hang out with your family and dog there. They have wine tastings one Friday a month during summer. It's really a delightful place to mix cultural pursuits and spend time in nature.

There's so much depth to Los Angeles. The creative power here is unleashed. It's about finding the subtleties and unexpected treasure troves. For example, there's a cemetery called Hollywood Forever that does movie screenings during summer. They do a fantastic Day of the Dead Festival, which is just extraordinary; everybody's dressed up in the Mexican tradition of the Day of the Dead, like those Grateful Dead album covers that had skeletons and roses. It's really steeped in a centuries-old tradition. And the whole cemetery turns into this alternative world.

The Siqueiros mural, "America Tropical," is another huge piece of our cultural plane. David Siqueiros was a brilliant Mexican muralist. Just like Diego Rivera's Rockefeller Center mural that was painted over, the same thing happened here. So after sixty or seventy years, the mural that he painted, which was very critical of capitalism and washed over, has been rescued. And now we're starting a visitors' center.

Barnsdall Art Park, 4800 Hollywood Boulevard, Los Angeles; (323) 660-4254; www.barnsdall.org

America Tropical Interpretive Center; El Pueblo de Los Angeles Historical Monument; 125 Paseo de La Plaza, Los Angeles; (213) 485-6855; www.americatropical.org

Hollywood Forever, 6000 Santa Monica Boulevard, Hollywood; (323) 469-1181; www.hollywoodforever.com

. . . .

Darin Moiselle, writer, executive producer and co-creator, *Wedding Band*

As a movie buff, the Cinerama Dome is my favorite theater. And through the years, they've kept it intact. Thank God. The architecture has always been striking.

I remember when I was really young and my mom was getting foot surgery. It was back when they used to keep you overnight for that. And my dad took us to see *The Hindenburg*. Great family movie when you're five about a guy blowing up a blimp. But I was really amazed with the screen which was designed to be in Cinemascope. The impact of the surround screen and that dome made the movie-going experience more unique without taking away from it. It only enhanced and made the typical largeness of a movie-going experience larger than ever. Even at that age.

ArcLight Cinerama Dome, 6360 West Sunset Boulevard, Hollywood; (323) 464-1478; www.arclightcinemas.com

....

Ken Levine, Emmy-winning writer, director, producer, play-by-play announcer for the Seattle Mariners, and author of *The Me Generation . . . By Me: Growing Up in the '60s*

My favorite place is Dodger Stadium. It's a great ballpark, even though it's fifty years old. It doesn't feel like fifty years old. And you know, the summer nights in Los Angeles. One of the great things about LA is that it cools off at night. So you can have a hot, warm, sticky day, and a lovely, cool evening. And it's a very great pastoral setting.

I remember the very first time I went to a major league game. I was eight years old, and the Dodgers had just come to LA. This was before they played in Dodger Stadium. They played at the Coliseum. My dad took me to a game, and I couldn't believe that the players whose names I knew and who I would follow on the radio and save their baseball cards, were there. They actually were there in uniform playing baseball, and all you had to do was buy a ticket and you could watch them. You could see them live. And that, to me, was thrilling. And as a kid, I saw Sandy Koufax and Hank Aaron, and Stan Musial and Willie Mays, all of these great baseball players.

Most kids dream about becoming ballplayers, but they reach a certain age where they realize, I'm just not good enough. And for me, I think that age was eight. So when the Dodgers came to town, I first heard Vin Scully I thought, oh, this is what I want to do. I can be a broadcaster. It's the only way that I can make it to the major leagues.

So I grew up going to Dodger Stadium as a kid, and through my young adult years, and I reached the point in the mid-thirties, I had always wanted to be a baseball announcer, and I figured if I don't pursue it now, I never would. During the day during this period, I was writing *Cheers*. But for about two years, every night I'd go to the upper deck of Dodger Stadium. And Dodger Stadium is kind of a wedding cake design. And I would go to the upper deck, which was truly above the timberline, and I would set up a tape recorder and a crowd mike and I would broadcast the games. Most sane adults don't do that.

And I would sit up there. The seats were non-reserved, so I figured if somebody was annoyed, that there was some skeezix trying to call a baseball game next to them, they could just get up and move over to one of the other aisles. If somebody was paying real good money for a good box seat, they wouldn't want some guy sitting next to them saying, "And the 1-1 pitch fouled away."

So I sat up in the nosebleed section and it was actually great, because there were like a lot of regulars. That's where all of the drunks and crazy people and guys with pinwheel hats sit. And a lot of them would come every night and after a while, a few would gravitate around me. I mean, this was Los Angeles and LA is so status conscious, and for people it's like hey, I have my very own announcer at Dodger Stadium.

So people would sit around me. The ballplayers were like ants at that height, they were so small. The guys around me would bring binoculars and they would check the bullpens and pass me notes as to who was warming up, because the bullpen was like in a different area code than where I was. They were all supportive.

It was funny because I was up so high, and I would be calling these pitches. I would say, "Oh, he's got a good backdoor palm ball working tonight with late action," and that sort of thing. And I couldn't even see the ball. It was just a blur. I'm talking about a four-seam fastball versus a two-seam fastball, like I could tell at that height.

I didn't have all of the statistics and things that you can get online today. This was back in 1986 and 1987, so I would just, make stuff up. This guy hit .450 in college, or he won a Tony for choreography in 1982. No one knows. But it was great fun, and I would do that night after night after night. And very slowly, I got better. That was my audition tape.

And eventually I sent tapes around and told people that I was looking to get a job in the minor leagues and I did. I got a job in Syracuse, New York, based on a tape of a Dodger game I did. But when I started, I was terrible. In fact, my first night, one of the ushers came down and offered to arrange a cab home for me. He thought I was totally drunk.

Now I'm announcing for Seattle. It's great because I've done a few games at Dodger Stadium. At one time, I was an announcer for the San Diego Padres. And I was doing a TV game. And going into an inning out of a commercial break, I had the cameraman point a camera on the upper deck, and when we came back from commercial, I said, "This is where I used to broadcast Dodger games." And then I had the cameraman slowly move down to find me in the press box and I said, "It has taken ten years to get from there down to here."

Gigi Levangie Grazer, best-selling novelist and screenwriter

I'm third generation LA. And I've grown to worship and adore my city over the years as I've traveled. My favorite thing is a late afternoon Dodger game sitting between home and first watching the sun set. There's the light at Dodger Stadium, the smell of the grass, the families who can still afford to go. It's a hodgepodge of everything that LA has to offer. From six-week-old babies to people in wheelchairs to the wealthy to immigrants. It's the most communal experience I think one can have in Los Angeles.

When I was a child, I went to Dodger Stadium a couple times through the Boys and Girls Club when I was a member of Boys and Girls Club in Hollywood. But, it's really more recent that I've grown to appreciate it. Like many things, we grow to appreciate more with age.

I also have Clipper season tickets right behind the players' bench and I always feel that I'm going to be called up any minute. If they need a point guard, I'm their man. I'm the guy. I'll go up there in my Manolos. I don't care.

The Clippers are much more family oriented because the Lakers have gotten so crazily expensive so only a select few can really afford it. So it's a little more goofy. It's definitely more democratic and has a small town feel. I mean, you're not going to see quite as many agents at the Clipper games. Okay, I love my agents. No complaints. The Clippers games is like *Cheers* for me now. I know everybody. I know all the security people and the ushers, the waiters, and it's so much fun.

I grew up wanting to live in Santa Monica and now I do. I love walking from my home in Santa Monica to the Palisades with the cliffs overlooking Santa Monica Beach. I look north and I see Cap d'Antibes. Well, it is just as beautiful. I think, I don't want to get on a plane for twelve hours.

I think there's no better place to raise my boys, specifically because they can play sports all year long. And LA is a true melting pot. The greatest learning experience that my children can have is how to be able to move between social classes, different languages, and understanding people from all worlds. That's something we definitely have here in LA. So my kids really do keep me here. Otherwise, I might be in Barcelona. You never know.

Los Angeles Clippers, Staples Center, 1111 South Figueroa Street, Los Angeles; (213) 742-7326, (888) 895-8662 (for tickets); www.nba.com/clippers

....

Robert Wuhl, actor, comedian, and Emmy-winning writer

Dodger Stadium is a terrific place and so is Edison Field (aka Angel Stadium) where the Angels play. These are two terrific stadiums. Different, but singular. I've been to just about every ballpark in the country and those are very good.

Dodger Stadium is pretty. The traffic to get to either of them is tough, but once you're in, the sight lines are always good. Considering now it's the second oldest ballpark in the National League after Wrigley Field, it's really held up incredibly well. They've put a lot of money into it and they're going to put more money into it. And Edison Field (aka Angel Stadium) has been redone twice now. They have good food, it's a beautiful ballpark, safe and clean.

Pauley Pavilion at UCLA just underwent its first facelift in about forty or fifty years. It's a great UCLA basketball arena and UCLA's going to have a terrific team. It's also a piece of history. It's like Kentucky basketball, Alabama football, or Notre Dame football. UCLA basketball, especially Pauley Pavilion, is the house that John Wooden built. So it's a very, very special place. I remember when I was a kid in college, I drove out from Texas to go to UCLA and sat there watching the great teams. I'll never forget that.

I'll tell you another great thing about Los Angeles and the West Coast in general: the football games start at 10:00 in the morning on Sunday. That is the greatest thing of all time. Anybody who is a sports fan loves the fact that football games start three hours earlier. Because you get up in the morning, have breakfast, and they're on.

Dodger Stadium, 1000 Elysian Park Avenue, Los Angeles; (323) 224-1507; www.dodgers.com

Pauley Pavilion, 555 Westwood Plaza, Los Angeles; (310) 825-2101; www.uclabruins.com/facilities/ucla-pauley-pavilion.html

Angel Stadium of Anaheim, 2000 East Gene Autry Way, Anaheim; (714) 940-2000; http://losangeles.angels.mlb.com

. . . .

Cassie Steele, actress, singer, songwriter

Working at such a young age, I always felt very much like a grown-up. I actually grew up when I moved away from my parents' house in Canada to the West Park Village apartments at the corner of Ohio and Butler Avenue in West LA. Now, this place is off of Santa Monica Boulevard right by the 405 freeway which has possibly the worst traffic I've ever seen.

So some may think this to be a less than pleasant spot to live. But on the contrary, it was the most exciting neighborhood I've ever been a part of (traffic included). There are plenty of art supply shops if you're the creative type. The very hip Floyd's 99 Barbershop attracts beautiful tatted folk. There are amazing restaurants, a farmers' market to get all the freshest veggies and fruit every Sunday afternoon.

While I was being shoved into responsibilities and pressures that I never knew existed, I found solace in Cacao Coffee Shop. All the coffees and hot choco-lates are delicious. The staff is wonderful, and it's open till 3:00 a.m. if you like an alternative nightcap. I've never frequented a place so often to be called a "regular," but there I was a permanent guest.

While my will and belief in myself was tested, by what seemed at that time as the heart-crushing auditioning process, I let my will break in another way at

Benito's Taco Shop. There are so many talented, beautiful, and creative people in this city, after being humbled, you deserve a taco. Or five.

And when I finally made friends that I'll cherish forever in my heart, Cafe Dahab hookah lounge was a perfect place to sit for hours around a hookah, laughing, talking, and sharing delicious appetizers, entrees, and desserts.

So much of who I am was born in that neighborhood that every time I pass through, the nostalgia is so strong, I almost turn onto my old street every time. And though my chest tightens to think those days are far past, no matter where I am in the world, the happiness of my memories there make me feel at home.

Floyd's 99 Barbershop, 11431 Santa Monica Boulevard, Los Angeles; (310) 231-7200; www.floydsbarbershop.com

Cacao Coffee House, 11609 Santa Monica Boulevard, Los Angeles; (310) 473-7283; www.cacaocoffeehouse.com

Benito's Taco Shop, 11614 Santa Monica Boulevard, Los Angeles; (310) 442-9924; and 7912 Beverly Boulevard, Los Angeles; (323) 938-7427; www.benitos.com

Cafe Dahab, 1638-1640 Sawtelle Boulevard, Los Angeles; (310) 444-0969; www.cafedahab.com

....

Sir Richard Branson, founder of the Virgin Group

I always like the Sunset Marquis. I've been going there for years. It was always the musician's hangout. There's just always a nice group of people there. They've got friendly rooms, a nice sort of casual restaurant area, and I always meet people who I haven't seen in years there.

Sunset Marquis, 1200 Alta Loma Road, West Hollywood; (310) 657-1333; http://sunsetmarquis.com

....

Gale Anne Hurd, film and television producer and restaurateur

I'm a fourth-generation Los Angelena. My family came here in the 1860s, so we have a long tradition in Los Angeles. And it's interesting that my first ancestors were married in the San Gabriel Valley in the mission church there. And I grew up on the west side.

But I have found perfection in Old Pasadena,

It takes me right back to the San Gabriel Valley. So it's returning to my roots in the 1860s. When I was growing up, I heard the Beach Boys' song, "Little Old Lady from Pasadena," and I had the feeling that it was a very uptight, insular community, and I found it to be anything but.

It's incredibly diverse especially culturally. We have the Norton Simon Museum, which is one of the great museums of the world. We have the Pacific Asia Museum. We have Huntington Gardens and Library nearby in San Marino. And then, of course, we have not only Cal Tech, one of the top universities in the world, but also Cal Arts, one of the top creative and artistic universities in the country.

And I love the historic, old downtown area in which I live. When our daughter went off to college, my husband and I chose to live in a condominium so that everything could be accessible by walking. I'm really part of this new return to living in an urban core.

When we met, my husband lived in New York. We wanted something that really had a downtown feel. The metro is four blocks from our condo. We have a fantastic bakery in our building, Euro Pane. And I actually own a restaurant in Old Pasadena called Vertical Wine Bistro, which is five blocks from our condo. And the ArcLight Cinemas are across the street.

Some of the finest paintings in the world—including a fantastic collection of Degas in the Norton Simon Museum—are within walking distance. There's a little cafe in the garden there. They've got a little pond and sculptures, and you can sit outside under an arbor and relax and enjoy the pond and the sculpture garden.

So literally, there is everything one could want without ever having to get into a car, From the metro, I can get to downtown Los Angeles. I'm hoping that the metro expands so that I can actually use public transportation predominantly.

Pasadena is also famous for the Rose Bowl. And I am a soccer fanatic. All the top soccer teams come and play in the Rose Bowl, which once again, is walking distance from our condo. So I've seen Barcelona play there. I've seen Real Madrid, AC Milan, Inter Milan. The soccer matches attract ninety-some-odd-thousand people of all ethnicities, of all cultural heritages. It's really a fantastic and vibrant community that hasn't been given its due. And it's a much cheaper place to live than on the west side.

The reason that I wanted to have a restaurant was essentially to have a place where I felt home in Pasadena, a home away from home. It's in a brick building that was built in 1906. And you walk into a courtyard in which you feel transported to New Orleans or Paris in my imagining. You walk up a wrought iron staircase and you enter a bistro that is my home away from home.

We have a fantastic chef, Laurent Quenioux, who's French, who was a finalist in the James Beard Foundation awards. I really love the corn fritters made with corn with salmon and crème fraîche. And we have a wonderful wine program. We're coming up on our sixth year anniversary. So our restaurant has become a second family, for people who work there and for our customers.

Norton Simon Museum, 411 West Colorado Boulevard, Pasadena; (626) 449-6840; www.nortonsimon.org

Pacific Asia Museum, 46 North Los Robles Avenue, Pasadena; (626) 449-2742; www.pacificasiamuseum.org

Huntington Botanical Gardens, 1151 Oxford Road, San Marino; (626) 405-2100; www.huntington.org

Euro Pane Bakery, 345 East Colorado Boulevard, Pasadena; (626) 844-8804

Vertical Wine Bistro, 70 North Raymond Avenue, Pasadena; (626) 795-3999; www.verticalwinebistro.com

ArcLight Cinemas, 336 East Colorado Boulevard, Pasadena; (626) 568-9651; www.arclightcinemas.com

Rose Bowl Stadium, 1001 Rose Bowl Drive, Pasadena; (626) 577-3100; www.rosebowlstadium.com

. . . .

Michael Barlow, producer, writer, and screenwriting professor, UCLA

LA is famously a city without a center, but I think downtown is becoming a center more and more. It's nice that you can take the subway downtown, go to Disney Hall and MOCA and take Angels Flight [a landmark funicular railway] down to the Grand Central Market. You walk through the market and can be at the Bradbury Building. It's an easy way to get a reading of now and then.

In the middle of cross-cultural urban mix, the Bradbury Building is very simply an amazing interior, famous from movies from *Double Indemnity* to *Blade Runner*. But it's worth its own special signature view and offers a remarkable sense of place and time—a view of the future in terms of the past. Given that LA is a city of contradictions, it is also the home office of the Internal Affairs division of the LAPD, which is cool.

The Bradbury Building is so beautifully designed and worth a trip downtown to see. But I think like most people, I came there first because of jury duty. The reason you're there, is you're at the LA courts and you have lunchtime. I had heard about the building for years, but I'd actually never been inside it.

You go up to the Grand Central Market directly opposite, get a couple of tacos at lunchtime, and then, walk in. But just going into the building, you get the sense of what an extraordinary dream of Los Angeles in the future was in 1893.

The Bradbury Building is someplace that I try to take anybody looking to see Los Angeles. The lobby is really special. The ironwork is incredible. It's a Los Angeles you don't expect—a kind of elegant, graceful enough, optimistic place. Also, it's a very, very human-scale building.

By contrast, Disney Hall is nine years old. It was a very controversial project. Frank Gehry had a major commission from the Disney family to build the thing. It kept running over and there were delays. Then finally, the Guggenheim Museum in Bilbao opened. And when that opened it became clear that this could be a great building.

This extraordinary free form building became almost an instant landmark. It's a great place to hear music as well. It's interesting that downtown Los Angeles, which was a place of barriers, is starting to become a place where things overlap, which is a very good thing. It used to be that nobody went on Broadway. And now it has become much more vital. The whole of downtown is coming alive in a way that it never has for the last forty or fifty years.

We now live in Hollywood just below Sunset and Vine and absolutely love it. It was a very dicey neighborhood fifteen years ago but it's interesting, partly because it's finally reviving. People are living in Hollywood.

We love the proximity of restaurants, farmers' markets, the fact that you can do so many things without getting into your car. We love the cultural mix. Hollywood's become a very vital place. Before, there were grand landmarks like Musso and Franks. And then there was tacky, tacky, tacky, tacky, tacky. Now there's kind of a tourist section of Hollywood Boulevard but also a lot of really useful little ethnic restaurants, coffee houses, a great farmers' market, Thai Town, ArcLight Cinemas and Amoeba Records—all of that within walking distance.

A lot of places you live in Los Angeles you feel like you're locked into one neighborhood. And this one is much more varied.

Bradbury Building, 304 South Broadway, Los Angeles; (213) 626-1893

Walt Disney Concert Hall, 111 South Grand Avenue, Los Angeles; (323) 850-2000; www.laphil.com

....

Michael Tilson Thomas, music director of the San Francisco Symphony, founder and artistic director of the New World Symphony,

I go to classic things in LA. When I'm downtown I always like to check in at the Bradbury Building. It's such an incredible, incredible structure. On the outside it looks just like an ordinary office building. Inside, it's the building that was used in the film *Blade Runner*. It's just amazing. It transports into a whole other era. Of the old LA restaurants I still check in at the Pacific Dining Car. I grew up in LA, and have memories of being in that restaurant as a kid with all sorts of amazing legendary folk from the old days. You go there for steak, big salads with seafood. That kind of food.

Bradbury Building, 304 South Broadway, Los Angeles; (213) 626-1893; www.bradburybuilding.info

Pacific Dining Car, 1310 West 6th Street, Los Angeles; (213) 483-6000; and 2700 Wilshire Boulevard, Santa Monica; (310) 453-4000; www.pacificdiningcar.com

....

Dave Barry, Pulitzer Prize–winning American author and columnist

I like to sit at the Beverly Wilshire Hotel with Ridley Pearson and have a vodka gimlet. That's the hotel where they filmed *Pretty Woman*. They make a great gimlet. I think the secret of that drink there is that it cost $83.50. I'm kind of a connoisseur. I drink gimlets and Ridley watches me drink gimlets.

Beverly Wilshire Hotel, 9500 Wilshire Boulevard, Beverly Hills; (310) 275-5200; www.fourseasons.com/beverlywilshire

....

Eric Ripert, chef and co-owner of the Michelin starred Le Bernardin, author, and television personality

My favorite hotel in Los Angeles is the Chateau Marmont. I've been going to LA for many, many years, and I always stay at the Chateau Marmont. I almost fly to LA just to stay at the Chateau. It has a different vibe. It doesn't feel like a hotel. It's a hotel that has a soul, obviously because it has seen many people passing by. But the rooms are basically large, nice, and beautiful. It's all like 1920s, 30s, 40s in terms of furniture. And the fridge in your kitchen is authentic from the 40s. You feel you're stepping into another era. But at the same time you basically have your computer and your flat screen TV and things like that.

   Sometimes, I don't even get out of the Chateau. It's almost like a retreat. It's very nice to have the garden surrounding the hotel. Very often I eat lunch and dinner in the garden. You can eat in that garden area. And I think it's very nice to be under the trees and bamboo. They do a very good breakfast. And I love their huevos rancheros. They have a good bolognese if you order room service. They have a legendary burger and fries. It's funny but as soon as I enter the Chateau I feel like I'm coming home. I don't know why.

Chateau Marmont, 8221 Sunset Boulevard, Los Angeles; (323) 656-1010; www.chateaumarmont.com

....

Duff Goldman, chef, owner of Charm City Cakes, Charm City Cakes West, Duff's Cake Mix, and host of Duff's FoodTube on Hungry

I'm relatively new to Los Angeles. I've only lived here for close to two years, and I've really found that I really love Venice Beach. And here's the thing: I didn't want to pick Venice Beach, because probably a lot of people will say Venice Beach. It's probably relatively cliché to say Venice Beach. I mean, it's like the most visited tourist destination in the world.

   But I have a reason why I like Venice Beach. And my reason is that it reminds me of Baltimore.

I moved to LA from Baltimore and, it was really hard to leave the place where I grew up and became who I am. Baltimore is a town that has such great community and is so fantastic. Then I come here and I love Los Angeles. I really love LA. It's very different. It's a bigger city. There are different rules and it's a different place. But there's something about Venice Beach that is very comforting to me. It just feels like Baltimore if Baltimore had a beach.

Here you get a great mix of wide-eyed tourists and really cool locals who own things like the Schultzies Bread Pudding stand and the Poke place. And then you have the other locals that really lend the place its sort of aura of, shall we say, mystique. There are things you can count on. Like every time there's that guy who plays the guitar and Rollerblades everywhere. And every time I've been to Venice Beach, my entire life, going back to the first time I came to California when I was in college, every single time I've come to Venice Beach, I've seen him. He dresses super crazy. He's got crazy hair. I think he has dreads, and he has a guitar amp strapped to his belt, and an electric guitar. And he Rollerblades up and down the boardwalk, shredding on his guitar like Eddie Van Halen shredding. And it's so funny because it's just so random. He wears shorts. Every single time. I've never not seen him.

Poke is a Hawaiian dish with big chunks of tuna. There's a little Poke stand, and right next to it, sharing the same kitchen is Schulzies Bread Pudding, where this girl, Schulzie, makes delicious bread pudding. It's right next to Muscle Beach.

Muscle Beach is an outdoor weight room and the tourists love it. You find them taking pictures of the bodybuilders, and everybody wants to look at 'em. Look at all these crazy humongous people with the huge muscles. I remember when I first saw it. I stood in front of it, and I was flexing. And my brother took a really goofy picture of me.

I love the idea of Muscle Beach because why does that need to exist? I guess I just wonder about what human emotion, what need people have who created Muscle Beach. I guess it's almost reverse voyeurism, where you'd want to work out in front of a lot of people. It's almost like exhibitionism. It's a very strange phenomenon. I mean, I don't know if it exists anywhere else.

I think it's really cool, because the people who you see at Muscle Beach are very serious. Those guys are really into lifting, or they're really into fitness, and they are pretty amazing. And so it leads me to wonder what drives these guys to want to go and lift there as opposed to Gold's Gym which is where I go, which is two or three blocks away.

Schulzies Bread Pudding, 1827 Ocean Front Walk, Venice; www.schultziesbreadpudding.com

Poke-Poke Place, 1827 Ocean Front Walk, Venice; (424) 228-5132; www.poke-poke.com

Muscle Beach, www.musclebeach.net

. . . .

Ken Burns, Academy Award–winning filmmaker

I love Santa Monica. I love walking along the beach and the pier. I love the attitude of the west side of Los Angeles. I love the energy and the people. I love strolling on the promenade there on 3rd Street and the restaurants. For many years, I always went to Sheila's on Main, which is Wolfgang Puck's place. But I am a great sampler. I have been known to just pick up stuff at Le Pain Quotidien then walk down to the ocean, and sit and eat it there. Or my friends who live in the district will say "Oh, we have a great seafood place for you."

If my kids were here they would say, "Dad, the best place is the zoo!" The Los Angeles Zoo, which because of its proximity to San Diego, is underrated. But the Los Angeles Zoo is one of the greatest zoos in the country. The San Diego Zoo is very famous and I love it. But when you don't have the time to schlep all the way down to San Diego, and you have your kids, you go to Griffith Park. And back behind it, near the Hollywood Cemetery is this amazing zoo. It has what you need in a zoo: the variety of animals, the beauty of the display, the wonder you see in your children's faces, and the wonder that you feel too, when you look at the majesty of nature, and all the variety that's been created. Human beings are the highest form, but maybe also the most narcissistic. You forget to regard the variety of all those species that reveal a handiwork bigger than us.

Los Angeles Zoo, 5333 Zoo Drive; (323) 644-4200; www.lazoo.org

....

Lou Diamond Phillips, actor

I have four daughters. So places like the beach and the zoo are huge. I love animals and they are fascinating to watch. For me, it's sort of amazing to watch my kids look up at a huge elephant or be amazed at the gorillas. The Los Angeles Zoo has done a wonderful job. There's a fairly new elephant enclosure. They seem to take amazing care of their animals. It's spacious, clean and set right there in the hills in nature. If I were a meerkat, I wouldn't mind being there.

Los Angeles Zoo, 5333 Zoo Dr; (323) 644-4200; www.lazoo.org

....

Patrick Dragonette, interior designer and founder, Dragonette Ltd.

Have you ever gone to a sporting event in LA? Have you ever gone to a Lakers game? It's spectacular. It's the best theater going. You should see the way a Lakers game opens. It's a whole show. The lights dim, the music swells, a cyc (or drape) drops down and they project over forty years of Lakers history on the cyc with a swelling orchestra and lights flashing. And all of a sudden the cyc drops to the floor and the whole team is inside. And the Laker Girls come up and gather up the scrim and it's the greatest show. It's fantastic. I'm telling you, you should see the way a Lakers game opens. The LA fans are just incredibly devoted fans. It's a lot of fun.

Los Angeles Lakers, Staples Center, 1111 South Figueroa Street; (310) 426-6000; www.nba.com/lakers

....

Gulla Jonsdottir, critically acclaimed architect and designer and founder, G+ Gulla Jonsdottir Design

An ideal Saturday would be to walk to Urth Caffé, on Melrose and have an almond cappuccino. They have good quality, organic coffee. The best in town. It's also Italian, and I love Italy. And then I would probably go back home, grab my car, and drive towards Malibu. I'm not much of a hiker, but once in a while, I hike Temescal Canyon.

Once you get to the top, you see the ocean and the views are quite stunning. You can walk by a waterfall coming back down, which is a hidden LA gem. I love the combination of waterfall, trees, mountains, and ocean view.

So after that excruciating experience to my muscles, I would go to the beach, relax and have a glass of rosé. Back on the Beach is the only restaurant that's actually in the sand. It's a good place to have a nice glass of wine or lunch, and just lay out on the beach, for an hour or two.

And since I'm in the neighborhood near Malibu, I love the Getty Villa. Actually it has one of the best secret lunch places in LA. The restaurant is just so quiet high up there, you feel like you're in Italy. You look at some old art, get inspired, and transported. The restaurant in the Getty is not that fancy and the food is delicious. You sit outside and are surrounded by all this art and gardens and sculptures.

I also like the Getty Center, which I actually worked on for about four years. After architectural school, I worked for Richard Meier and it was my first project. The Getty Center was designed on a thirty-inch grid, so everything is based on thirty by thirty dimensions and geometrically just perfect. It takes you away from chaos and creates order and peacefulness within the architecture and the spaces. And I like their traveling shows. Sometimes they have live music outside and a cocktail hour. And the views are amazing.

Urth Caffé, 8565 Melrose Avenue, West Hollywood; (310) 659-0628; www.urthcaffe.com

Back on the Beach, 445 Palisades Beach Road, Santa Monica; (310) 393-8282; www.backonthebeachcafe.com/cms

J. Paul Getty Villa, 17985 Pacific Coast Highway, Pacific Palisades; (310) 440-7300; www.getty.edu/visit/see_do/ eat_shop.html

The Getty Center, 1200 Getty Center Drive, Los Angeles; (310) 440-7300; www.getty.edu

. . . .

Geraldine Knatz, PhD, executive director, The Port of Los Angeles

My favorite place is the LA Waterfront down in the harbor in San Pedro. Even though a lot of people think of LA as a large coastal city, the longest stretch that the city of LA actually has on the water, on the Pacific Ocean, is down in the harbor in San Pedro. It is the largest seaport in the Western Hemisphere.

The public viewing area is way out in the outer harbor. The harbor is super sized. It's larger than life. The scale and the magnitude of the ships that pass right by you, the Vincent Thomas Bridge and the cranes. It is unmatched anywhere in Los Angeles. There's a spectacular view of the super-sized ships and cranes, and machines. It is really majestic.

I first discovered the harbor when I was a student at USC doing research, and I never left. It was fascinating. I was drawn to the ocean. And I came to California to become a marine biologist. I started doing research in the harbor, and I just loved the place so much. It's so fascinating, I stayed there my whole career.

Most people don't know about it, but every once in a while I run into someone in LA who says "Oh yes, we drive down to the outer harbor every month and we just sit there, and watch the ships coming in and out." You would basically take the harbor freeway to it dead ends, and then exit at Harbor Boulevard. You drive all the way down. Follow the signs to Berth 69/70. And there's a public area there. You can park and there's a walkway, a little pier you can walk out and sit on. It's right by the oldest warehouse in the port, which is historic and it has cute little gargoyles on it, and the water spouts. It was built after the turn of the century. It is probably the prime viewing area for looking at the harbor, seeing the lighthouse, and the ships come in.

San Pedro is a part of LA that's unique. It was settled by Croatian and Italian fishermen. People have stayed for generations. There are so many different varieties of foods. You can eat your way from one end to the other. But the public viewing area to watch the ships come in is spectacular.

I like going early in the morning when there's a couple cruise ships in and it's still dark. Our cruising season is really in the winter here. So, in January I'll come to work and it's still pretty dark. And you come over the bridge, and see a couple of cruise ships, and it's still dark out and it's just lit up with the lights.

But you can come down at night too. There are actually a lot of places to sit and watch. You get off at Harbor Boulevard, like you're taking the boat over to Catalina Island. Park like you're going to Catalina and go into the terminal. You can buy a glass of wine, and go outside. Even if you're not taking a trip to Catalina, you can buy beer and wine at the little bar. You can sit outside right underneath the bridge and watch the ships go by, and have a glass of wine in your hand because the liquor license covers the whole area. There are lots of tables, chairs, and benches right on the edge of the harbor.

People can also see the USS *Iowa* in the harbor. It's the last remaining Iowa-class battleship and opened to the public this past July; it's the only one that had a bathtub for Roosevelt. It's on permanent display. On Friday, Saturday, and Sunday, on the way to the outer harbor, there's a year-round craft market at the Port of Los Angeles called CRAFTED with people selling jewelry, ceramics, baked goods, and all kinds of things. So if you get off at Harbor Boulevard, it's one thing after another. First you hit the USS *Iowa*. Then you hit CRAFTED. Then you hit the outer harbor where you can stop and watch the ships.

I have a nice office with a view of the harbor. I could be in a meeting with my staff, and even though a lot of us have worked around the harbor all our lives, when a big ship is coming up the main channel, we stop, and we all look out the window.

CRAFTED at the Port of Los Angeles (Open Friday through Sunday only); 110 & 112 East 22nd Street, San Pedro; (310) 732-1270; http://craftedportla.com

USS *Iowa*, 250 South Harbor Boulevard, Berth 87, San Pedro; 877-446-9261; www.pacificbattleship.com

. . . .

Art Streiber, celebrity/portrait photographer

When I was a kid, I went to the LA Coliseum and saw my very first football game with my uncle. Both USC and UCLA played there. And Stanford, which was my grandfather's alma mater, would play once a year. So when Stanford came to town, I would go once a year with my family.

I also went to the Super Bowl at the Coliseum when the Miami Dolphins played the Washington Redskins when I was twelve. Being at the Super Bowl was incredibly exciting. And then as I got older, I actually attended Stanford and I worked the sidelines of one of the Stanford/USC games as a photographer when I was shooting for the school paper

The Coliseum is old school. It's grand. It was built for the 1932 Olympics. The closing ceremonies of the Olympics in 1984 ended there. It doesn't feel like a modern stadium, much to its dismay now. I would love to see the stadium renovated and modernized. I'd love to see a pro team back at the Coliseum, but I think if that happens, it's going to happen downtown. But the Coliseum is still evocative for me because I'm a huge history fan, especially a California history fan.

The place is a big cement bowl, but on a fall Saturday or Sunday the Coliseum can be a pretty magical place. Magical for me because I love college football and I have these memories associated with it. And most recently, I did a portrait of the new USC head football coach, Lane Kiffin, for *Men's Journal*. Walking through the tunnel from which the players emerge. I hadn't done that since I was a kid marching with the Stanford band. And being able to drive my truck into the tunnel when we photographed Coach Kiffin was amazing. Like so many visceral things that we all experience, it all comes back to our childhood. And that's the case for me with the Coliseum.

Los Angeles Memorial Coliseum, 3939 South Figueroa Street, Los Angeles; (213) 747-7111; www.lacoliseumlive.com

....

Amadea Bailey, contemporary abstract expressionist painter

My favorite thing to do in LA is visit the Broad Contemporary Art Museum at the Los Angeles County Museum of Art (LACMA). The three-story building, which was built in 2008, is a 60,000-square-foot space that mostly shows contemporary art.

There are many reasons why I love this place. It brought such a breath of fresh air to the LA County Museum. It's an incredible modern contemporary building designed by Renzo Piano. There's something really magical about it. There's a stairway that you can walk up on the outside up to the top floor. It has these huge amazing elevators that are something like twenty-one feet by sixteen feet with tall glass so when you're going up you can see out.

The building is also very fun. All the trim is hot red. The Museum of Contemporary Art actually reminds me a little bit of the feeling I get when I'm in Paris. When I go to the Pompidou Center, which is such an out of the box building. I get that feeling of something different, and contemporary. I love that the LA County Museum has contemporary architecture next to the older buildings.

The other amazing thing there is a fantastic installation by an LA artist, Chris Burden. It's called Urban Light and consists of about 202 restored cast iron, antique street lamps. It's so dramatic. And although I'm a full time artist I have also been dancing for thirty some years. I've actually been there with a few dancers and we always end up wanting to dance through that structure because it's like a forest of city street lamps.

Broad Contemporary Art Museum at LACMA, 5905 Wilshire Boulevard, Los Angeles; (323) 857-6000; www.lacma.org

. . . .

Tom LaBonge, Los Angeles Council member, 4th District

If you only had one hour to be in the city, the absolute best spot in Los Angeles is the Griffith Observatory. I recommend going at the end of daylight, when the city transforms from day to night. And there's the illumination above the city.

The Griffith Observatory sits on the hillside of Mount Hollywood about one thousand feet above sea level. There's a wonderful walking deck around this Art Moderne classic 1935 building. It was in *Rebel Without a Cause* with James Dean. It's been a star in many movies.

To understand the universe, you go inside to the Hall of Science. But to understand Los Angeles, walk around the deck and experience the view. For a greater view climb up about a half-hour hike up to Mount Hollywood, 1,645 feet above sea level.

From the Griffith Observatory, to the northwest is the iconic Hollywood sign. To the west you see the Santa Monica Mountains and canyons. To the far west you see the Pacific Ocean, and on the south, on a clear day, you see the underbelly of the Vincent Thomas Bridge in San Pedro. Further to the southeast is the Cleveland National Forest and Saddleback Peak.

Due east you'd see San Gregorio, which is right at the foot of Palm Springs. And then, as you look to the northeast there's the beautiful San Gabriel Mountains and the Angeles National Forest.

I grew up in Los Angeles not far from the observatory in a big family of seven brothers. We hiked all over Griffith Park. Now in the last thirty-two years, I have hiked that location almost every day. I'm in love with the spot. It brings greatness to an individual. You have this great view of the city. There are massive mountains that are foothills that drape around. There are four national forests that you can see from the observatory. Four national forests. What city has more than one?

From this spot, you're at the greatest public park, Griffith Park, which is over 4,500 acres. And you're at the greatest address: 2800 Observatory Drive. You're right there on top of the world. To me, it gives me freedom. This is the roof of Los Angeles. You walk up to the roof and you're in nature. There's wind and the beauty of nature. It's all there.

Griffith Observatory, 2800 East Observatory Road, Los Angeles; (213) 473-0800; www.griffithobs.org

. . . .

Hannah Simone, actress (*New Girl*)

There's an amazing place called Zankou Chicken and they have the most fantastic chicken schwarma. It reminds me of living in the Middle East. So I get a schwarma to go.

I love going up to the observatory in Griffith Park. I'll eat the schwarma there and take in the view. The city is absolutely beautiful from above.

Zankou Chicken, 7851 West Sunset Boulevard, Los Angeles; (323) 882-6365; www.zankouchicken.com

Griffith Observatory, 2800 East Observatory Road, Los Angeles; (213) 473-0800; www.griffithobs.org

. . . .

Ilene Angel, award-winning songwriter and author of the book *In Search of George Stephanopoulos*

My favorite place in LA is the Agape International Spiritual Center in Culver City. My friends first took me there years ago, long before the DVD *The Secret* came out, which featured Agape's founder, Dr. Michael Bernard Beckwith.

When I first went there, it was for a Sunday "early-bird" service that began before 7:00 a.m.—I kid you not. And the place was packed! When I entered the building, I didn't know quite what to expect. Was this a religion? A cult? What?

I was immediately struck by the diversity of those in attendance, which was greater than any I'd ever witnessed in any kind of religious service anywhere. I took that as a good sign of things to come.

There was a point in the service during which new visitors were welcomed. We were asked to stand, which made me a little nervous, but then, Dr. Beckwith, who is small in physique, but huge in presence, began, "Welcome to Agape. We recognize you. We know who you really are . . ." I think that's the point when I reached for the Kleenex.

Agape is a community of people dedicated to being "a beneficial presence on this planet." It offers classes, has a thriving musical and artistic environment, and its outreach to charities and causes both in the immediate vicinity of its LA location and worldwide is truly astounding.

Agape became a special and sacred place for me that day, a place of unity in a divisive world, of peace in an all-too-often chaotic world, a sanctuary without judgment or condemnation, a place of spirituality without the confines of any religious doctrine. It inspired me and still does by its mere existence.

Agape International Spiritual Center, 5700 Buckingham Parkway, Culver City; (310) 348-1250; www.agapelive.com

....

Martin Cooper, president, Cooper Communications

One of the major things that makes this city unique is the entertainment industry. For the last century, emanating more from Los Angeles than any other single place, have been all of these creative arts: film, radio, television, and all the way to online games. That creates a society where there's always something new and exciting. This is the home of entrepreneurialism. It's not the head of corporate America. It's the head of the creative arts for the whole world. And I think that lends an innate excitement. To me favorite places synthesize this. They include two places where I worked, Walt Disney Productions and the Playboy Mansion. They're all about the fantasy that is Los Angeles.

Disneyland was constructed to be a place where people could leave their cares behind them. It's designed for the whole family. It's not just a kid's place. It's not just an adult place. It's deliberately sealed off from the rest of the world.

When I was there, there was a big berm, which is a huge earthen mound around Disneyland. And they were going to build a hotel across the street. We used to talk about visual intrusion, meaning that from inside Disneyland, if we didn't build the berm high enough, you could see the hotel. And that would be a visual intrusion into this fantasy world of Disneyland. I love the fact that it deliberately separates itself from the world. Disney started building it in July of 1954, and it opened on July 17th of 1955. On the opening day, Walt Disney said, "As long as there is imagination left in the world, Disneyland will never be completed." I like that idea that a commercial venture is driven by imagination.

I've probably been on every ride fifty times, and my favorite thing to do is to sit on a bench on Main Street and watch people. It's the best people-watching place in the world. Why is that? They're happy. They're looking forward to the next adventure that they're going to have there, whether it's the Jungle Cruise ride, or the Matterhorn, or whatever it might be. And they're without their masks and inhibitions that most of us carry around with us all the time.

The best time to go is when the park first opens. Preferably on a weekday, but it's more crowded on Saturday than on Sunday. So I like to be there early when the park opens on a Sunday. Everything is clean and fresh and you're enjoying it almost as if for the first time.

Disneyland Park, 1313 Disneyland Drive, Anaheim; (714) 520-5060; http://disneyland.disney.go.com

....

Hans Ulrich Obrist, contemporary art curator, critic, and historian and director of international projects at the Serpentine Gallery

My favorite place in Los Angeles is the Museum of Jurassic Technology, which the artist David Wilson founded. Lawrence Weschler wrote a book which describes the beauty of this place. It's an artist-run museum, and a sort of late-twentieth-century analogy to the Sir John Soane's Museum, which is a nineteenth-century museum in London.

The Museum of Jurassic Technology has a complexity of narratives so it's a museum which artists love. When I went to LA for the first time all the artists told me about this museum. The artist Raymond Pettibon took me there. It's a very magical museum.

From outside you think it's a very ordinary house, but inside are all these different depictions. There are strands of an anthropology museum, a natural history museum, a museum of mankind. All these dimensions are mentioned. But you realize that they have artistic fiction. There's a blur of fiction and reality. You're not in a monumental museum where you basically have to find your own way. You're in a house with rooms. And it's very special to walk through these rooms and learn about all these strange stories. It's a storytelling device.

Normally people invent a novel to tell a story. Here we have an artist developing a house museum as a device for new narratives which are not lineal. And it's lovely that LA has a brother or sister museum to Sir John Soane's Museum. There are many interesting connections between London and LA, because of the art scene. In fact, my single most favorite thing in LA are the artists. There's an amazing arts scene and amazing artists. And how interesting that an artist even founded a museum.

The Museum of Jurassic Technology, 9341 Venice Boulevard, Culver City; (310) 836-6131; http://mjt.org

....

Fred Armisen, Emmy-nominated actor

I love downtown LA. I love Silver Lake and Echo Park. And my favorite place is the Museum of Jurassic Technology. It's the most beautiful place. And it may be one of my favorite places on earth. I love everything you do in there. Even the sound of it is very curated. You have to go to the website to see what I mean.

When I was a kid, my dad took me to LA on a trip. And I loved Universal Studios and show business things. I wanted to be Lon Chaney, the 1920's silent film horror star. I still get those feelings. That's not gone. I love it all.

The Museum of Jurassic Technology, 9341 Venice Boulevard, Culver City; (310) 836-6131; http://mjt.org

....

Jerry R. Schubel, PhD, president and CEO, Aquarium of the Pacific

My favorite place, of course, is the Aquarium of the Pacific. It's not only my favorite place because I work here but it really redefines what the modern aquarium can and should be. It combines live animal exhibits with the ability to tell big, important stories of the changing relationship that people have with the earth, the ocean, and how that relationship is affecting marine life. And with Hollywood close by, the master storytellers and filmmakers, it gives us an opportunity to do things that other aquariums don't have to the same extent.

The other thing that I really love is that the ports of Long Beach and Los Angeles are joined at the hip even though they are separate ports. They are the largest container port complexes in the United States. They account for about 50 percent of the imports of finished goods to the nation.

I love going into these ports, especially on boats, and watching the magnitude and the majesty of the movements of these big ships and the containers. The grace with which they are all handled is almost musical in nature. The size of the ships and cranes, and the gracefulness with which the goods are moved is like a ballet. It's hard to describe.

The best time to visit is in the evening when the lights are on and it's a magical experience. I don't think that we take full advantage of these ports as a visitor attraction. They are quite remarkable.

You see the huge container ships moving in and out of the port. You see them being guided by tugs, putting them up against the piers. You see cranes lifting these containers off ships. They are able to unload a huge ship in hours where it used to take days.

There are places where you can drive and overlook the port from observation places. You can even drive over the Gerald Desmond Bridge and look down upon the site of the activity that takes place. I think it's worth driving over that bridge. When you go over the Gerald Desmond Bridge and look off to the left, you see the Port of Long Beach. To the right you see the Port of Los Angeles.

People can also take a cruise to see them. We have something called Urban Ocean that goes into the Port of Long Beach. I believe the Port of Los Angeles also has some cruises. They are usually a couple of hours long and quite special.

Aquarium of the Pacific Harbor Tour, www.aquariumofpacific.org/education/info/harbor_tour

....

Margy Rochlin, award-winning journalist who writes for print, online media, and radio

I have a lot of favorite places in LA and one of them is the Culver City pool. It's a true Olympic-size swimming pool and the best deal in town. You can't buy a grande caramel macchiato at Starbucks for how much it costs to get a card and go. ($4 per visit for nonresidents, $50 for a 15-visit card.)

It has an incredibly nice atmosphere. When you start going to the pool and become a regular, you see the same people all the time. They are so interesting and different. One of the guys at the pool is the piano player at Mastro's Steak House. Another guy teaches literature of the American West at UCLA. The people are so lovely.

Anybody can go to the pool. You don't have to be a member. You can pay as you go. When it's really hot, it's always several degrees cooler, or when it's really cold it's several degrees warmer. There's a solar heating system that powers up the pool. You can call up and ask for the water temperature, or if it's full or empty and they'll tell you. People love the kids who run it so much they bring them boxes of doughnuts.

Another favorite place is a really wonderful bike shop in Venice called Bicycle Ambulance. You can rent a bike to go bike riding on the Santa Monica bike path which takes you all the way to Palos Verdes. Or they'll repair your tires or fix your bike, and they are incredibly inexpensive.

The Culver City Municipal Plunge, 4175 Overland Avenue, Culver City; (310) 253-6680; www.culvercity.org/Government/PRCS/Recreation/Aquatics.aspx

Bicycle Ambulance, 2212 Lincoln Boulevard, Santa Monica; (310) 395-5026

....

Nick Karno, environmental prosecutor, city attorney's office, Los Angeles

One of the complaints about LA is that it doesn't have a city center. They're trying to do a downtown but it's very balkanized. In fact, LA is a lot of different cities just woven together.

But that said, you can go to all these diverse parts and have completely unique and interesting experiences that are very different than other parts of the city. And actually that makes it very unique.

Have you seen the Pixar animated cartoon movie *Up*? In the story, everybody is trying to buy this guy's house because there's a development all around it and he won't sell. Picture huge buildings all around this tiny little two-story craftsman house. And that's exactly the restaurant Off Vine. It's basically a two-story craftsman house surrounded by honeysuckle and vines.

The food is amazing California cuisine mixed with a little bit of comfort food—grilled fish with some asparagus and maybe sweet potato. It's sort of traditional American, but has a California touch, which is usually a lot of healthy greens and vegetables.

Off Vine is a very unique place. I almost don't want to go there too much. I've only been, maybe five to seven times, but usually it's because I'm saving it for something special like Valentine's Day, where I really want to do a romantic dinner. You have to tell them to do the chocolate soufflé ahead of time because it's really, really incredible.

Once you're done eating in this house in the middle of Hollywood, you walk a few blocks and you're at the Pantages Theater, which is really old: LA art deco at its height. They did something like a multi-million dollar renovation and modernized the whole stage. From what I understand, the largest theater on Broadway in New York City has about 1900 seats, and the Pantages holds 2700. So it's a massive theater. A lot of the art deco is wood-carved, gold-plated, and takes your breath away when you walk in. Los Angeles actually has a number of theaters that are getting remade. Downtown on Broadway, there's the Los Angeles Theatre and the Orpheum. They don't make theaters like that anymore. A lot of movies have been shot there because they're such spectacular old theaters. It really takes you back in time.

Off Vine Restaurant, 6263 Leland Way, Los Angeles; (323) 962-1900; www.offvine.com

Pantages Theatre, 6233 Hollywood Boulevard, Los Angeles; (323) 468-1770; www.broadwayla.org

....

Betty Buckley, Tony-winning and Emmy-nominated actress and singer

I lived in the Chateau Marmont the whole time I was doing the TV show, *Eight is Enough.* And in those days the hotel was like a rock and roll dorm.

In fact, my little Yorkshire Terrier, Rags, who lived with me there, is buried in the front garden of the Chateau Marmont. She is buried underneath what used to be the Marlboro Man big billboard on Sunset Boulevard. Actually, at that time she died, I wasn't staying there. But I wanted Rags to be buried in that garden right underneath that sign, because the whole first year of *Eight is Enough* I lived in a suite that overlooked Sunset Boulevard. For years I lived on the sixth floor. Robert De Niro was in room 64 and I was in room 68. And I would pass him all the time in the garage. It was, "Hi, Robert," "Hi, Betty."

My brother, Norman, is a TV director in Los Angeles and directs shows like *Gossip Girl, Pretty Little Liars, Rizzoli & Isles,* and a myriad of othes. He said, "You can't do that. You can't bury a dog in a public place." And I said, "I'm going to do it."

And so my friend and I went tromping through the hotel lobby and the staff said, "Hi, Betty." And I'd say, "Hi, ya'll." And we went out to the garden and tried to dig a hole with a rock, which was absurd. So I went to the basement and got a shovel. Nobody questioned me because I'd lived there forever. In fact, I still have 12 pieces of luggage and boxes in storage at the Chateau Marmont of clothes from the late 70s and early 80s. And every time I go there, they ask, "Do you want your boxes?" and I say, "No, that's okay." But one of these days I'll get them and auction them off on eBay. The boxes contain things like trashy lingerie and clothes from the 70s. I thought that I was a rock and roller—or I aspired to be. And here I was playing an American mother on a TV show.

I went back through the lobby with this shovel. We went out to the front, dug the grave for Rags, sang some hymns and told Rags stories, and buried her there. So it's a really important place for me.

I always stay at the Chateau Marmont. My brother, Norman, says, "You might want to find a new place to abide in LA?" and I say, "No." This is my home away from home.

I think of the people I met there and the adventures I had. One day I was at the pool, hanging out and this little kid started drowning in the pool. His parents' backs were turned and so I jumped in the pool and saved him. I didn't know who they were. But years later I found out I saved Rufus Wainwright.

I knew everybody at the Chateau Marmont. I used to hang out with my friend, John Belushi. We met when we were just starting out and we were buddies and hung out. I remember a night that Belushi called and said, "Buckley, do you want to go meet the Rolling Stones?" and I said "Absolutely!" So he came to get me and we went on this adventure to the house of the Rolling Stones, up in Laurel Canyon someplace. It was one room to the next room to the next room with each Rolling Stone and his entourage playing pool or hanging out, listening to music or whatever. It was a really fun time. I really love that place and have a great deal of affection for it.

Chateau Marmont, 8221 Sunset Boulevard, Hollywood; (323) 656-1010; www.chateaumarmont.com

....

Nancy Davis, founder, The Nancy Davis Foundation for Multiple Sclerosis

One of my favorite places in Los Angeles is the ballroom at the Hyatt Regency Century Plaza Hotel in Century City. It truly is a gorgeous space not to mention the largest ballroom in the city—and has been the scene of our annual Race to Erase MS Gala Fundraiser for over a decade.

Each year I am amazed by the incredible generosity and giving spirit of our attendees who help us raise vitally needed funds for MS research to help us find a cure for the 2 million people who suffer from this autoimmune disease. Amazing and legendary performers have graced the Century Plaza stage not only for our event but the hundreds of other amazing events that take place—all in the wonderful celebration of curing diseases and healing our planet. Magic takes place at this remarkable venue and the generous people in our city who congregate to support our Race gala each and every year truly inspire me and give me hope that we will win our Race to Erase MS!

Hyatt Regency Century Plaza, 2025 Avenue of the Stars, Los Angeles, (310) 228-1234; http://centuryplaza.hyatt.com

Jean-François Piège, chef and owner of the Michelin-starred restaurant Jean-François Piège, Brasserie Thoumieux and Hotel Thoumieux

I love the atmosphere of the Chateau Marmont. It's both chic and calm and I adore eating the pancakes at breakfast. They are so light and not heavy. In fact, I put the chef's pancake recipe in my book.

My wife and I had never heard about the Chateau Marmont before. But a friend recommended that we go. We didn't know about the history. It was a great surprise. The first time we arrived at the hotel, it was 5 a.m. and dark outside. The hotel seemed gothic and very strange. But we slept for four hours and then experienced the sunlight and fell in love with the hotel.

Also, the light in LA is so different and intense than in Paris. At night, it's just a little cold.

I also love walking along Melrose Place. It's an incredible and big street, with vintage and antique stores and small shops. It reminds me of a boulevard in Paris.

Chateau Marmont, 8221 Sunset Boulevard, Hollywood; (323) 656-1010; www.chateaumarmont.com

Max Casella, actor

When I was living in Los Angeles, the New Beverly Cinema was my home away from home. They have double features. The films are always interestingly paired. It could be films by Kurosawa, Ingmar Bergman to new movies by Tim Burton. They would play Ed Wood with Barton Fink. They have the best popcorn. At the time I went it was $5 (now it's $8) to watch great movies in a wonderful movie theater. It's my favorite thing about LA.

The New Beverly Cinema, 7165 Beverly Boulevard Los Angeles, (323) 938-4038; www.newbevcinema.com

SAUNTERS, SAILS, RIDES, HIKES & DRIVES

 When you drive along PCH, there's one road that wraps around the coast. And if you time it at sunset, you see the most beautiful sunset over the Pacific Ocean and maybe pull into a restaurant nearby to grab a bite to eat.

—Ryan Seacrest, host of American Idol, "American Top 40 with Ryan Seacrest," and "On Air with Ryan Seacrest"

Marvin Braude was a conservationist and avid bicyclist from Chicago. As his daughter, Ann Braude, explains, "my grandfather used to tell me if I ever wanted to get married I'd better not do it on Sunday morning because my parents would be bike riding." When Marvin and his wife Marjorie honeymooned in Yosemite, they became so enchanted with the mountain landscape. They ultimately moved to Brentwood in the early 1950s and lived up in the hills in the Santa Monica Mountains.

In fact, conservation inspired Marvin Braude's launch into public life. During the 1960s, he discovered plans for freeway development when the newspapers printed a map of a freeway that would go across the Santa Monica Mountains. He could see those mountains from the window of his house. Convinced that the plan was a bad idea, Braude was inspired. He went to a council hearing at City Hall, thought, "I could do that," and ran for city council. He remained on the council for thirty-two years.

Nearly every Sunday before the cars hit the streets, you could find Marvin Braude, Marjorie, and their two daughters on their bicycles. "We lived in LA, the automobile city, and my parents were dedicated to nature," says Ann Braude. "It was just a real spiritual connection for them." But back then, both LA and Santa Monica didn't allow bicycles on the boardwalk after 9:00 a.m. (except in winter). Of course, that didn't stop the Braudes. "My dad knew every little back way and had all these circuitous little roads and detours," she offers. "He knew just exactly where to go to find the routes with no traffic. We rode in alleyways. You had to be an explorer because there were no designated bicycle paths."

Understanding that bicyclists were a silent constituency and weren't represented, Marvin Braude saw a need for change. "A part of his dream was that everyone should have access to the incredible experience of riding on the beach and riding on the California coast," explains Ann Braude. So one Sunday morning in 1968, he invited cyclists to ride with him to help bring attention to the need to create a bike path. Close to four hundred people showed up to peddle a total of twenty-one miles from Venice to Playa del Rey and back.

By 1972 Marvin Braude and the many bicycling bandits got their wish. That year, the first section of bike path opened from Santa Monica to Washington Street in Venice. Today it spans a total of twenty-two miles. The trail runs mostly along the majestic beachy shoreline from Pacific Palisades, through Santa Monica, Venice, Marina del Rey, Playa del Rey, Manhattan Beach, Hermosa, Redondo—all the way to the City of Torrance. "He just wanted the bike path to go on forever," says Ann Braude. "When it wasn't very busy, my parents used to ride down the bicycle path holding hands. To me, that path represents my parents' love for each other and for the city that they gave their lives to."

After many, many years of riding on the bike path that he so adored, Marvin Braude passed away in 2005. But on July 23, 2007, the bike path that Braude dreamed of and worked to create was renamed The Marvin Braude Bike Trail. Ann Braude spoke at the dedication of the bicycle path sharing how her father would head to the beach in Santa Monica from his office in City Hall. "He often told me that no day was ever wasted if you saw the sun set over the ocean. Of course, what he really meant is that no day was ever wasted if you saw the sun set over the ocean from the bicycle path."

. . . .

Cheryl Tiegs, *former supermodel and designer*

My favorite place to go is Will Rogers's State Park. There's a big polo field and Will Rogers used to live there.

The trails go up, up, way into the mountains. It's a ten mile hike and it is arduous. It's not easy to go up, up, up, up and it's long. But it's so magical. Sometimes you are crossing a bridge. Sometimes you are in foliage that you have to brush aside. There are all these trails. There are oak trees and flowering trees. Every time you turn a corner there's just something that's new and special.

I always go with a friend. I would never do that hike alone. In my backpack are Westwood sandwiches from Nate 'n Al, a famous deli in Beverly Hills.

Westwood sandwiches are turkey with coleslaw on rye. And I treat myself to a bag of potato chips, and always have a bottle of water. And at the end of this long trail is a beautiful oak tree. I put out a lightweight blanket and just lie down and look up at the sky to the oak tree. That's where I have the picnic. If you climbed up twenty feet farther you can climb up and see the city. But I'm just very happy to forget about the city for a day.

And then I have to do the walk home, but it is lovely. It's one of the best things I can do. I can't wait to always do it again.

It's not ten easy miles. It's hard. It's uneven ground so you really have to watch yourself. Then sometimes the plants are very sweet and you just brush them aside. It's very gentle. That's what LA is all about: going up in the hills, getting away from the city, and going on a really good hike.

I moved to LA when I was five so it's where I grew up. I was just in Minnesota, New York, and Toronto and I'm telling you I just was jonesing to come back to LA where the sky is blue and the sun is warm.

Will Rogers State Park, 1501 Will Rogers State Park Road, Pacific Palisades; (310) 454-8212; www.parks.ca.gov

Nate 'n Al, 414 North Beverly Drive, Beverly Hills; (310) 274-0101; www.natenal.com

. . . .

Usher, Grammy-winning singer, songwriter, actor, and founder of Usher's New Look Foundation

My favorite thing about LA? My bikes! My Ducatis. I love them. I ride them all over the city. I'm the guy with the red wheels.

. . . .

Kellan Lutz, actor

There's a lot of beauty in California. You can get away. You can drive an hour any direction. You can be in San Diego. You can go on up to Santa Barbara. I snowboard also, so it's great to be close to Mount Baldy, which is forty-five minutes away. It's not the most amazing, but for a half-day trip, you can just do it easily. There's Lake Arrowhead to Jet Ski. I'm a big hiker and I love the ocean. I live by the water so it's always fun going out there. I've been stand-up paddleboarding. There's Griffith Observatory to hike. There's so many paths up by the observatory, so many paths. So I go there, or I hike up Malibu.

What brought me to LA was that my father's always lived in LA. I wanted to go to college. I got a full ride to Chapman University, which is an amazing beautiful school in Orange County. I went for chemical engineering and football. I had left Arizona, left my nests that my mom had made, and I packed up my nice truck that I saved money up to have, put all my keepsakes in the bed of it, and drove. I remember hitting downtown when I believe the 101 hits the 10 freeway. And there's something like twelve different overpasses going over each other. I was just, whoa, this is big. This is a big city. But I wasn't scared. I was just thrilled for this new moment in my life.

I started modeling before I started acting and so I always knew I loved being in front of the camera. I never thought I was a pretty or a handsome dude who could have a modeling career. I just knew I had personality. When I first fell into acting, I started going to acting classes and found it very therapeutic. I was a middle child so I found a way to just get stuff off my chest and in an indirect way.

Then I got into the actual work, and I just fell in love with acting. And the great thing about it is I don't mind if I never win an Oscar. I never had the dream to be an actor. But it's great to look back at previous work and see my growth as an actor. And it's great because you can work with better actors and better directors, and there's never a ceiling.

Griffith Observatory Hike, Fern Dell Drive (off Los Feliz), Los Angeles

. . . .

Ryan Seacrest, host of *American Idol,* "American Top 40 with Ryan Seacrest," and "On Air with Ryan Seacrest"

I like driving down PCH. When I was a kid I grew up watching the show, *Chips.* Remember the show, *Chips*? You'd see them every once in a while going down PCH in that shot. It's still a dream come true to be driving along the beach in a car. When you drive along PCH, there's one road that wraps around the coast. And if you time it at sunset, you see the most beautiful sunset over the Pacific Ocean and maybe pull into a restaurant nearby to grab a bite to eat.

What can you not love about LA? My job is there, the weather is fantastic, the fact that the *American Idol* stage is ten minutes away. It would be tough to live somewhere else. Having all that near is good.

. . . .

Guy Webster, renowned photographer

I have fifty motorcycles, so I ride to coffee shops throughout LA and all over California. At least twice a week, I go to a place called 3 Square in Venice on Abbot Kinney and sit outside at one of the two tables. The bakery goods are fabulous. But they have a five-grain scone, which I love and it's healthy. They have good coffee. It's one of my favorite places.

I've always loved Venice. I love the energy, the crazy people of which I am one, and it's my home. I really enjoy the ambiance and the people on Abbot Kinney and all the streets surrounding the Venice area. I love the boardwalk. About once a week, I'll go down to the boardwalk and have lunch and watch all the people. In fact, we were working on a magazine here for years called *Wet Magazine,* which came out in Venice. It was a very famous magazine for graphic art back in the 70s.

I believe the boardwalk in Venice is used in so many movies and commercials. It has palm trees, roller skaters, Rollerbladers, crazy people, fat people, skinny people, black, white, gray, you name it, everything is there. It is the ultimate of the LA experience because everybody takes buses down there, and it's a cross section of the people of LA.

LA in the old days was really about "Angel's Flight." Angel's Flight is a tram you take from lower LA to higher LA, and it gets you up the hill. It is called Angel's Flight because it takes you up to heaven, That was THE place that you showed people because LA was downtown LA.

But when LA spread out to the beach, and to Venice, people started moving west. It's as far west as you can go, and everybody wants to live there. Now rich people have moved in and taken over, but that's OK. There's always change, and people always move towards the beach. Where you could buy a house in 1929 for $3,000 in Venice, it's now $3 million. That is not an exaggeration.

....

Nancy Silverton, chef, author, and co-owner of Osteria Mozza and Pizzeria Mozza

I've often heard it said that Los Angeles is not a great walking town like Paris or New York. And they're right. But Los Angeles, on a Sunday morning when traffic is lightest, is a great driving city.

It is a town built for a car. If there is another city in the world more designed for a car, I don't know it.

So my Los Angeles is the Sunday drive. I love to get in my Porsche, put the top down and take off with the love of my life, my boyfriend of nine stupendous years, the honorable Sir Michael Krikorian, for a random cruise through my city.

Ideally I'm on the road by 10 a.m., and most of the time I don't even plan where I'm going. Just get in the car and drive, and then figure out where to go. That is part of the beauty of Los Angeles, anywhere you point your car can lead to a fascinating mini escape.

I've ended up thirty miles away on Palos Verdes Drive speeding around a coast that seems like Highway One. On the right of the windy road are multimillion-dollar hilltop houses and on the left is the mighty Pacific where wave after wave crashes against the jagged boulders below. That island in the distance is Catalina.

I sometimes stop in San Pedro before taking the bend around the coast. There is a mom and pop market there called Busy Bee that has the best meatball sandwich in town. It's easy to find the market; there's usually a line snaking out the door.

I've driven twelve miles south and toured the Watts Towers. I've seen the spirals several times and every time I marvel at their intricate beauty and at the determined spirit of its creator, an Italian immigrant named Simon Rodia.

Just about seven, eight miles east of my house is almost like another country, East LA. A Sunday cruise down Whittier Boulevard (the street that practically invented cruising) is like going to Guadalajara. Mariachis, pandelarias, taquerias, mercados line the boulevard. A few blocks south is the Nuevo Estrada housing projects which boast a dozen national award-winning murals painted during the height of the 1970s Chicano Movement.

Like my city, my drives are full of contrasts. The week after driving though Watts and South Central, I might be on Mapleton Drive in Holmby Hills, probably the most exclusive street in Los Angeles. Some of the homes are so big, you can't even see them through their extensive landscaping. One of the "homes" is called "The Manor" and is fifty-six thousand square feet, which is almost as large as Delaware!

Getting even closer to my home, only four miles north, is the winding enclave Lake Hollywood. With a name like that you'd think it would be a local landmark, but I'd bet most Angelenos don't even know where it is. It's easy to get lost amid the windy streets, and that's part of the enjoyment of the drive. No hurry. Just cruising and sightseeing in basically my backyard.

I love the diversity of these neighborhoods, not only in the people, but in the architecture. On one single block there can be so many different styles of homes. These are not tract neighborhoods.

I've driven up Mandeville Canyon, a rustic version of the more well known Laurel Canyon, and it seemed like I was so far away from the city, even though I was just three or four miles away from UCLA in Westwood Village.

Just when I think I know the entire city, there are enclaves in Silver Lake and Echo Park that I'm surprised to stumble upon.

That's part of the charm of the city and the Sunday drive, Though I've lived almost my entire life in Los Angeles, I almost always find a place on these drives I've never seen. It's an adventure to discover somewhere new in a place you lived for fifty years. That's my Los Angeles. Always fresh. Whether it's changing or still the same.

Busy Bee Market, 2413 South Walker Avenue, San Pedro; (310) 832-8660

....

Hugh Jackman, Emmy- and Tony-winning, Golden Globe–nominated actor, and singer

I love Runyon Canyon. It's the middle of the city. It's a place to walk up to the top and has a great view.

Frances Fisher, actress

Before I moved to LA, someone told me that Los Angeles was like a cow farm, while New York was condensed milk. That was his impression. And it's true because everything's so spread out here. You can have a house, trees, grass, and a one-story experience.

When I first arrived, I was sleeping on a blowup mattress in my brother's tiny one-bedroom place in Burbank. He had the bedroom and I was in the living room. We then moved to a little house in Manhattan Beach, right on what's called the Strand, which is a walkway and bike path that goes along the ocean.

The Strand is beautiful. I could look at the Pacific Ocean everyday. You can walk, bike or roller-skate on it. And I really got into roller-skating. It was a fun place to live because I was close enough to Los Angeles to drive in for meetings or work. Then I could come home and look at this great expanse. I would go to the beach at night, especially during a full moon and nobody would be on there. I'd just walk and hear the waves come in. It was idyllic.

I like to hike in Runyon Canyon which is near my house. It's a great walk because you can see the Hollywood sign and it overlooks all of downtown LA. I always run into people I know up there and it's a great walk for the dog. It tends to be very busy in the mornings and late afternoon.

If I have even more time, I go to Fryman Canyon with my friends because there are a lot more trees and it's a little prettier. It's lush. It's subtle. You feel that you're in the woods but you're right in the middle of LA.

Jane Fonda, Academy Award–, Golden Globe–, and Emmy-winning actor

I only moved recently back to LA. I like to walk Runyon Canyon. I like taking walks in the hills. It's convenient and it's a good walk and it's about an hour and a half.

Sanaa Lathan, actress

I love going hiking. I like to walk with my dogs at Runyon and Fryman Canyons. I actually like Fryman Canyon because it's less crowded. I love being in nature. No matter how stressed you are or what you're going through, by the time you are done walking over the mountain, it's like you can breathe again. Also, I'm one of those people who likes to drive. I like getting in my car. Sometimes I'll drive for no reason. And I love that you have the beach right there.

Edward Mady, general manager, The Beverly Hills Hotel

On any given Saturday or Sunday morning or both, I'll hit the coffee shop at the Beverly Hills Hotel and enjoy breakfast there. It's one of those iconic hangout places and you'll never know who you run into. And then I head to Runyon Canyon.

When I have an opportunity to unplug, I like hiking. The exercise is good. You can get up to 675 feet in elevation depending on what path you take. One path takes you to a higher elevation. The other is not as high but still you get good exercise. The views of the city are awesome when you don't have any marine layer.

Or sometimes I plug into my iPhone and just enjoy the views. Other times, just enjoy the quiet of the day. Usually it's hot as heck. You always have a ton of people walking their dogs. And if I go with someone, we'll have a dog counting contest. And whoever wins doesn't have to buy lunch. You say, "okay, we're going to count to 75 dogs today," and whoever is closer to the number doesn't have to buy.

I once did an interview for NPR at the hotel. I was asked, who are some of the famous people who have visited? We don't talk about our customers. But I said if we were to walk around, I'm sure you're going to see people that you might recognize. So that's what we did.

So we were walking out the door, and who do we run into standing at the door waiting to be seated? Jane Fonda. And clearly that's who the interviewer saw. As we walked out of the Polo Lounge, and walking downstairs, Diane Keaton tapped her on the shoulder and asked, "do you know which way the hairdresser is?" And then we continued to walk and she discovered a third famous person was walking from the pool back towards the lobby. In any event all you have to do is walk around.

Byata Cousins, casting producer, Doron Ofir Casting

My favorite thing to do in LA is hit up Runyon Canyon. This is the one spot in the city where you can find anyone and everyone from all walks of life. I work as a casting director and many times I have to recruit people for shows. I am always recruiting, so I sometimes approach people who I see on the mountain. I have no problem approaching anyone at any time. I'm a New Yorker. And so all at the same time, I am meditating, exercising, and working.

I hike up Runyon at least three times a week, sometimes in the morning with my eleven-month-old baby strapped on my back and then again at night after a hard day's work. Sometimes I bring my hubby along and our hike becomes a family affair. Not to toot my own horn, but the three of us together definitely turn some heads on that mountain. He's a gorgeous Jamaican Italian man and I am a Russian Jewish New Yorker with lots of style and swagger. And to top it all off, throw our cute little baby Luca in the mix. We are the stars of the Canyon!

Runyon Canyon Park, 2001 North Fuller Avenue, Los Angeles; (323) 666-5046; http://runyoncanyon-losangeles.com

....

Mark Ruffalo, Academy Award–nominated actor

Bronson Canyon doesn't feel like LA. I just like it. It's very peaceful. It's beautiful. There's a little bit of water trickling there. And my kids grew up in that park.

Bronson Canyon, 3200 Canyon Drive, Los Angeles; (323) 666-5046; www.laparks.org

....

Arlene Nelson, Emmy-nominated cinematographer and director

There's nothing better than living in a city with quick, easy access to nature. For me that means hopping on my mountain bike and riding along the Ballona Creek Bike Path. This seven-mile path starts at Syd Kronenthal Park in east Culver City and extends to the Coast Bike Path along the Strand beach in Playa del Rey.

The path hugs the creek with a challenging but manageable terrain of hills and slopes. I am endlessly fascinated by the salt- and freshwater birds like sandpipers (my favorite), and ducks, gulls, geese, grebes, and loons that can be found along there.

The path cuts through several neighborhoods that are so different from each other. It varies in scale and height unified by the natural beautiful native California plants and of course the water flowing through the creek—sometimes plentiful and sometimes sparse but always tranquil. The path is oddly quiet as it winds its way to the Pacific.

I really dig the murals that brighten all the natural landscape like the "Rivers of the World" mural on the entrance ramp at Duquesne Avenue and the "Postcards From Ballona" mural on the parking lot retaining wall behind the library on Overland as you enter the bike path.

Winter, spring, summer, and fall, the Ballona Bike Path is a place where I go to exercise, clear my head, or just enjoy, with my husband and daughter or alone. I am grateful to have this right down the block from the city where I live.

Ballona Creek Bike Path, Syd Kronenthal Park, east Culver City (National Boulevard) to the Pacific; www.ballona creek.org/index.php/bike-path-info or www.labikepaths.com/bike-paths/ballona-creek

....

Chynna Phillips, singer, songwriter, member of Wilson Phillips, and
Billy Baldwin, actor

Chynna Phillips: We have very sentimental, sort of melancholy feelings about Santa Monica. We had a condo in Santa Monica where we spent the first three years of our relationship. We love walking up and down Montana, passing the little shops and eating at all the little restaurants there.

Billy Baldwin: I love that story about how you wrote "Hold On."

Chynna Phillips: Me, Glen Ballard, Carnie [Wilson], Wendy [Wilson] had written the track, the music, to "Hold On." And Glen gave us each the track and said, "Go home, listen to it. If you come up with any ideas, come back tomorrow with them." So the whole way home from work, I just kept playing the song over and over again in my head and I had this melody.

I thought, how can I put this melody into words? So I sat in front of my mom's house in LA and got out my legal pad. I had recently gone through a very dark time and I decided that I was really at a turning point or a crossroads. And I decided that I was going to take the righteous path of light, positivity, forgiveness, and all that stuff. Instead of focusing on the negative and doing things that I knew were self-destructive.

So I had this theme, hold on for one more day, in my head. When I was sitting in front of my mom's house, I just kept playing the track over and over and over again until I wrote the entire song from beginning to end, lyric and melody.

Billy Baldwin: How long did that take?

Chynna Phillips: A couple of hours. And then the next day I went into the studio and I sang it down for them, and everyone was so excited. They thought it was a real winner but we recorded it a year and a half, two years later.

We've received such amazing fan mail. People saying, "you've helped me through my divorce, through the death of my son, through losing everything." Amazing letters. That song just lives on. I don't know what it is. It's bigger than me. It just keeps going. It has legs of its own. I was nineteen or twenty, just a young girl.

I think everyone can identify with the idea if oh, if I could just stay positive or if I could just refrain or sustain from this one thing for one day . . . one more day, I can handle that. If you told somebody, "you can't do this for six months, or for a month," then people start to second guess themselves. But for one day, anybody's capable of refraining for a day.

Billy Baldwin: Some people just assume, I being one of them, that it was inspired by relationships and love, and a breakup, a broken heart. But it was rooted in a different type of a struggle. And for somebody who's only nineteen-years-old, to have that kind of perspective on your life already.

Chynna Phillips: I had to get sober when I was nineteen-years-old because I was abusing drugs by the time I was thirteen, fourteen-years-old. So, it was very profound for me. It was therapeutic for me to write that song.

Billy Baldwin: It's cool that you wrote the song for yourself and then shared it with everybody else. And it wound up being so identifying for people and they could relate to it.

Chynna Phillips: I guess in some ways, LA makes me think of that time in my life. Those were some beautiful years in my life when we were writing and recording that record. It was just a very profound, very meaningful time in my life. It was a super creative time. I would sit at the piano and write for hours at a time every day.

Montana Avenue, Santa Monica; www.montanaave.com

....

Jon Cryer, Emmy-winning actor

I love Griffith Park. I bike around there. It's a little bit of Old Hollywood. You have Forest Lawn there. You have the Hollywood sign on one side. You have Griffith Observatory. You have the zoo. And it's all in one place.

I like LA because it's beautiful. I love Old Hollywood, and I love what's wonderful and stupid about showbiz. It's a dumb industry, let's face it. But you also get to be around incredible and talented people. You do silly things and get paid marvelously and it's hard to argue with that.

Forest Lawn, 1712 South Glendale Avenue, Glendale; (800) 204-3131; www.forestlawn.com

Griffith Observatory, 2800 East Observatory Road, Los Angeles; (213) 473-0800; www.griffithobservatory.org

Los Angeles Zoo, 5333 Zoo Drive, Los Angeles; (323) 644-4200; www.lazoo.org

Kelly Lynch, actress

My favorite thing to do in Los Angeles is to walk into Griffith Park and get lost. Without a doubt. Griffith is the largest city park in the United States. It's much bigger than Central Park. And it's incredible to have this urban setting and there you are with deer and bobcats. There you are in the middle of nature, miles and miles of it.

Gabriel Macht, actor

I love the hikes in Griffith Park. They're beautiful. In fact, there are over five hundred hikes there. It is really our Central Park in LA. And it has tennis courts, pony rides, golf courses and beautiful beautiful views of downtown LA and long beaches in Santa Monica. You can be on top of the mountain and look down into the valley and the city of Los Angeles at the same time. The scenic views are gorgeous.

Charles Brunner, environmental engineer, author, and world-renowned lecturer

Three evenings a week, for at least the past forty years, the Sierra Club has been conducting mid-week walks through Griffith Park. Starting just before sunset, we meet at the upper parking lot and look down on a flat tableau of short, tightly packed houses with tall office buildings visible in the Hollywood area, and more downtown. As the sun fades into twilight and lights appear, the landscape changes to one of real beauty. It's hard to make out individual buildings but there are lights everywhere. It looks magical. That is my favorite place to be in LA. Walking through Griffith Park in the early evening with dozens of others, looking down on a city slowly showing its beauty.

Marion Cotillard, Academy Award– and Golden Globe–winning actress

I love going to the beach and I love Griffith Park. It's a very large park within the city. You have raccoons and all sorts of animals. I really like it.

Carol Bishop, artist, educator, and author

My LA fix is, and has always been, Griffith Park. Maybe it's even a parallel to New York to have a huge area that pulls you away from the intensity of the city. Of course, our intensity is the traffic. I know people say that LA doesn't have much area to walk in, but that really isn't true. Since I live in Hollywood, I've always been able to walk, or take the metro.

Griffith Park can be accessed from both the valley and Hollywood sides. It contains treasure after treasure. The Hollywood sign at one end is not exactly part of the park, but to me, it's one of the perfect icons. It's not only historic, it encompasses the ideas of what Hollywood is. It's advertising, because it started out as an advertisement. It's the idea of celebrity. It doesn't really have a functional purpose. And so many symbols emanate out of that sign, its stories and myths. These ideas are really collapsed into that icon.

Going farther into Griffith Park you can hike, go to the zoo, take a pony ride. There are horse trails, animals, and even old sets. For example in the Bronson Park section, there's the caves that people can go into and get a sense of where all the very early silent films did their sci-fi stuff. We have the old abandoned original zoo, we have a real zoo, we have a carousel.

LA has a history and most people aren't really aware of it. You have both rich and poor. When my kids were growing up they hung out with one kid who lived in a castle and another kid who lived in a car. So that diverse human element always interests me.

LA is a place of very unusual architecture. In the 60s, it became almost a magnet for young people that were in the movie business or artistic fields, and so a lot of them renovated houses, or put down roots here. We have one of the great Frank Lloyd Wright houses just down the street, which is the Hollyhock House. We also have the Ennis House, the Schindler House. We have the work of Neutra, Lautner. We have the Case Study houses.

We've had a lot of fantastic houses that were taken down early on because one of the quirks of Los Angeles was tear it down and put up something new. Historically there had been these fantastic old structures in Venice and along the beach that were taken down. The Garden of Allah or many of the great early movie hangouts were taken down. The Ambassador Hotel was taken down. A number of people became incensed so now there's a big conservation group. So many of the houses that people don't even recognize as being important, especially the mid-modern from the late 1930s to the early 60s, luckily have been preserved. People have been on the case.

Griffith Park, 4730 Crystal Springs Drive, Los Angeles; (323) 913-4688; www.laparks.org/dos/parks/griffithpk

. . . .

Gina Marie Lindsey, executive director, Los Angeles World Airports

My favorite thing to do, besides going to Hollywood Bowl, is biking along the beach and up San Vicente Boulevard in Santa Monica.

San Vicente is a fabulous boulevard that goes through Santa Monica to Brentwood. It's a very wide boulevard with a beautiful median in the middle, dividing the two traffic directions. And there are delightful segregated bike lanes on either side. It goes through a lot of old, wonderful residential neighborhoods. So, it's beautiful and yet you're getting exercise.

I combine trails. I do the beach trail, also called the Strand, and then go up to San Vicente Boulevard. I get off the beach and head inland on San Vicente. So, you can get the best of both worlds.

On San Vicente Boulevard you pass mostly old, lovely, very expensive and very nicely designed houses, and then you'd get up to the little business community in West Brentwood, where I usually stop and have breakfast at Le Pain Quotidien. I can get soy latte and an egg white omelette there. Then I turn around and go back and that gets me about a thirty-mile bike ride.

San Vicente bike route, www.laparks.org/info/west_la_biking.htm

. . . .

Gail Midgal Title, Esq., entertainment and media attorney

If you want to realize just how colorful LA is, go down to Venice Beach and the big boardwalk there. You see people roller skating with transistors at their ears, smoking pot, selling new clothes, selling old clothes. Right alongside them, you have yuppies drinking cappuccinos in cafes. Then there's the muscle people pumping iron and the volleyball players in the sand. You can find just about every element of LA there.

I first saw Venice Beach when I was thirteen years old. Moving to LA from Chicago, I was just agog. I thought, what is this place?

I went to Wellesley, a women's liberal arts college near Boston, and then to Berkeley for law school. After seven years in places where everyone smugly looked down at LA, I became one of them. I couldn't imagine coming back. LA seemed to have no culture, to be arid in every way. But it isn't a cultural wasteland now. There's wonderful theater, a quality symphony, and a lot of intellectual people to spend time with.

I came back to LA for family but, after a couple of years, I realized that I love this city because it's a total meritocracy. It doesn't matter where you came from, what your parents did or where you went to school. When I was there, Boston was very stratified. There were limitations to what you could do if you weren't a Boston Brahmin. If you didn't go to Harvard, there were firms that you couldn't join. San Francisco was the same.

But LA doesn't care. Whatever your ambition, you're given an opportunity to succeed. That's what brought my dad out here and I think it's still true. If you're an excellent lawyer, you can even become a partner at a hoity-toity law firm. So that's what I love most about LA—that it's such an open society.

Venice Beach, Ocean Front Walk, Venice; http://venicechamber.net or www.laparks.org/venice/venice.htm

....

Tova Laiter, film producer and founder, Avida Entertainment

Sometimes on Sundays I like to walk around Lake Hollywood. It's basically a reservoir. At one time you could go all around, but they closed one part of it and never really quite opened it. So you have to get off at one of the exits or come back the way you came. As I go around, I see water and water and more water from the reservoir which otherwise doesn't really exist in LA. And then I come to a bridge and see the Hollywood sign in front of me. And there are swans. And it's a very lyrical, peaceful, beautiful place that really transports you because Los Angeles is not known for its waterways, lakes, swans, peace and quiet. To stand on that beautiful, ornate bridge and look at the Hollywood sign right in front of you is really stunning.

Lake Hollywood Reservoir, 2600 Lake Hollywood Drive, Hollywood

....

Dayle Reyfel, actress, playwright, and producer of *Celebrity Autobiography*

I moved to Los Angeles from New York City and love both cities for so many different reasons. When I am in New York, I sometimes feel the city's energy often decides what my day will be like. However, in LA, it's all up to me! One of my favorite "up to me" getaways is the Hollywood Lake (in Toluca lake). It's beautiful, quiet, serene and has a stunning view from the bridge. The forty-five minute walk feels like a mini vacation.

Lake Hollywood Reservoir, 2600 Lake Hollywood Drive, Hollywood

....

Patrick Dragonette, interior designer and founder, Dragonette Ltd.

I was a New Yorker through and through. I grew up in Ohio and I moved to New York when I was eighteen years old. I never thought I was going to live anywhere but New York.

But in 1991, the economy took a big dive. The piano bar that I had managed closed after seven years. Two weeks later, my partner who worked for an interior designer for six or seven years, also found himself unemployed.

My best friend had lived in New York and had since moved with her husband to Los Angeles, Bel Air no less—to a beautiful, beautiful setting. And we were on the phone one day. And I said to her, "I'm unemployed and so is Charles and I don't know what we're going to do." She said, "well if you're going to be unemployed, you might as well do it in Los Angeles because the weather is certainly better." I thought, she's absolutely right. It's time for a change. I hung up the phone, turned to Charles and said, "do you want to move to LA?" And he said, "are you serious?"

We had enough free miles accumulated that we could take a trip out, stay at her house in Bel Air, which I knew was not going to be a reality for us. But then we decided that was it. We were going to go ahead and shake things up and move to Los Angeles. So, we loaded everything in our car, rented a U-Haul, we got cat Valium for our kitty and drove across the country.

We got out here and had a lot of resistance. I thought this place just doesn't make any sense and you can't walk around. And I've got to drive a car, are you kidding me? I mean, I left Ohio when I was eighteen so I drove a car once a year when I went home at Christmas. I was terrified. I used to make Charles drive everywhere. I certainly wasn't going to drive on the freeways and now, by the way, I love them.

I remember very clearly one day when it was in the winter. Winter in Los Angeles of course means 72 degrees and blue skies, possibly rain. And I was on Santa Monica Boulevard in the Beverly Hills area and heading east. I remember looking into my rearview mirror, which of course was to the west, and there was this magnificent snow-capped mountain range. And I almost had an accident. I thought, that's always been there but we don't get to see it that often unless we get great rain or the Santa Ana winds blow in and clear everything out. I thought, you know what? This is just an incredibly beautiful place to live.

It's not that I plan trips to drive there, but when I'm on Mulholland, it's just the most gorgeous spot to drive around. You get the valley on one side with spectacular views. You pretend like you're in Monte Carlo in a race car, driving those crazy turns, ups and downs and blind corners. It's extremely exhilarating. But the thing that's so beautiful is the view. You see the valley. You see the other side of Los Angeles.

You're up on a ridge, Mulholland is a ridge, and you see the entire valley at your feet. During the day, it's green, beautiful and you see great architecture. During the day it's impressive. But at night, when it's nothing but a sea of lights, it's absolutely mesmerizing. At night, especially when the air is clear, it's filled with sparkling beautiful light that just twinkles and glows. I'm a big romantic at heart so I love those images.

I believe that Mulholland was one of those places we visited and took a drive on before we lived here. Those are images that I always have that are essentially LA. It's in guidebooks and there's a reason. I always tell people who haven't been here before, when they come to LA, not to discount all of those things that are considered touristy. There's a reason they're touristy, because they're awesome. You want to see the Hollywood sign. You want to drive Mulholland. You want to go see Grauman's Chinese Theatre and the footprints and handprints. You want to see the Walk of Fame. Whenever I have visitors, I make sure they do all of those things and nobody is ever disappointed. Because they're special. It's quintessentially Los Angeles.

I found my path moving to LA. It's everything that I want. It's everything that I enjoy. It's where I make my living. If I was still in New York, who knows if I would still be working in a piano bar. Being here opened my eyes to other possibilities.

. . . .

Dan Klass, humorist, actor, pioneering podcaster, and author

Whenever I need a break from "normal" Los Angeles, I try to head over to Los Feliz ("the happy"). Los Feliz is a section of LA between Western Avenue and the LA River, along the base of Griffith Park, where my wife and I lived when we first got married. It was the perfect place for us, because I had somehow convinced her to move to LA from Greenwich Village, and Los Feliz seemed the best place to live if I wanted to keep her off the eastbound flights.

Being a New Yorker, she needed to walk. So, we did. We'd walk from our apartment, up Waverly Drive, past the . . . what do you call a place where nuns live? A "nunnery"? We'd walk up past the nun . . . and along to the bridge over Hyperion Boulevard where you stand at the edge of Los Angeles and look out over all of, well, Glendale.

Back along Hyperion, past the small but immaculate reservoir, past the tiny cottages Walt Disney built for his animators back in the Snow White days (Mickey Mouse was born in Los Feliz), past the high school where Danny told Sandy "You're the One That I Want," and across the unlikely white cement gothic bridge named for the Bard of Avon. We'd browse hipster T-shirts and retro knickknacks, eventually hit a restaurant and see a movie at one of the two theaters in the neighborhood. Vintage theaters. Vintage but renovated, one all in Egyptian kitsch.

It's such an essential part of Los Angeles, and yet a perfect escape from it, its own universe, detached from the sprawl and caught in its own multiple time-warps. It's a hodgepodge of the oldest and the newest, the site of the most heinous ends and the most illustrious beginnings, with the observatory looming over it, pointing Los Angeles to the other stars.

The Vista Theatre, 4473 Sunset Boulevard, Los Angeles; (323) 660-6639; www.vintagecinemas.com/vista/vistacontact.html

Shakespeare Bridge, connects Franklin Avenue to St. George Street.

John Marshall High School, 3939 Tracy Street, Los Angeles; (323) 671-1400; www.johnmarshallhs.org

Disney cottages, the 2900 block of Griffith Park Boulevard, Los Feliz

....

Mehdi Eftekari, general manager, Four Seasons Hotel Los Angeles at Beverly Hills

After a day of work or on the weekends, I love to drive on a portion of the Pacific Coast Highway. It's one of the best forms of relaxation because you're driving right along the beach. You can go to small beaches south of Los Angeles and head to Newport Beach. Or you can drive north from Los Angeles up to Malibu. The enjoyment is to take your time and really digest what you see.

Every portion of the highway is different. Venice Beach is an eclectic melting pot, with bodybuilders, street vendors, and musicians. Driving through Santa Monica, I pass the Santa Monica Pier. Then there's Malibu and Zuma Beach. And if I go farther I can see Little Hawaii where people do windsurfing. It just all depends on how much time I have on my hands.

A little bit after Sunset Boulevard, the traffic really dies down. I have less lights and driving all the way past Malibu, Zuma and beyond is so beautiful. And there are many great restaurants like Geoffrey's.

The newest restaurant is Nobu Malibu. The owners put twenty million dollars into designing it. It hangs right over the ocean with the waves crashing into the beach. You see this pristine, clear beautiful water that starts from a very turquoise color. Farther on it seems to become darker and bluer. Beyond that, you see Catalina Island and if you're angled correctly, the Channel Islands.

Nobu Malibu, 22706 Pacific Coast Highway, Malibu; (310) 317-9140; www.noburestaurants.com/malibu

....

Ella Thomas, actress, model, and producer

At Coldwater Canyon Park, I take the path that leads to the right. Wood chips crunch under my Asics-clad feet. The morning air still has a cool dampness that the rising sun will soon enough evaporate. I reach up and gently pull a single leaf from one of the eucalyptus trees that line the path, crush the petal between my two hands, and inhale the scent deeply. The woods around me are alive and birds sing out clear and bright from the surrounding trees.

Sometimes if you listen closely, you can hear the snapping of branches as a doe or, on rare occasion a buck, makes their way through. This place reminds me of home, it reminds me of my mom. For the next three miles, I leave everything behind and revel in the simple beauty.

This is my sanctuary. This is my Los Angeles.

Coldwater Canyon Park, Tree People, 12601 Mulholland Drive, Beverly Hills; (818) 753-4600; www.treepeople.org

....

Cristin Milioti, Tony-nominated actress

Topanga Canyon is one of the most beautiful parts of the world. You drive up these winding roads and there's wildflowers and birds and you see valleys and mountain and the ocean—everything. It smells like an herb garden it's amazing up there. Driving up to Topanga Canyon, you feel like you are leaving the world. It's nice to go at sunset, although it's hard to get back down those roads. Or go early in the morning when the sun is coming up and everything is glistening. You can walk it too, but when I was filming there, I drove it every day.

Topanga Canyon Boulevard, Top of Topanga Overlook, 3400 North Topanga Canyon Boulevard, Topanga; www.lamountains.com

. . . .

Eugene Pack, Emmy-nominated writer, actor, producer, director, and co-creator of *Celebrity Autobiography*

When I first moved to LA, someone told me it was important to establish your "hike of choice." It could be Runyon Canyon, the Santa Monica Mountains, Lake Hollywood, up and down the escalator of the Beverly Center. Try them all—and try to pick one they suggested. I fell instantly in love with Fryman Canyon, also known as Tree People.

You can get there via Laurel Canyon or Coldwater. And once you park, leave the phone in the car and officially enter. The paths have it all—winding trails, breathtaking views, endless peaks and valleys. You can run it, stroll it, brisk walk it . . . you can make the experience whatever you want, depending on your mood, energy level, or what you're listening to on your iPod. I've seen snakes, deer, celebrities—and they all keep to themselves. I've been caught there in the rain. I've seen the sun set and rise. There's no better place to grab peace of mind. I always feel better after spending an hour with nature in Fryman Canyon.

Fryman Canyon, 8401 Mulholland Drive, Studio City; www.treepeople.org

. . . .

Lucy Hale, actress (*Pretty Little Liars*) and singer

I like hiking at Fryman Canyon. It's one of the lesser known hikes. So I take my dog and just chill out. The weather is obviously gorgeous year-round so I can go pretty much any time of year.

The hike is not too strenuous, but it can be if you run it. You get to the top and can see so much of Los Angeles. It's relaxing and really beautiful.

I'm from Tennessee. And when I arrived in LA, I had never seen traffic like that before. It was a completely different lifestyle. It was really fast-paced. But I like the fast-paced-ness of LA. It seems everyone is here for a purpose. It's exciting.

Fryman Canyon, 8401 Mulholland Drive, Studio City; www.treepeople.org

....

Peter Theroux, translator of ten novels from Arabic and author of *Translating LA: A Tour of the Rainbow City* and *Sandstorms: Days and Nights of Arabia*

I chose Forest Lawn Glendale as a favorite place in LA. It is a serious drive from my home, which is down in Long Beach, but worth every minute of the drive, because I can easily spend half a day there losing myself in another world. Actually, two other worlds, this one and the next.

I think every Angeleno takes visitors to see the glorious cemetery/theme park which is Forest Lawn Glendale, but the guilty pleasure is going there alone. It is a perfect offbeat destination for visitors, and a versatile one. It contains history (the chapel where Ronald Reagan married Jane Wyman), legend (Walt Disney tomb), beautiful vistas, and—for serious readers, for whom a tourist visit to a cemetery is too twee—the inspiration for Evelyn Waugh's *The Loved One*. And just consider that in this place, the adjacent graves of Elizabeth Taylor and Michael Jackson are a mere footnote.

At the entrance, you are greeted by the world's largest iron gates—twice as wide and five feet higher than the ones at Buckingham Palace. You gaze at a fifty-foot-high marble pylon on which The Builder's Creed is engraved. You view colossal reproductions of Michelangelo's *Moses* and *David*, and nearly two dozen Last Suppers by every Old Master as you wander in and out of the classical Roman buildings, Babylonian crypts, English courtyards, and rolling American lawns.

And then the theme park subdivisions: Babyland and Lullabyland, the Court of Freedom (look for Walter Elias Disney's garden-like grave here—there is music piped in), the Triumphant Faith Terraces, the Court of David, the Court of the Christus, and much more. You might smile or get misty eyed, but if you actually cry or snicker, you have missed the point. This is where you walk and lose yourself in the silence and acres of statuary—none of it famous and nearly all replicas, so no need to think arty or historical thoughts. You might spot the grave of a great scriptwriter but not a great author. Here, the dozens of marble cherubs celebrate infant lives, not famous sculptors. The pharaonic-style mausoleums celebrate big Hollywood egos. Death, where is thy sting? Not here!

This place could not exist anywhere else in the world—not Dubai, not Europe, not Florida, least of all the Bay Area. It epitomizes the Los Angeles I love to death. The combined Museum and Gift Shop—the final stop on the tour—beats the stuffings out of anything you have ever seen. After a few hours contemplating death, serenity, tragedy, startling kitsch and poignant kitsch, after enjoying the Californian blue sky, warm sun, and classical vistas that perfectly express my idea of Heaven, you deserve a chuckle.

You can only hold it in so long as you wander through the knickknacks, racks of 3-D postcards, oh, and the replicas of Ghiberti's doors to the Baptistry in Florence. But then you come upon—surprise!—replicas of the British crown jewels, and the startling head of an Easter Island monolith, and you have to think, What the . . . ???? It was at this point in the museum, a few years ago, that my brother Alex and I had the longest fit of stifled, tearful laughter that I ever experienced. I think it was the Easter Island head that set us off.

We staggered around whimpering, trying to find a remote corner where we would not offend the kindly museum staff with our sobbing mirth that threatened internal organ damage. Considering the joy and the tears, the surrounding cemetery, the gentle sunshine, the ethereal surroundings—and I actually had my next of kin handy!—I could have done a lot worse than dying right then and there. Maybe next time.

Forest Lawn, 1712 South Glendale Avenue, Glendale; (800) 204-3131; www.forestlawn.com

. . . .

Graham Russell, Grammy-nominated co-founder of the band Air Supply, musician, songwriter, and singer

I love driving down Sunset to be quite honest. When we first arrived in the US in 1977, it was July Fourth. We drove down Sunset. That's the first thing that we did. I always remembered that. We were driving in a limousine and it was just beautiful.

Sunset Boulevard is really what Los Angeles is all about. It's the main road going east to west and if you're driving west in the evening, you get the sun in your face. You see all the billboards, the restaurants, all the rock and roll clubs in Hollywood. The street goes all the way down out to the beach. It's a beautiful road.

It takes about an hour to drive down it. But it's gorgeous because the weather's always great. The light's beautiful.

Back then, I remember right outside our hotel was a billboard with Bette Midler across the street and it was huge. It was for Divine Miss M. You don't ever see those billboards in other places. They're usually only found in Los Angeles. This had been my first time in the United States. I loved it. I thought yeah, I could live here.

One of my favorite restaurants in LA is the Bombay Palace in Beverly Hills. I love good Indian food. I actually cook it too. Bombay Palace is excellent, probably the best in Los Angeles. I like the chana masala vindaloo, which is vegetarian but it's really hot. Really spicy.

Bombay Palace, 8690 Wilshire Boulevard, Beverly Hills; (310) 659-9944; www.bombaypalacebeverlyhills.com

. . . .

Peter Greenberg, Emmy-winning travel expert, author, host of the Peter Greenberg Worldwide Radio show, and CBS News travel editor

To me, LA is eighty-six separate incorporated cities in desperate search of a community. If you're going to survive, let alone succeed in Los Angeles, you have to find that community that works for you. Otherwise, it's lost with a capital *L,* and I'm not talking about freeways. I'm just talking about lack of community. You've got to find that community.

For me, my community is to get on my boat and sail about forty-one miles southwest and that will take me to Catalina. It is part of LA County. And you never go on a weekend because that is the zoo. You go Monday through Thursday. It is even better to go Sunday, because everybody is coming back when you get there. I take my boat from Sunday to Thursday, and you get a mooring right in Avalon, and your pulse rate goes down. And you can bicycle. You can do everything. It is just a great way to get back on your feet.

You can see a lot of stuff there. First of all, it is actually the setting of a lot of the old Zane Grey westerns. There were never animals over there, so they actually brought a lot of animals over. You'll still see bison there in the middle of the island.

You can rent mini mokes. They are little jeeps. You can zip all around the island because it is all run by the Catalina conservancy.

If you really want to have fun, take the ferry over and spend the night at the Wrigley Mansion. The Wrigley Mansion still has about six or seven bedrooms. It was the original mansion of William Wrigley when he owned the Chicago Cubs. In fact, the baseball field is still there where they used to do their spring training. He would sit up at the top of the mansion with his binoculars, and if he didn't like the way the ballplayers were playing he'd say, "Have the ballplayers come up and see me." They would have to run all the way up to see him. The ball field is still there which is really nice.

Catalina is the one place in Los Angeles County where I can guarantee you the air is clean. And it is the one place that you sleep the best. They even have a very strong antipollution movement in the harbor. When you bring your boat into the harbor, and people don't know this, the harbor pilot boards your boat, goes into every one of your bathrooms, and drops special capsules in your toilets. If you are stupid enough or ignorant enough to pump your waste out of the boat, they are neon tablets, and your boat lights up like a Christmas tree and you're banned from the harbor for two years. So guess what? Since they put that rule into effect, it is one of the cleanest harbors in Southern California.

My magic hour there, most people would say sunset. No. For me it is sunrise. It is the time when you think the best. When I was growing up I never trusted anybody who got up early. Now I'm one of those guys who gets up early, and I understand why. I get up around four-thirty in the morning every day. So I beat the sunrise by at least an hour depending on whether it is Daylight Savings Time. There is nothing like sitting on the bow of your boat at that hour of the morning with no interference whatsoever and just looking out. You can solve all the problems in the world in that one-hour-and-a-half.

The first time I saw Catalina was on a weekend and I said, "I'm never coming back on a weekend. I'm coming back during the week," and I was right. I'm a big fan of the off-season. I'm a big fan of going to Catalina before the summer, and I'm a big fan of going to Catalina in February and March. I believe the off-season is a myth. If you travel in the off-season you have a much better experience.

I didn't choose LA. I was assigned to LA. I was sent out there to be the West Coast correspondent for *Newsweek* when I was twenty-one. It was the hottest bureau in the system. We had the best stories. It wasn't just entertainment. In fact, half of Watergate was reported out of California. The whole Nixon White House was out in San Clemente. All of those guys that worked for Nixon, they had all gone to USC and worked for Disney. All those guys whether it was Ron Ziegler or Haldeman. They're all Southern California boys. So I was at the right place at the right time to cover all those stories. I covered nine states, so I covered Gary Gilmore in Utah and Howard Hughes, you name it. For me, what could be better than doing that as a journalist?

Plus, the thing about Los Angeles that kept me there is that you're never more than twenty minutes away from the beach, the mountains, the desert, or just outright craziness. As in nuts. If you want to find craziness in Los Angeles, you're only twenty minutes away from anything. If you want to go down and watch people get crazy in Venice, you can do that. Or if you want to do anything, it is the most amazing smorgasbord.

Catalina Island, www.catalinachamber.com

....

Ezra Doner, production, finance, and motion picture distribution attorney

The special thing about Saddleback Butte State Park is not the park. It's the butte. It's that particular mountain. The park is in a wonderful and mysterious desert environment in the Antelope Valley. The mountain is so much larger than you think. You can see it when you set out to walk. On a clear day, when you climb up to the top of the peak, the stop lights, buildings, and cross streets seem to recede. You look out and you don't see anything but the same mountainous landscape. You don't see signs of human habitation. It is truly the unspoiled West.

Saddleback Butte State Park, Avenue J and 170th Street East, Lancaster; (661) 946-6092; www.parks.ca.gov

Jeff Klein, hotelier and owner of the Sunset Tower Hotel and the City Club Hotel

I'm a runner so I like to drive to Santa Monica and go for a run on the beach towards Malibu. It's a very pretty run. And if you're not a runner, there's also a really nice bike path.

You pass so many interesting things. On the Santa Monica Pier, you see a little mini carnival with a Ferris wheel. There's all these kids eating ice cream cones with their parents, and a lot of stimuli. There are some beach clubs right on the beach. So you run by them and see all these fancy people in their private clubs getting served by butlers. And then there's the Annenberg Center, which used to be Marion Davies's private home on the beach. It's a beautiful old house. But now it's a public place, which is also a wonderful place to spend the afternoon. There's a public pool, you have to reserve a seat though, because it's very popular.

I'm a member of Equinox. There's a wonderful Equinox gym a block away from the beach to take a shower. And then I drive five minutes over to Venice Beach and I have dinner at Gjelina on Abbot Kinney. The food is so damn good. It's very fresh. It's very unpretentious. The pizzas are delicious. It's very market-driven. The chef goes to the market and picks out what's good that day, so it changes a lot.

My place, the Sunset Tower, is a building with a tremendous amount of history. A lot of people, from the Gabor sisters to Elizabeth Taylor to Diana Ross to Howard Hughes to Frank Sinatra, all lived here. It used to be an apartment building and was converted to a hotel in the 80s. It's a very special art deco building with incredible architecture and floor to ceiling rounded windows.

Nobody would design this building today. You wouldn't make a rounded building. You would build a square. It doesn't economically make sense to have, for example, rounded windows. But people were not as concerned with the efficiency of space in 1929 when this building was built.

The Sunset Tower Hotel is special aesthetically in terms of history and in a Hollywood heritage point of view. It's a very private place. There is no formal club, but it feels clubby, like an eating club from the 30s. It's subtle, sophisticated, and elegant, which is sort of rare in this town. Usually, this is an over-the-top town with fire pits in the middle of rooms with Buddhas everywhere.

At the Tower Bar, there are wood-paneled walls, a pianist playing the piano and a bassist to accompany. It's dinner only. The terrace is off the pool and open for breakfast, lunch, and dinner. It's a very breezy indoor, outdoor space that people love as well. There are little cabanas. It's just very cool. The waiters are men in white coats and black ties. It's very old school.

Both spots have their own energy. People have meetings there. A lot of movie deals have been made in both rooms. So many celebrities come to celebrate their movies. They'll say to me or their waiter, "You realize this movie got made here, I wasn't sure I was going to do it. But I met with the director for dinner here." There's a lot of that, which is really nice.

Gjelina, 1429 Abbot Kinney Boulevard, Venice; (310) 450-1429; www.gjelina.com

Sunset Tower Hotel, 8358 Sunset Boulevard, West Hollywood; (323) 654-7100; http://sunsettowerhotel.com

. . . .

Annie Gilbar, best-selling author, TV and Internet entrepreneur, and founding editor of many magazines

It's Mulholland. It's always been Mulholland.

The extraordinary top of the world views, the clear air, the warm breezes, being on top of the mountain and seeing the entire world of Los Angeles spread before me anywhere and everywhere I look. The winding open roads in contrast to the gridlock below, the sandy hillsides colliding with lush green.

And, Mulholland is freedom.

When I first arrived in Los Angeles to begin my master's at USC (quantitative study of Middle East terrorism, no less) on a blue and blindingly bright January day, I rented a convertible. A Mustang (have never owned anything other than a car with the open top since). I drove it to the top of Beverly Glen. I pulled over, parked it there, and just sat for hours. The Santa Ana winds were at full force; with the 86 degree weather, it seemed that I had dropped into the middle of the most beautiful wonderland of desert—but a desert the likes of which I had never seen.

Everywhere I looked I saw mountains—some were snow topped!—and masses of houses dropped into the middle of pieces of green, and palm trees and flowers as far as I could see, which was pretty far. On top of the world, I thought; I had found the top of the world and I was going to stay there.

I didn't know then, but I soon came to find out, that Mulholland, my symbol of my new city, represented freedom not only to drive those curves in any direction, my long blond hair flying in every which way, blasting the Beach Boys (that sure was LA music, compared to my Bach in New York); it was the freedom to do anything. In the world I came from you had to have a pedigree and a history and connections and, oh yes, tons of money. Los Angeles gave me—gave all of us then—the freedom to do anything, try anything, make a mark.

You could be a part of the new, create a museum (I was a part of two) and meet an architect and build a house on a mountain (did three of those), get your children into the best private school without your name being Rockefeller (two kids and two schools, thank you very much). You could make your dream come true—of working at a magazine (too many to count) and then actually running more than one, finding the most extraordinary creative talents to make your dream a success. You could begin programs for children at the Philharmonic, support community groups in a way which made a hands-on difference, jump into the art community which seemed world class even though it was, then, just applauded locally. And contrary to local lore, you didn't have to be a part of the film community, nor any old timers community, to make your mark and be happy. And, oh yes, you could eat outside every day of the year.

To this day, forty years later, whenever I need peace, whenever I want to get away for even just a few minutes, and just for the hell of it, I drive up to Mulholland. Top down in my car (that has never changed), music blasting (really blasting—this time Maroon 5 and Paul McCartney and Gloria Estefan—I never get tired of rocking to "Hotel Nacional"), I take those curves up the canyons and reach the top in just minutes, my blond hair still long and still flying.

I am at Mulholland. I am happy. I am Los Angeles.

....

Sylvia Lopez, Emmy-winning journalist and co-anchor of KCAL 9's weekday newscasts

I'm a big fan of live music and Big Band tunes, but anchoring the 9:00 p.m. nightly news doesn't give me many opportunities to indulge that. One big exception is Johnny Vana's Big Band Alums. Every Tuesday morning at Las Hadas Mexican Restaurant in Northridge, this seventeen-piece orchestra jams for two hours. These guys are amazing. They're all veterans of well-known bands from the 30s, 40s, and 50s. Dancers pack the floor doing West Coast swing and jitterbug. I take my dad, and we both bliss out. Everyone is so happy! I think the music does that. It's like entering another era for a couple of hours.

Johnny Vana's Big Band Alumni, www.vanabigband.com

Las Hadas Mexican Restaurant, 9048 Balboa Boulevard, Northridge; (818) 892-7271; www.lashadasrestaurant.com/Home.html

....

Mark Mothersbaugh, Grammy-nominated and Emmy-winning composer and artist

Sunset Boulevard will always be the place that reminds me of how Los Angeles might be the most successful version of "the American Dream" in the whole country. I remember my band driving from Ohio and pulling up to the Whisky and feeling electricity at seeing the name Devo on the marquee.

The first "star" I met in Hollywood was Wild Man Fischer, looking homeless standing in front of Guitar Center. And just as we shook hands, I noticed something brown and sticky was all over his fingers. I washed my hand off at the open air taco joint next door, and to this day don't know what that stuff was.

Sunset Strip is still a place that attracts people from all over the planet, to come looking for something, coming to say something, and I was one of them. I walk on the street and imagine different times both past and future, and look up at the Whisky marquee most every day and see names I don't recognize of bands and performers whom I probably will never hear of again. But I feel a unity in the fact that once upon a time, I was standing on that stage singing with my band, and dreaming the same American dream.

Whisky A Go Go, 8901 West Sunset Boulevard, West Hollywood; (310) 652-4202; www.whiskyagogo.com

Guitar Center, 7425 Sunset Boulevard, Hollywood; (323) 874-1060; stores.guitarcenter.com/Hollywood

Scott Allen, general manager, Hyatt Regency Century Plaza

I'm really drawn to water and the beach. So without question, my wife and I have a favorite activity. We have a little Audi TT convertible, and drive up PCH, pretty much every Saturday. Top down. By the ocean. We stop wherever we feel like it. We don't really have plans. If we see a little fish taco shop we'll stop and have a little lunch. We enjoy that type of oceanfront casualness.

Unfortunately, in 2010 my wife was diagnosed with breast cancer. After she was diagnosed, we literally went to the beach and sat in the sand. We have a pretty strong faith. So we just sat there, watched the waves, and talked about how we were going to get through the breast cancer fight together. That's probably the most memorable thing for us in Los Angeles, sitting on the beach, just south of Santa Monica. And we just walked and talked our way through the diagnosis and what we were going to do about it.

The water gives us clarity. We watch the birds, the water, we listen. It's just the two of us. When we take the TT up and down the coast, the convertible is a little noisy so you really can't hear the outside noise, and it's just about her and me spending time together. And we have five children. So the idea of having a car that only holds two wasn't by accident.

Julian Sands, actor

One of my favorite pleasures in LA is hiking in the canyons. Whether it be Fryman or Franklin Canyon or farther afield up in the San Gabriels; Mount Baldy and Iron Mountain and, of course, the Santa Monica mountains all the way through Malibu Park and Topanga Park. The great outdoors is what I love about Los Angeles; the elements, the geophysical properties, the confluence of mountains, desert, and sea. The big sky. It's wonderful. I must have been up Mount Baldy about two hundred times, so I think that's a real favorite. And I like it in winter. Winter conditions make it a bit more interesting.

When I first went to Los Angeles, it was 1986. *Room with a View* was out and because of that my agents were very keen for me to go and take meetings in Los Angeles. And that's why I went out there. But it was also to see friends and curiosity.

I'm a great traveler. I love travel and had never been to the west coast of America. When I got off the plane, and I thought, *Oh wow, I love this sky.* The light, the scents. People back in New York had prepared me for smog, ugliness, deprivation, dereliction.

I remember I saw this white mountain. Crikey—nobody told me there were mountains that close to LA. It felt like you could reach it. But it was some years after that I actually went to the Sierras, up to the Mount Whitney region. And then I started going to the San Gabriels when I was doing a play downtown at the Mark Taper Forum, *Stuff Happens* by David Hare. I thought, *Well, where can I go that is close to the theater and pop on?*

I've also found great, really interesting people in Los Angeles. Everyone's come from somewhere all over the world. It's a great watering hole. There's much more culture available than I'd been prepared for by friends in New York, where it's a much more obvious melting pot of culture. In LA you have to work a bit to find it.

Mount Baldy, Angeles National Forest; (909) 982-2829; www.mtbaldychamber.com

. . . .

David O. Russell, Academy Award– and Golden Globe–nominated director, writer, and producer

Franklin Canyon is pretty gorgeous. You can usually see some interesting people hiking there. And you see apiaries—where bees live—all these boxes with thousands of bees in them. You hear this humming zzzzz and you can see all of LA. It's a great hike.

Franklin Canyon, 2600 Franklin Canyon Drive, Beverly Hills; (310) 858-7272

....
Amy Schiffman, literary manager at Intellectual Property Group (IPG)

One of the things that I missed terribly when I moved here was the constant company of pedestrians on the sidewalks of New York. In Santa Monica in those days, before the renovation of the Third Street Promenade, now a popular pedestrian mall, people rarely walked on the street, even during broad daylight. And they certainly never communed on the sidewalk the way we did in New York.

In sunny Santa Monica, if people were walking, they were singular pedestrians, in coordinated workout gear, carrying water bottles, checking their pulse rates. At night there was absolutely no one on the street. The only excuse to be out was to walk the dog, and then as now, I was, alas, dogless.

Then, after a few months in Santa Monica I discovered the bike path. This is one place where Angelenos commune. On bikes, freed of the controlled, air conditioned environment of our cars, we revert to our better, more spontaneous nature. We breathe in the crisp air off the Pacific, and exercise, sweat, smile and wave at one another as we fly past. The bike path starts at the northern end of Santa Monica, near Pacific Palisades. Here the beach is narrow, so for a while you are riding quite close to the surf. Then the beach widens as you pass the beach clubs (both swanky private ones and the new populist Annenberg Beach House), and the scalloped edge of surf recedes.

For a few minutes, when the path passes underneath the historic Santa Monica Pier, you're in a dark and sketchy tunnel, in gloomy contrast to the brightly lit amusement park above. After you pass the pier, a pedestrian path parallels the bike path, and there's a cluster of shops selling souvenirs, restaurants with bad overpriced seafood, hotels and apartment buildings. Here there are crowds of people walking as well as biking in both directions.

In the Ocean Park neighborhood, the beach gets wider, and the shops disappear. Here there is lots of white sand between bike path and the ocean. The view opens up, the crowd thins, and there's a sense of infinite possibilities. Between beach and street there's a wide swath of green park where large families picnic and kids play soccer. And on the east side of the park are two lone apartment towers, developed in the 1960s, which are now prized for their great views of the beach and the Pacific.

This is where I come to work out problems and release anxiety. I come down for a ride when I'm worried about my job or trying to sort through a personal dilemma. If I have time, I ride all the way down through Venice to where the bike path winds through a city park and then through the hodgepodge harbors of Marina del Rey. I feel at home here, with all the wacky, smiling, sweating riders, sharing the communal highway that is the bike path. This is a true cross section of the people who make up LA, a city that I have come to love, and where it seems I have decided to stay.

....

Denise Flanders, general manager, Hotel Bel-Air

My favorite thing to do in Los Angeles is taking a long bike ride along the pacific coast. Having come from Chicago, I think I appreciate LA's perfect weather more than most. I usually start at Manhattan Beach and ride fourteen miles down the coast to Palos Verdes.

The Marvin Braude Bike Trails, runs from Will Rogers State Beach in the Pacific Palisades to Torrance County Beach at the base of the Palos Verdes Peninsula; www.bicyclela.org

....

Adrian Salamunovic, co-founder DNA 11/CanvasPop, the company creates DNA portraits for celebrities

If you're visiting LA, grab a rental bike and ride it down bike path. You have to do it. And on the way back, stop at Silvio's, a Brazilian-inspired little surf spot, which is located on the pier in Hermosa Beach.

For less than twenty bucks, you can grab yourself amazing barbecued chicken on a fresh salad, called Ipanema salad. It's an awesome meal at the end of a bike ride. Watch the sunset go down on the pier. It's the perfect date or perfect way to end an LA day.

Silvios, 20 Pier Avenue, Hermosa Beach; (310) 376-6855; www.silviosbbq.com

Leven Rambin, actress

I love going to Beachwood Canyon— hiking up there near the Hollywood sign. I used to live right on that street. And so, every morning I would wake up and run the whole thing. You can go to Burbank on the other side of the mountain if you want to.

I never did that, but you can see it. It's beautiful and really quiet, and there are sometimes horses, It feels a little bit remote. It's in the middle of Hollywood, but it's so much quieter than Runyon, and a lot more mellow than a lot of the canyons.

If you want to appreciate nature, and just be quiet, like what a hike was meant to do, it's just so beautiful. You get up to this certain point and it's so high. You see all these beautiful valleys with trees. You get up there, and you feel so peaceful. It's so quiet. It's a hidden gem.

Beachwood Canyon, North Beachwood Drive, www.beachwoodcanyon.org

Brit Marling, actress and writer

I love the Beachwood Canyon hike. It's great because you can get up right behind the Hollywood sign and be up and over LA. You see all the way to the ocean, all the way downtown and to the observatory. It's a beautiful hike. I do that one a lot.

Beachwood Canyon, North Beachwood Drive, www.beachwoodcanyon.org

Christopher Reynolds, *Los Angeles Times* travel writer and author of *SoCal Close-Ups*

I head to Beachwood Canyon, directly beneath the Hollywood sign. Then I roll straight up Beachwood Drive, a mostly residential street that wriggles past an increasingly affluent procession of homes. (Some of them were part of the original Hollywoodland development that the sign was created to promote in the 1920s.)

I keep going even after the road dwindles to dirt, and wind up at Sunset Ranch, where dozens of horses are stabled. For forty dollars, I get an hour's guided ride.

Kids are okay if they're eight or older. The best time to begin is just before sunset. Not only do I get a different and uncrowded view of the Hollywood sign, I get an exhilarating introduction to the hills, which feel more rural than you'd ever imagine.

And as the sun sets, I get a full-on Technicolor panorama. Most days, I see a distant sliver of the Pacific, the sky goes orange, the hills and your fellow riders go into dramatic silhouette, and a vast grid of city lights starts twinkling at my feet. Then, to keep it all real, I get a little whiff of horse manure. That's Hollywood for you.

Sunset Ranch, 3400 North Beachwood Drive, Hollywood; (323) 469-5450; www.sunsetranchhollywood.com

....

Susan Feniger, chef, restaurateur (Susan Feniger's Street, Border Grill), cookbook author, radio and TV personality

My girlfriend, Liz Lachman, and I live up in Crestwood Hills, a tucked away neighborhood. In LA you can find these great neighborhoods everywhere. It's just a great old community which started after World War II by musicians who moved from New York and bought up this property. So all the homes are all not too big. They're very environmental. They have almost all glass. Our house feels like a tree house.

There's a park, Crestwood Hills, near where we live, and one of my most favorite things is going there early in the morning with our two Golden Doodles, Augie and Chewbacca or Chewie. It ends up being more about playing with the dogs in the park. Oftentimes two or three neighbors are also there. It's all ranges of people. One is a law professor. Another gentleman is in his eighties; he's a contractor. And we have the most interesting political discussions at 7:00 in the morning, just walking around this park where the dogs can run and play. It's pretty dreamy.

The other times, there's a day camp that's open during the summer. And Liz and I go walking there. If you go early enough in the morning before any of the kids arrive, you see goats, horses, and chickens. It's not any fancy thing. It's just a long path or you can just walk up into the hills. And the most amazing thing in LA is to be where you can walk in the canyon in the hills and have incredible views of the ocean.

Crestwood Hills Park, 1000 Hanley Avenue, Los Angeles; (310) 472-5233; www.laparks.org/dos/parks/facility/crestwoodHillsPk.htm

Jenny Wade, actress (*Wedding Band*)

I grew up in Eugene, Oregon, where camping and hiking and fishing were a huge part of my life. I had lived in Los Angeles for so long and it's beautiful, but I had never really had a true nature experience that could emulate what I had in Oregon.

And then I discovered Hermit Falls.

At the edge of the Angeles National Forest just past the big spread-out homes in Arcadia on the 134, you hit the base of the mountain and start climbing up, You wind and wind and wind up the side of the mountain. It's really off the beaten path and so quiet and a good two miles into the heart of the mountain and the view is incredible.

The actual falls and it's relatively small. There are two big cliff-like rocks that people gather on. There are also natural slides that are smooth that you can actually slide down into the water. The water is really clean, cool, and flows beautifully.

The reward of the hike is that you feel like you're at a natural amusement park. And there's space to sunbathe afterwards as long as you don't go on the weekend. Go on a Monday or Tuesday afternoon when kids are in school, you'll have lots of space. It's peaceful and beautiful. The hike back up the hill to the parking lot is not so terrible either. You're soaking wet so you're already happy and feeling relaxed.

Hermit Falls, Angeles National Forest, Chantry Flats Road, Arcadia

Tena Clark, Grammy-winning composer, lyricist, and CEO/chief creative officer for DMI Music & Media Solutions

LA kind of closes in on you sometimes as far as the rat race is concerned. One of my favorite things to do is to drive up the 210 highway and up through the Angeles Crest forest. It is a beautiful drive. There's a lot of great places to just sit and reflect. I use that as kind of a decompression sometimes.

It's very mountainous terrain and as you get higher and higher, you see the cedar trees and beautiful views. There's a lot of great hikes too. On the weekends, it's busy, but if you go up during the week, you can really find some great solitude. There's a hike that my little girl and I, well she's twenty-five now, still visit.

Actually, when my daughter was home with her husband over last Easter, we did a hike. It's also right in the Pasadena area and called Chantry Flats. You find waterfalls. The shortest hike you can do is about two miles into the mountains and two miles back. You see this huge waterfall and no one would ever expect this in Los Angeles.

Angeles Crest Forest, 701 N. Santa Anita Avenue, Arcadia; (626) 574-1613; www.fs.usda.gov/angeles

Chantry Flats, 2201-2299 Forest Route 2N40; La Canada Flintridge; (626) 574-1613

....

Merle Ginsberg, fashion writer, television personality, senior writer, *Hollywood Reporter*

One of the great things in LA is the various dog parks and hiking trails. Nichols Canyon is my favorite. I have a friend and he takes his dogs there. It's where he and I really have amazing conversations and we tend to go at dusk.

You walk very, very fast and when you get to the top you can't even believe how high up you are. You walk very, very quickly and you don't pay attention and suddenly you say, oh my God, I can see the whole city, it's amazing. There's a lot of dust and dirt around, and everyone is in hiking clothes and you really feel like you're in some national park. And then you go down and get into your car, you change your clothes, and you can go to some really sophisticated place.

Nichols Canyon, Trebek Open Space, 2500 Nichols Canyon Road, Los Angeles

....

Dr. Ava Cadell, love guru, media therapist, author, and founder of LoveologyUniversity.com

One of my favorite places in Los Angeles is Laurel Canyon Dog Park, a vast doggie wonderland for small and big dog people. There's plenty of open space for them to run their hearts out and a special fenced off area for small doggies. Plus there are picnic benches where you can relax, while you let your dog loose and watch them having fun.

sea. The big sky. It's wonderful. I must have been up Mount Baldy about two hundred times, so I think that's a real favorite. And I like it in winter. Winter conditions make it a bit more interesting.

When I first went to Los Angeles, it was 1986. *Room with a View* was out and because of that my agents were very keen for me to go and take meetings in Los Angeles. And that's why I went out there. But it was also to see friends and curiosity.

I'm a great traveler. I love travel and had never been to the west coast of America. When I got off the plane, and I thought, *Oh wow, I love this sky.* The light, the scents. People back in New York had prepared me for smog, ugliness, deprivation, dereliction.

I remember I saw this white mountain. Crikey—nobody told me there were mountains that close to LA. It felt like you could reach it. But it was some years after that I actually went to the Sierras, up to the Mount Whitney region. And then I started going to the San Gabriels when I was doing a play downtown at the Mark Taper Forum, *Stuff Happens* by David Hare. I thought, *Well, where can I go that is close to the theater and pop on?*

I've also found great, really interesting people in Los Angeles. Everyone's come from somewhere all over the world. It's a great watering hole. There's much more culture available than I'd been prepared for by friends in New York, where it's a much more obvious melting pot of culture. In LA you have to work a bit to find it.

Mount Baldy, Angeles National Forest; (909) 982-2829; www.mtbaldychamber.com

. . . .

David O. Russell, Academy Award– and Golden Globe–nominated director, writer, and producer

Franklin Canyon is pretty gorgeous. You can usually see some interesting people hiking there. And you see apiaries—where bees live—all these boxes with thousands of bees in them. You hear this humming zzzzz and you can see all of LA. It's a great hike.

Franklin Canyon, 2600 Franklin Canyon Drive, Beverly Hills; (310) 858-7272

fact that once upon a time, I was standing on that stage singing with my band, and dreaming the same American dream.

Whisky A Go Go, 8901 West Sunset Boulevard, West Hollywood; (310) 652-4202; www.whiskyagogo.com

Guitar Center, 7425 Sunset Boulevard, Hollywood; (323) 874-1060; stores.guitarcenter.com/Hollywood

....

Scott Allen, general manager, Hyatt Regency Century Plaza

I'm really drawn to water and the beach. So without question, my wife and I have a favorite activity. We have a little Audi TT convertible, and drive up PCH, pretty much every Saturday. Top down. By the ocean. We stop wherever we feel like it. We don't really have plans. If we see a little fish taco shop we'll stop and have a little lunch. We enjoy that type of oceanfront casualness.

Unfortunately, in 2010 my wife was diagnosed with breast cancer. After she was diagnosed, we literally went to the beach and sat in the sand. We have a pretty strong faith. So we just sat there, watched the waves, and talked about how we were going to get through the breast cancer fight together. That's probably the most memorable thing for us in Los Angeles, sitting on the beach, just south of Santa Monica. And we just walked and talked our way through the diagnosis and what we were going to do about it.

The water gives us clarity. We watch the birds, the water, we listen. It's just the two of us. When we take the TT up and down the coast, the convertible is a little noisy so you really can't hear the outside noise, and it's just about her and me spending time together. And we have five children. So the idea of having a car that only holds two wasn't by accident.

....

Julian Sands, actor

One of my favorite pleasures in LA is hiking in the canyons. Whether it be Fryman or Franklin Canyon or farther afield up in the San Gabriels; Mount Baldy and Iron Mountain and, of course, the Santa Monica mountains all the way through Malibu Park and Topanga Park. The great outdoors is what I love about Los Angeles; the elements, the geophysical properties, the confluence of mountains, desert, and

This dog park is near and dear to my heart as I used to take my beloved Romeo, a rescue Pomeranian, with me regularly. Though he preferred to hang out with the humans rather than the canines. I'm convinced that he thought he was a person! We spent many hours of entertainment each week socializing with other dog owners and their furry friends. The park is loaded with singles exercising their flirting skills, celebrities escaping from the paparazzi with their happy hounds, and dog lovers from all over LA. This place is hands down the best dog park I've ever visited.

Laurel Canyon Dog Park was featured on the TV series *Entourage* as a pickup place, so don't be surprised if you get hit on with some original lines like, "I came here looking for a little tail, did you?" Or "Is it warm in here, or are you in heat?" But my favorite is, "my dog wants to meet your dog, but is too shy."

Laurel Canyon Dog Park, 8260 Mulholland Drive, Studio City; (818) 769-4415; www.laparks.org/dos/parks/facility/dogparks/laurelcyndogpk.htm

Kim Marshall, founder and owner of The Marshall Plan

When I moved here and was single, an old friend said, "you should meet us to go hiking on Saturdays at the Paseo Miramar Trail." I thought, I love the idea. It's five minutes from my house. It's a tough hiking trail in the middle of nowhere in Pacific Palisades.

I'm talking about mountain lions, deer, snakes, coyotes. It is so magical, Some days the mist is out, it looks like Ireland. Other days it looks like the desert. What else is hilarious is that in LA, people don't speak to each other because they're never on the street. They don't walk anywhere. So, in small town USA, people say "Hello, good-morning," when they pass you in the street. In LA, one of the only places people do that is on the Paseo Miramar Trail. It's because you're in nature, you're not all made up. It doesn't really matter how you look.

I have seen so many celebrities hiking around there. It is the place to go on Saturday mornings. When you end up on the top plateau over the ocean, you can see Century City, and downtown. No one who comes to LA and just visits for business would ever even know that existed. It's two hours up and back, if you go at a clip.

The morning of my wedding, I invited everyone who was coming to the wedding to hike the trail. We packed backpacks with champagne, orange juice, bagels, and cream cheese. And everybody met up at the top, and sat and had Mimosas and bagels. Someone was videotaping. They went around to everyone and said, "Say your name, you made it to the top." It's not easy. It's pretty much uphill. The first half hour is way uphill, but then it gets okay.

The fun thing about LA is that you're twenty minutes from any party, even if you're not invited. Mentally it's nice to know that you're twenty minutes from the Oscars, I mean literally. In the grocery store you can see Julia Louis-Dreyfus shopping. And it doesn't matter. The woman who makes coffee at our grocery store says, "I've waited on Steven Spielberg." But in LA, it's cool just to say . . . "whatever."

Paseo Miramar Trail, 899 Paseo Miramar, Pacific Palisades

....

Rocky Malhotra, chairman, SuperMax Corporation

I travel all over the world, but I love to go to the top of the Paseo Miramar Trail.

Apart from the fact it's a great workout on a Saturday or Sunday, you feel so close to nature. I have a spiritual connection there. You get an unbelievable view of the Pacific and the wonderful coolness coming out of the ocean. You feel serene, quiet, and peaceful. And the irony is it's minutes away from the madness of the business world, your office. There aren't many cities where you can have that instant contrast.

I like to visit the trail before 11:00 a.m. Or I'll go just before sunset when you get the views of the ocean and see the sun coming down, dropping like a ball. Within seconds it's gone but it really puts you in touch with the universe. We get so busy and get stuck with conference calls, meetings, e-mails, and traveling. You need that moment to come back to God.

Paseo Miramar Trail, 899 Paseo Miramar, Pacific Palisades

....

Jill-Michele Meleán, actress

Working in this fast-paced judgmental crazy TV/Film business can be hectic. I want to always love what I do so I have found a way to balance this magical thing called life. Just thirty minutes away from the heart of Hollywood is the picturesque Malibu Creek State Park. My favorite thing to do in Los Angeles is to escape the smog to this place of nature. I love hiking, pretending I'm a rock climber, and surrendering to the calmness of the creek. Malibu Creek also allows you to explore historical terrain that has been the outdoor set to many famous television shows and movies such as *M*A*S*H* and *Planet of the Apes*. Oh, and the cell phone signal is really bad so I'm forced to connect to the environment instead of my Wi-Fi.

Malibu Creek State Park, 1925 Las Virgenes Road, Agoura; (818) 880-0367; www.malibucreekstatepark.org

....

Bernard Markowitz, MD FACS, Clinical Professor of Surgery, David Geffen School of Medicine at UCLA

My favorite places in Los Angeles center around my two daughters and their athletics. They are both dedicated soccer players and equestrians. I love to photograph them competing. The soccer fields and equestrian centers they play on and ride in throughout Los Angeles and Southern California are where I most enjoy spending my free time. There is nothing better to see than their glowing faces after winning a soccer game or getting the blue ribbon for an equestrian event.

Two of my favorite places are the fields at the Veterans Administration where the girls play and practice soccer and Sullivan Canyon where they train as equestrians. Sullivan Canyon is a beautiful throwback to old Los Angeles. It's a pristine protected area, where, in addition to horseback riding, you can take a hike and appreciate a gorgeous pocket of nature in the heart of the west side of Los Angeles.

MacArthur Field on the West Los Angeles VA property is many acres of manicured lawn where dozens of youth soccer teams practice and play their games. It is a sight to watch all the kids practicing in the same area at once.

Sullivan Canyon, 1640 Old Oak Road, Los Angeles; (310) 454-5905; www.access-scpa.org

....

Karen Zambos, designer and owner, Karen Zambos Vintage Couture

Even as a little girl growing up in the Midwest, I remember being drawn to fashion. It was never simply the clothes, or the latest trends that fascinated me. I loved diversity and the more eclectic the better. I loved discovering long dresses worn with a pair of vintage boots. I noticed how retro prints were being reinvented on new fabrics. So it's no wonder that Los Angeles, the "anything goes" city with only one fashion rule (the Oscars are a "black tie" event) would lend me the inspiration and become home to my own fashion line.

Like any city, if you don't seek out and visit your places of refuge, the noise, the crowds and traffic can wear on you, and block you creatively. When I need to clear my head, I love hiking Temescal Canyon. The views are stunning and I always leave full of inspiration. With my business headquartered downtown, I love to sneak away from the office to spend an hour walking around MOCA. Even among the permanent collections and grounds, I always discover something new.

For wine tasting, I make the drive to Los Olivos. It's so close, any Angeleno would be crazy not to consider it a "local" favorite. And last but not least, my favorite restaurant by far is Laurel Hardware. I love this city. It has been kind to me. I love calling Los Angeles home.

Temescal Canyon, Temescal Gateway Park, Sunset Boulevard & Temescal Canyon Road, Pacific Palisades; (310) 454-1395

Los Olivos Meat Market, 437 South Victory Boulevard, Burbank; (818) 843-4299

Laurel Hardware, 7984 Santa Monica Boulevard, West Hollywood; (323) 656-6070; www.laurelhardware.com

. . . .

Paul Herman, actor and part of the Ago restaurant team along with Robert De Niro, Bob and Harvey Weinstein, Ridley Scott, Michael Mann, John Lovitz, Lawrence Bender, Gianni Nunnari, Christopher Walken, and Agostino Sciandri

There are trails like Temescal Canyon which are so beautiful and invigorating. And you don't see many people on them.

When climbing up Temescal, take the left trail to Skull Rock. Keep going to the top, almost up to Topanga Canyon. As you're going around every turn you see a panoramic view of the Pacific. You get a better glimpse of the ocean and you say, "Wow." And then as you go another 50 feet you come to another turn and you're that much higher. The view is even more breathtaking and gets better and better. When you get to the top, it's jaw-dropping. Everything is laid out before you.

From that vantage point, you see the Southern California coast in every direction. You see everything from Malibu to Santa Monica to Manhattan Beach. Santa Catalina and Palos Verdes are in the distance. A couple of islands, Santa Barbara and St. Nicholas, are 50 miles out. But on a clear day you can see them too. Because of the curvature of the earth, you see below the curve as you get higher. So you see islands that you can't see when you're standing on the beach.

I opened the restaurant Ago with a team of friends. I'm no chef. I stay out of the kitchen. I'm sort of what you might say, the social director. You never know who will pop in there. I figure, why would I go somewhere else? Pretty much everybody comes by. There's a private back room where Marlon Brando would have dinner and we have the best outdoor patio in Los Angeles. You get a good Italian meal and a lot of ambiance.

Temescal Gateway Park, 15601 Sunset Boulevard, Pacific Palisades; (310) 454-1395

Ago, 8478 Melrose Avenue, West Hollywood; (323) 655-6333; http://agorestaurant.com/

....

Zane Buzby, comedy director of over 200 sitcoms and founder of The Survivor Mitzvah Project, a non-profit charity helping Holocaust Survivors in Eastern Europe

As I took root here, performing in bands and acting in films segued into directing film and then producing and directing television. I became more in synch with the LA clock. I rise early and by 9:30 p.m. even I'm asleep. Or yawning. But sunrise in LA is perfect from atop Mount Washington (also known as NELA), where I live. Minutes from downtown LA, Pasadena, Silver Lake, and Echo Park, Mount Washington is the best-kept secret in Los Angeles.

I have a killer view and you can too by making your way up to the top of West Avenue 37. Park on the ridge by lover's leap, and you are looking right through the downtown skyline, past Dodger Stadium's ridge of palm trees to the beaches and beyond, all the way out to Catalina in the west, OC in the south, and the snow-capped Sierras Madres and the San Gabriels to the north. Winter is the best time. The air is fresh and visibility crystal clear. It's also a great place to watch the sunset as all of Los Angeles spreads out in a carpet of brilliant lights for as far as the eye can see, in all directions. Also, it's the single best place in LA to watch fireworks on July 4th. Why pay to go to a fireworks show when you can see fireworks at Dodger Stadium, Disneyland, downtown, Santa Monica and everywhere else—all at the same time—all for free? It goes on for hours. Bring a shaker of martinis and some fresh chicken burritos from Taco Fiesta on Avenue 43 and Figueroa.

Taco Fiesta, 4501 North Figueroa Street, Los Angeles; (323) 223-5478

....

Lorraine Bracco, Academy Award-, Emmy-, and Golden Globe–nominated actress

I like to go to Malibu and walk my dog on the beach. My dog loves it. I call her Malibu Barbie. She loves the ocean. This dog is in heaven.

Malibu beach, www.malibucity.org

INDEX

Abbot Kinney Festival, 139
Abbot's Habit, 88–89
Abramson, Richard, 23–24
Adams, Patrick J., 50
Aero Movie Theatre, 143–44
Agape International
    Spiritual Center, 202–3
Ago, 41–42, 257
All'Dai, NiRé, 84, 179–80
Allen, Scott, 245
Alves, Camila, 81
American Rag, 153
American Tropical
    Interpretive Center, 182
Ammo, 72–73

Amoeba Music, 53–54,
    118-19
Andersen, Thom, 123
Anderson, Erika, 6
Anderson, Robert S.,
    19–20
Angel, Dan, 63–64
Angel, Ilene, 202–3
Angeles Crest Forest,
    251–52
Angelini Osteria, 86
Angel's Flight, 218
Angel Stadium of
    Anaheim, 187
Animal, 81, 111

Annenberg Community
    Beach House, 4–6
Anthony, La La, 90
AOC, 111–12
Apple Pan, The, 58–59, 66,
    118-19
Aquarium of the Pacific
    Harbor Tour, 205–6
ArcLight Cinemas, 189–90
ArcLight Cinerama Dome,
    182–83
Area, 158–59
Armisen, Fred, 205
Aroma Coffee & Tea
    Co., 100

Cinerama Dome
Courtesy of Pacific Theatres/ArcLight Cinemas

Arroyo Chop House, 93-94
Astro Burger, 57
Austin, Stephanie, 135
Axe, 96-97

Babalu Cafe, 88-89
Baby Blues BBQ, 37
Back on the Beach Cafe,
    88-89, 197
Bailey, Amanda, 200-1
Baker, Dylan, 83
Baldwin, Billy, 223-25
Baldwin Hills Scenic
    Overlook, 127
Baldy, Mount, 245-46
Ballona Creek Bike
    Path, 223
Barlow, Michael, 190-92
Barneys New York, 137
Barnsdall Art Park, 117-18,
    181-82
Barry, Dave, 192
Bartnett, Anne, 121
Basche, David Alan, 54
Batt, Bryan, 67-68
Bay Cities Italian Deli &
    Bakery, 88-89
Baywatch, 1-3
Bazaar by José Andrés,
    The, 97-98
Bea Bea's, 51, 63-64
Beacher's Madhouse, 126
Beachwood Cafe, 98
Beachwood Canyon, 249
Beau Rivage Restaurant, 13
Beech Street Cafe, 134
Bellamy, Edward, 164
Benito's Taco Shop,
    77-78, 188

Bennett, Tracie, 13
Bergere, Jenica, 175-78
Beso Hollywood, 90
Beverly Gardens Park,
    24-26
Beverly Hills Art Show,
    The, 139
Beverly Hills Farmers'
    Market, 133-34
Beverly Hills Hotel, 15-16,
    149. *See also* Fountain
    Coffee Room at the
    Beverly Hills Hotel, The
Beverly Hot Springs, 131,
    150-52
Beverly Wilshire Hotel, 192
Bicycle Ambulance, 207
Bikram's Yoga College of
    India, 151-52
Bishop, Carol, 226-27
Black, Jack, 73
Blair, Selma, 148-49
Bleu, Corbin, 105
Bloom, Richard, 175
Blucas, Marc, 37
BOA Steakhouse, 83
Bob's Coffee & Doughnuts,
    91-92
BodyFactory, 57
Bombay Palace, 238
Bonann, Greg, 1-3
Book Soup, 148-49
Borden, Bill, 87-89
Bow Wow, 51
Bracco, Lorraine, 257
Bradbury, Lewis, 164
Bradbury Building, 163-64,
    190-92
Branson, Richard, 188

Braude, Ann, 213-14
Braude, Marvin, 213-14
Braun, Scooter, 83
Brentwood Country Mart,
    The, 140, 160-61
Brien, William, 24-26
Broad Contemporary Art
    Museum at LACMA,
    200-1
Broad Stage, The, 89, 165
Brody, Adrien, 40
Bronson Canyon, 222
Brownstein, Carrie, 50
Brunner, Charles, 226
Bryan Kest's Power
    Yoga, 131
Buckley, Betty, 209-10
Buffalo Club, The, 88-89
Burns, Ken, 195
Busy Bee Market, 219-20
Buzby, Zane, 100-101, 161,
    257-58

Cacao Coffee House, 188
Cactus Taqueria, 45
Cadell, Ava, 252-53
Café Dahab, 188
Cafe Dulce, 118
Café Gratitude, 73-74, 86
Cafe Stella, 113, 135-36
Café Tropical, 60
Cafe Vida, 134
Caffé Delfini, 88-89
Caffe Roma, 41-42
California Science
    Center, Space Shuttle
    Endeavour, 178-79
Cambor, Peter, 125-26
Cannon, Nick, 64

Capital Grille, 35, 37
Carbon Beach, 18–19
Carney's, 96
Carpenter, David R., 122
Casa Vega Restaurant,
    70–71
Casella, Max, 211
Catalina Island, 238–39,
    240
Cecchetto, Cheryl, 95
Celebrity Autobiography,
    103–4
Chain Reaction!, 122
Chait, Bill, 30–31
Chandni Vegetarian
    Restaurant, 88–89
Chanel, 149–50
Chantry Flats, 251–52
Charles, Josh, 66
Chastain, Jessica, 1
Chateau Marmont, 68,
    107–8, 148, 193, 209–11
Cheban, Jonathan, 56–57,
    126, 153
Cheese Store of Silver
    Lake, The, 135–36
Chenoweth, Kristin, 79
Chevalier's Books, 156–57
Chez Jay, 83
Chiba Japanese
    Restaurant, 48
Chimo, Tracee, 86–87
Chmerkovskiy, Valentin, 95
Ciara, 66
Cinefamily, The, 111
City Spa, 135
Clark, Chris, 120–21
Clark, Tena, 93–94, 251–52
Cleo Restaurant, 169, 172

Coffee Corner, The, 91-92
Coldwater Canyon Park,
    Tree People, 234
Compagno, Natalie, 129–30,
    157–59
Conant, Scott, 48–49
Cooks County
    Restaurant, 33
Cooper, Martin, 203–4
Corcos, Gabriele, 86
Costin, Glynis, 160–61
Cotillard, Marion, 226
Cousins, Byata, 222
Covina Bowl, 65-66
CRAFTED at the Port of
    Los Angeles, 199
Craig's, an American
    Restaurant, 32–33,
    89–90
Creativity (performance
    space), 103–4
Crestwood Hills Park, 250
Cryer, Jon, 225
Culver City Municipal
    Plunge, The, 207
Culver Hotel, 127

Dahan, Jerome, 147–48
Daichan, 42
Dan's Super Subs, 75–76
Dan Tana's, 66, 119
Danza, Tony, 32
Dash Clothing LA, 132
Davis, Nancy, 210
Dear John's, 126–27
De Line, Donald, 69–71
Disney cottages, 232-33
Disneyland Park, 204
Divino, 94

Dodger Stadium, 183–85,
    186–87
Doner, Ezra, 99, 240
Dorothy Chandler Pavilion,
    44–45, 71
Doughboys Cafe &
    Bakery, 85
Douglas, Illeana, 90–92
Dr. Hogly Wogly's Tyler
    Texas BBQ, 39
Dragonette, Patrick, 196,
    230–32
Dreyfuss, Richard, 37
drives and walks, 212–57
Dumas, Debi, 144–45
Du-par's, at the Farmers'
    Market, 80–81

Eames House, The, 173-74
East India Grill, 84-85
e.baldi, 57
Eftekari, Mehdi, 233
Egglesfield, Colin, 52
El Carmen, 159
El Chato (Taco Truck),
    51–52
El Compadre
    Restaurant, 87
El Conquistador Mexican
    Restaurant, 46–47
El Floridita Cuban
    Restaurant, 49–50,
    105-6
El Matador Beach, 7–8
El Pueblo de Los
    Angeles Historical
    Monument, 182
Emmerich, Noah, 11–12
Entre Nous, 158–59

Enzo & Angela Restaurant, 64
Euro Caffe, 144
Euro Pane Bakery, 189–90

Fairchild, Barbara, 119–20
Farmers Market, The, 80–81, 91–92
Father's Office, 22
Feinstein, Michael, 53–54
Feniger, Susan, 250
Ferguson, Jesse Tyler, 135–36
Figaro Bistrot, 84
Fiore, Kathryn, 33–37
Fisher, Frances, 74
Flanders, Denise, 248
Flicka, 155
Floor Plan, 158–59
Flore Vegan, 53–54
Flower, Chloe, 89–90
Floyd's 99 Barbershop, 187–88
Fonda, Jane, 221–22
Forage Restaurant, 50
Forest Lawn, 225, 236–37
Fountain Coffee Room at the Beverly Hills Hotel, The, 69–71, 167, 172, 221. *See also* Beverly Hills Hotel
Frankies on Melrose, 32
Franklin Canyon, 246
Fraser, Neal, 30, 78–79
Fratelli Café, 95
Fred Segal (boutique), 138–39
Fryman Canyon, 148, 221, 235

Garay, Olga, 67, 181–82
Garcetti, Eric, 17
Gartin, Christopher, 145
Genghis Cohen, 101
Genwa, 79
Gervasi, Sacha, 77–78
Getty Center, The, 197
Getty Museum, The, 174
Getty Villa, 88–89, 173–74, 197
Gilbar, Annie, 242–43
Gilbar, Lisa, 96
Ginsberg, Merle, 71–73, 111–12, 136–37, 252
Gjelina, 44–45, 52, 241–42
Goda Yoga, 141
Gogosha, Julia, 117–18
Goin, Suzanne, 140
Golden Bridge Yoga, 138
Goldman, Duff, 193–95
Goldschmied, Adriano, 113
Gomez, Selena, 27
Gorham, Christopher, 78
Grace, 30
Graham, Heather, 131
Grauman's Chinese Theatre, 168, 172, 232
Grazer, Gigi Levangie, 185–86
Greenberg, Peter, 238–40
Greenblatt's Deli, 77
Greer, Chad, 84–85
Gregg, Clark, 66
Griffith Observatory, 201–2, 225
Griffith Observatory Hike, 216–17
Griffith Park, 67, 226–27
Groban, Josh, 43–44

Groundlings Theatre & School, The, 108–9
Grove, The, 140
Guitar Center, 244-45
Gurmukh, 137–38

Haden, Pat, 13–14
Hale, Lucy, 235
Hallberg, David, 71
Hal's Bar & Grill, 88–89
Hammer Museum, 166–67
Hardin, Melora, 15–16, 150–51
Harry's Berries, 134
Hennessey + Ingalls, 141
Herman, Paul, 256–57
Hermit Falls, 251
Hewitt, Jennifer Love, 129
Hills, Kimba, 145–46
Hillstone, 66
Hoffman, Dustin, 165
Hollywood Bowl, The, 119–22
Hollywood Forever, 116–18, 182
Hollywood Palladium, 109–10
Hollywood Roosevelt Hotel, 60–62, 172
Hotel Bel-Air, 112–13
House, Sharon, 21–22
Howard, Ken, 32–33
Huckleberry Bakery and Cafe, 44–45
Hudgens, Vanessa, 132
Hugo's, 52
Huntington Beach, 5
Huntington Library, Art Collections, and

Botanical Gardens, 13–15, 27, 93
Huntington Meats, 152–53
Hurd, Gale Anne, 188–90
Huston, Angelica, 44
Hyatt Regency Century Plaza, 210

Il Tramezzino, 56–57
Improv West Theatre & Training Center, 109–10
Inaka, 40
India Sweets & Spices, 150
Ink., 54
Intelligentsia Coffee & Tea, 113, 135–36
Interim Cafe, 88–89
Iowa (battleship), 199
Irby, Michael, 38–39
Ismail, Mohan, 150
Itacho Izakaya and Sushi, 31
Ivy, The, 90, 149
Ivy at the Shore, 68, 85
Izaka-Ya by Katsu-Ya, 62

J. Paul Getty Museum, The, 174
J. Paul Getty Villa, 88–89, 173–74, 197
Jackman, Hugh, 220
Jacobson, Max, 100
Japanese Garden, The, 16–17
Jar, 42
Jarecki, Nicholas, 135
Jerry's Famous Deli, 90
Jewel, 33
Jitlada, 51–52
Joan's on Third, 78, 158–59

Joe Rivera's Focus (Center) Fitness, 96–97
John Marshall High School, 232–33
Johnny Rockets, 90
Johnny Vana's Big Band Alumni, 244
Jonsdottir, Gulla, 69, 196–97

Kameon, Judy, 14–15
Kardashian, Kim, 132
Karno, Nick, 116–17, 207–8
Katana Restaurant, 90
Kazan, Lainie, 151–52
Kazu Sushi, 82
KCRW radio, 72–73
Keaton, Diane, 222
Kelly, Claude, 52
Kendrick, Anna, 29, 38
Kimball, Paige Morrow, 55–56, 174–75
Kind, Richard, 92–93
Klass, Dan, 20–21, 232–33
Klein, Jeff, 241–42
Knatz, Geraldine, 197–99
Koi, 81
Kramers Pipe and Tobacco Shop, 144–45
Kreation Kafe, 22
Krisel, Jonathan, 98
Kristof, Nicholas, 3
KyoChon Chicken, 110–11

LaBonge, Tom, 201–2
La Fonda Supper Club, 127
Laiter, Tova, 115, 229
Lake Hollywood, 219, 229
Lake Shrine Temple, 180–81

La-Louisanne Cajun Creole Restaurant, 42
Landau, Susan B., 142–43
Landis' Labyrinth Toy Shop, 155–57
L & R Salon, 158–59
Lane, Laura, 115–16
Langer's Delicatessen-Restaurant, 58-59, 99
Lansbury, Angela, 64
Lanter, Matt, 100
Largo at the Coronet, 108–9
LA Rowing Club, 6
La Scala Beverly Hills, 57–58
La Serenatade Garibaldi, 70–71
Las Hadas Mexican Restaurant, 244
Lathan, Sanaa, 221
Laurel Canyon Dog Park, 252–53
Laurel Hardware, 256
Lehrer, Mia, 26–27
Levine, Ken, 183–85
Lillien, Lisa, 82
Lindsey, Gina Marie, 228
Ling, Lisa, 42
Little Dom's, 50
Little Next Door, 158–59
Little Tokyo, 118
Liu, Lucy, 31
Lobis, Josh, 134
Loggia, Audrey, 43
Loggia, Robert, 43
Long, Justin, 111
Long Beach Antique Market, 145–46

Looking Backward
(Bellamy), 164
Lopez, Sylvia, 244
Los Angeles Clippers,
    Staples Center, 186
Los Angeles County
    Museum of Art
    (LACMA), 200–201
Los Angeles Lakers, 196
Los Angeles Memorial
    Coliseum, 199–200
Los Angeles River, 17, 26–27
Los Angeles Zoo, 195, 225
Los Feliz Municipal Golf
    Course, 22
Los Liones Canyon,
    Topanga Canyon State
    Park, 24
Los Olivos Meat
    Market, 256
Loteria Grill, 84–85
Lucques, 62
Ludwig, Alexander, 5
Lulu Cocina Mexicana,
    88–89
Lunsford, Loris Kramer, 62
Lutz, Kellan, 106, 216–17
Lynch, Kelly, 225
Lyons, Brooke, 44–45

Macht, Gabriel, 226
Mackie, Anthony, 42
Madeo Restaurant, 47
Mady, Edward, 221–22
Main Street Farmers'
    Market, 44–45
Malhotra, Rocky, 254
Malibu beach, 257
Malibu Country Mart,
    146–47

Malibu Creek State Park,
    254–55
Malibu Kitchens & Gourmet
    Country, 8
Mandeville Canyon, 219
Manhattan Beach, 21
Manhattan Beach Bikram
    Yoga, 141
Manhattan Meats, 19
Mapleton Drive, 219
Marciano, David, 22–23
Marielas Taco, 84
Markowitz, Bernard, 255
Marling, Brit, 249
Maroulis, Constantine, 172
Marshall, Kim, 253–54
Marston's Restaurant,
    93–94
Martinez, Ana, 60–62
Martinez, Carol, 178–79
Marvin Braude Bike Trail,
    The, 213–14, 247–48
Mar Vista Farmers'
    Market, 154
Mascis, J, 143
Mastro's, 79
Matthews, Thomas, 84
Mazar, Debi, 86
Mazeau, Dan, 174
M Café, 38, 59, 60, 80
McCormack, Eric, 31
McDonald, Audra, 133
Meikco, 48
Meleán, Jill-Michele, 254–55
Melrose Avenue, 133
Meltdown Comics &
    Collectibles, 109–11
Menchie's, 63–64
Metchek, Ilse, 106, 139
Mikawaya, 118

Milioti, Cristin, 234
Miller, Lauren, 81
MI Westside Comedy
    Theatre, 109–10
Moiselle, Darin, 182–83
Moller-Islas, Erica, 126–27
Monastery of the Angeles
    Cloistered Dominican
    Nuns, 178–79
Montana Avenue, Santa
    Monica, 223, 225
Montgomery, Janet, 62
Morgan, Jeffrey Dean, 62
Morgan, Piers, 19
Morrison, Jennifer, 47
Morrison, Mark, 7–8
Morrow Kimball, Paige,
    55–56, 174–75
Mothersbaugh, Mark,
    244–45
Mount Baldy, 245–46
Moynihan, Bobby, 110
Mr. Chow, 153
Much, Elizabeth, 101
Mulholland Drive, 231–32,
    242–43
Muscle Beach, 176, 194–95
Museum of Contemporary
    Art, Los Angeles
    (MOCA), 44–45
Museum of Jurassic
    Technology, The, 204–5
Musso & Frank Grill, 33–35,
    37, 168–69, 172

Nate 'n Al, 56–57, 215
natural areas, 1–27
Nawab (of India), 88–89
Nelson, Arlene, 223
Nelson, Candace, 166–67

Newman, Laraine, 103, 108–10, 133–34
New Beverly Cinema, The, 211
New Stone Age, 158–59
Ne-Yo, 73, 133
Nichols, Chris, 65–66
Nichols Canyon, 252
Nicholson, Mark, 5–6
nightlife, 102–27
99 Ranch Market, 150
Nissenbaum, Offer, 123–24
Nobu Malibu, 81, 233
Noodle Stories, 145
North Woods Inn, 65–66
Norton Simon Museum, 189–90
Nuart Theatre, 105

Obrist, Hans Ulrich, 204–5
Off Vine Restaurant, 208
O'Hare, Denis, 60
OK, 158–59
Old Town Pasadena, 93
Olympic Spa, a Korean Day Spa, 133, 157
101 Noodle Express, 98, 99
Original Los Angeles Flower Market, The, 142
Osteria Mamma, 59
Osteria Mozza, 59, 108, 110

Pacific Asia Museum, 189–90
Pacific Coast Highway (PCH), 213, 217, 233, 245
Pacific Dining Car, 192
Pacific Palisades Farmers' Market, 134
Pack, Eugene, 103–4, 235

Palisades Park, 21–22
Palmeri Ristorante, 43
Pann's Restaurant & Coffee Shop, 65–66
Pantages Theatre, 208
Papazian, Martin, 96–97
Paradise Cove, 20
Paramount Pictures (Paramount Studios Tour), 163, 166–68, 172
Park's BBQ, 79
Pasadena City College Flea Market, 145–46
Paseo Miramar Trail, 253–54
Patinkin, Mandy, 131
Patrick's Roadhouse, 87, 89
Patterson, Ryan, 155–57
Patys, 31, 63, 64
Pauley Pavilion, 187
Paves, Ken, 58
Peninsula Beverly Hills, 124
Perry, Tyler, 83
Phillips, Chynna, 223–25
Phillips, Lou Diamond, 196
Phins Water Sports Club, 6
Piano Bar, 84–85
Piège, Jean-François, 211
Pinkberry, 144
Pinkins, Tonya, 81
Pink's Hot Dogs, 37
Pizzeria Mozza, 35, 37, 110
Playa del Rey, 20–21
Plumb, Eve, 80–81
Point Dume Natural Preserve, 23–24
Poke-Poke Place, 194–95
Polkadots & Moonbeams, 158–59

Pollack, Zach, 29–31, 51–52
Polo Lounge, The, 46
Porta Via, 124
Port of Los Angeles, 199
Pressed Juicery, 140
Primitivo, 154

Rabineau, Steve, 4–5
Rainbow Bar & Grill, 118–19
Raitt, Bonnie, 55
Rambin, Leven, 249
Rancic, Giullana, 85
Randolph, Da'Vine Joy, 78
Ray's and Stark Bar, *28*, 71–72, 73, 95
Real Food Daily (West Hollywood), 38, 101
Red O, 69
Red Rock Bar & Eatery, 124
Reed, Marco, 180–81
Reel Inn, 88–89
Reiner, Alysia, 54
restaurants, 28–101
Retta, 124, 140
Reyfel, Dayle, 103–4, 230
Reynolds, Christopher, 249–50
Rice, Luanne, 12–13
Riggi, Chris, 73
Ripert, Eric, 193
Roberts, Doris, 59
Rochlin, Margy, 207
Rockwell, 113–14
Roger Room, 114
Rolston, Matthew, 167–72
ROOM 5 (performance space), 104
Room at the Beach, 147
Roscoe's House of Chicken and Waffles, 73

Rose Bowl Flea Market, The, 145–46

Rose Bowl Stadium, 93–94, 189–90

Rose Cafe & Market, 88–89

Roxy, The, 122–23

Ruffalo, Mark, 222

Runyon Canyon Park, 220–22

Russell, David O., 246

Russell, Graham, 237–38

Russell, Sam, 181

Rustic Canyon Winebar and Seasonal Kitchen, 89

Ryan, Amy, 40

Ryan, Debby, 122–23

Saddleback Butte State Park, 240

Saks Fifth Avenue, 149–50

Salamunovic, Adrian, 114, 173–74, 248

Samson, Steve, 30–31

Samy's Camera, 142–43

Sands, Julian, 245–46

Santa Monica Airport, 125–26

Santa Monica Beach, 1, 7, 10–12

Santa Monica Farmers' Market, *128*, 140, 160

Santa Monica Outdoor Antique & Collectable Market, 145–46

Santa Monica Pier, 3, 175

Santa Monica Stairs, 8–10

Santa Monica Swingers Diner, 43–44

Santee Alley, 161

San Vicente bike route, 228

Sarandon, Susan, 105

Sauce on Hampton, 88–89

Schaler, Karen, 75–76

Schiffman, Amy, 247–48

Schubel, Jerry R., 205–6

Schulzies Bread Pudding, 88–89, 194–95

Schwartz, Stephen, 97, 98

Seacrest, Ryan, 213, 217

Segal, Kirsten, 94, 138–39

Self-Realization Fellowship, Lake Shrine Temple, 180–81

Shakespeare Bridge, 232–33

Shannon, Michael, 42

Shannon, Molly, 4, 155

shopping, 128–61

Shutters on the Beach, 15–16, 148

Sidibe, Gabourey, 85

Silverton, Nancy, 218–20

Silvios, 248

Simmons, Gene, 45–46

Simone, Hannah, 202

Simple Things Sandwich and Pie Shop, 158–59

Skoll, Jeff, 67

Smith, Patti, 129

Smits, Jimmy, 10–11

Soda Jerks, 174–75

Soho House, 36–37

Solstice Canyon, 12–13

Son of a Gun, 81

Soot Bull Jeep, 79

Sotto, 30–31

Soul Cycle, 132

Space Shuttle Endeavour, 178–79

Spago Beverly Hills, 95

Spelling, Candy, 47

Spheeris, Penelope, 16–17

SPiN LA at The Standard (Downtown LA), 105

Splichal, Joachim, 142

Springer, Jerry, 57

Sprinkles Cupcakes, 36–37

Steele, Cassie, 187–88

Stevens, Fisher, 80

Stevie's Creole Cafe and Bar, 64

Stewart, Elizabeth, 143–44

Stiller, Ben, 163, 165–66

Strand, 220

Streiber, Art, 112–13, 199–200

structures, 162–257

Stuhlbarg, Michael, 105

Sugarfish by Sushi Nozawa, 48

Sullivan Canyon, 255

Sun Cafe, 55

Sunday Night Jazz nights, 106, 122–23

Sunset Boulevard, 237–38

Sunset Marquis, 136–37, 188

Sunset Ranch, 249–50

Sunset Tower Hotel, 67, 69, 241–42

Surfas, 135

Sushi Park, 47–49

Swerve, 158–59

Swingers Diner, 43–44

Taboo Hair Care, 158–59

Taco Fiesta, 257–58

Temescal Canyon, 256–57

Temescal Gateway Park, 256–57

Tennenbaum, Andrew R.,
     18–19
Terroni Restaurant, 78
Teru Sushi, 152
Theroux, Peter, 236–37
Thomas, Ella, 234
Thoms, Tracie, 113–14
3 Square Cafe & Bakery, 217
Tiegs, Cheryl, 215
Tigerman, Gabriel, 33–37
Tilson Thomas, Michael, 192
Title, Gail Midgal, 228–29
Toast Bakery Cafe, 158–59
Topanga Canyon
     Boulevard, 234
Topanga Canyon State
     Park, 24
Topanga State Beach, 4–5
Torihei, 51–52
Toscana Restaurant, 43
Tower Bar, 67, 69
Tracht, Suzanne, 152–53
Trails Cafe, The, 59
Traveler's Bookcase, 129–30
Trico Field, 149
Troubadour, 122
Trucks, Toni, 110–11
True Food Kitchen, 38–39
Truetone Music, 143
Two Boots, 101

UCLA Marina Aquatic
     Center, 6
Upright Citizens Brigade
     Theatre, The, 108–10
Urth Caffé, 196–97

Usher, 216
USS *Iowa,* 199
U Studio Yoga, 131

Valderrama, Wilmer, 49–50
Venice, 217–18
Venice Beach, 193–94,
     228–29
Vernieu, Mary, 154
Versailles, 40
Vertical Wine Bistro,
     189–90
Village Gourmet Cheese
     and Wine, 62
Villaraigosa, Antonio R., 165
Vincenti Ristorante, 148
Virbila, S. Irene, 160
Vista Theatre, The, 232–33
Vitale, Ruth, 40–42, 107–8,
     149–50

Wade, Jenny, 46–47, 251
walks and drives, 212–57
Walt Disney Concert Hall,
     44–45, 191–92
Walter, Steve, 118–19
Watts Towers Arts Center,
     165, 219
Wayward Beach, 121
Webster, Guy, 217–18
Westfeldt, Jennifer, 67
West Hollywood Monday
     Farmers' Market, 74
Whiskey A Go Go, 244–45
White, Shaun, 7
White, Vanna, 103

Whitman, Mae, 157
W Hollywood presents
     Sunday Night Jazz
     nights, 106, 122–23
Will Geer Theatricum
     Botanicum, The, 117
Williams, Allison, 140
Williams, Cindy, 76–77
Will Rogers State Beach,
     1–3
Will Rogers State Park, 215
Wingstop, 35, 37
Wuhl, Robert, 58–59, 145,
     186–87
Wyman, George, 164

Yamashiro, 115–16
Yamashiro Farmers
     Market, 145
Yang Chow, 35, 37
Yoga Works, 131
Yogurtland, 144
Yoon, Sang, 24, 98–99

Zadan, Craig, 90
Zambos, Karen, 255–56
Zankou Chicken, 35–37, 202
Zanzabuku, 123
Zelda's Corner Deli, 55–56
Zeman, Jacklyn, 146–47
Zimmer, Constance, 59
ZJ Boarding House, 147–48
Zuma Beach, 7, 13
Zwick, Edward, 8–10

ABOUT THE AUTHOR

Jeryl Brunner is a writer and journalist whose work has appeared in *O* magazine, *Huffington Post*, *Every Day with Rachael Ray*, *National Geographic*, *Traveler*, *Travel + Leisure*, *Delta Sky*, and *In Style*, where she was a staff correspondent for many years. She is also the author of *My City, My New York: Famous New Yorkers Share Their Favorite Places*. She has interviewed hundreds of celebrities, including Meryl Streep, Julia Roberts, Madonna, and George Clooney. She lives in Manhattan. Visit her at www.jerylbrunner.com.